Clear Red Water

Clear Red Water

Welsh Devolution and Socialist Politics

Nick Davies
& Darren Williams

Francis
Boutle
Publishers

First published by Francis Boutle Publishers
272 Alexandra Park Road
London N22 7BG
Tel/Fax: (020) 8889 7744
Email: info@francisboutle.co.uk
www.francisboutle.co.uk

Clear Red Water: Welsh Devolution and Socialist Politics
© Nick Davies and Darren Williams, 2009

ISBN 978 1 903427 44 6

Contents

Dedicated to our dear friend and comrade, the Rev. David 'Dai' Morris (1930–2007), lifelong campaigner for socialism, peace, social justice, and self-determination for Wales; Member of the European Parliament; founder-member and chair of Welsh Labour Grassroots. All those who knew him – throughout Wales and far beyond – will always remember his passion, eloquence and good humour.

Foreword

Reading this book is a delight tempered with shame for me because my appreciation of the philosophy and pioneering work of the Welsh Assembly Government (WAG) was so deficient. How could I have missed so many of the achievements of the WAG?

This is a splendid time to top up my knowledge banks. We are on the brink of the Obama revolution. Political certainties are collapsing and the world economy is convulsed. Welsh Labour is receptive to fresh ideas that challenge the superficial canards of New Labour. The Labour movement has been hurt by bewildering self-destructive polices from Westminster. On the gravest error, the Iraq War, the Labour party in Wales had their objections silenced by bureaucratic procedure. An explosion of anger from a lifelong Labour supporter, Professor Peter Hennessy, in January 2009 illustrates the depth of the wound. In answer to a question on why the Labour cabinet did not insist on seeing the full advice on the legality of the war, Peter said:

> We need to know the degree to which they did or did not test out this lit-tle shrivelled opinion. Did anyone ask for a fuller one? Under the Ministerial code they are meant to have the full Attorney General's legal opinion but they did not get it, did they? I have a suspicion not one of them spoke up. An injection of water would have stiffened those bastards' backbones.

This is the authentic exasperated anger at the wayward drift of New Labour from our core values. Our subservience to America's neo-cons was our foulest hour. Many opportunities have been neglected and much of the value of Labour's electoral victories were dissipated in fruit-less meandering into political dead ends. Happily, Labour in Wales has embarked on its voyage across the clear red water.

Nick Davies and Darren Williams reveal the divergence between Classic Labour and New Labour. In Wales, Labour has clung to the party's traditional values, avoiding much of New Labour's perverse shift to the false gods of fashionable modernisation: (Hobson's) choice, 'contestability' and the supremacy of the market. With commendable objectivity the authors have chronicled the chosen paths of Welsh Labour.

The Welsh Assembly has sought an equality of outcome rather than an equality of opportunity. Consumerism is rejected in favour of a collective voice. Mark Drakeford, the guru of Welsh Labour, argues that 'Services that are reserved for poor people very quickly become poor services' but universal services can be the 'glue that binds together a complex modern society'. Free school breakfasts are provided in Wales for all pupils, not just for those stigmatised as needy. Unfortunately Welsh Labour's passage across the red water encounters some treacherous rocks. The inbuilt conservatism of officials and the retentive neurosis of Welsh MPs are formidable obstructions. The institutional inertia of the civil service mandarins has passed almost unchanged from Westminster to Cardiff. Davies and Williams write:

> The policy of delivery of profound change to the marginalised is entrusted to officials schooled in the arts of deliberate administrative adjustment, ensuring that that anything remotely radical or ambitious passes through a series of filters that serve, all too frequently to mitigate its impact.

Some Labour MPs have perpetuated their traditional role as a drag anchor on devolution. In 1950 only five Welsh MPs backed the call for devolution. Some MPs campaigned to sabotage party policy in the two referendums. The recent alleged slow motion implementation of Legislative Competence Orders has reinforced the suspicion that MPs feel threatened by the movement of power down the M4 to Cardiff. Loss of Welsh parliamentary seats is the likely outcome of the evolution of Welsh autonomy. Nothing concentrates the mind more than the prospect of an approaching P45.

A small group of MPs remain in denial of devolution. Speaker Betty Boothroyd intervened in the first year of WAG to block MPs' questions on matters that had clearly been devolved to Cardiff. The shock of the election of non-Labour AMs in Llanelli, Islwyn and the Rhondda in 1999 still reverberates. A renewed bid for the hegemony of MPs over AMs was recently made on the basis that more votes are cast in general than in assembly elections. Why stop there? On that argument, MPs should also determine council and European parliamentary decisions. Welsh MPs' attempts to obstruct the *One Wales* coalition agreement were emphatically rejected by the party in Wales. But fear that coalition would dilute Labour's radical policies were unfounded. On health the coalition government has strengthened the commitment to 'move purposefully to end the internal market' by merging the functions of trusts and Local Health Boards.

Support for WAG policies has been unreliable and spasmodic in the greater party. Sniping from London ministers still undermines the independence of decision-making. There is permanent irritation at Westminster that a Labour-controlled body can stray from the revealed truth of the fashionable, often short-lived, nostrums of New Labour. It was a courageous Welsh decision to reject PFIs and the instant political gratification they offered. WAG policies will deliver better value and a fully publicly owned NHS in the long term.This is in the tradition of the founding father Aneurin Bevan. Prolonging the existence of Community Health Councils has been a popular success that reflects the respect for patient involvement. I recall the pride of Ron Davies when he added the word 'sustainable' to the Government of Wales Act. We are one of only three nations in the world to have a duty of sustainable development enshrined in our constitution. The Assembly has redefined sustainability as:

> Improving people's quality of life and well-being, while using environmental resources sustainably, so that development does not compromise the quality of life of future generations.

To their great credit the Welsh Assembly Government has earned universal praise for its imaginative pursuit of practical sustainable policies that are 'the single organising principle for all parts of the public sector.' The hope is that our global footprint could be reduced to that of a 'one planet nation'.

The leadership of first minister Rhodri Morgan has been the inspiration for the loyalty to 'Classic Labour'. In two major speeches he has differentiated Welsh Labour from New Labour. Rhodri's recipe for Wales is more 'participative than passive' and the role of the state as a force for good in politics. It's refreshing that the Welsh government has the stated aim of Welsh socialism for the 21st century. This is founded on Welsh working class idealism exemplified by Chartism and the immense achievements of the 1945–51 Labour government.

The present political turmoil has undermined the laissez-faire nostrums of Thatcherism and Blairism. Light touch state intervention has allowed the market to gorge, exploit and pillage. The future is malleable and it will be receptive to a freshened socialist creed. Nick Davies and Darren Williams have produced a fair-minded thorough account of the ambitions, achievements and failures of the limited Welsh home rule that we enjoy. Even those who are in daily contact with the microsurgery of nation building will learn a great deal from their account of the struggle for a distinctive Welsh way to challenge the third way. Rightly, they complain of the widespread lack of understanding and promotion of the achievements of WAG. News from WAG is dominated by media-encouraged ephemeral crises and rows. The daily trivia obscures the big picture that is brilliantly presented here.

Welsh Labour has demonstrated that a practical alternative exists to the policies pursued by New Labour in England. Welsh Labour Grassroots has developed as the thinking conscience of the labour movement in Wales. It will greatly influence the direction of Welsh politics in the advance towards a brave new Wales.

Paul Flynn MP

Preface

This book makes the case for a democratic socialist agenda in Welsh politics today. In so doing, it endorses much of the governmental programme pursued by Welsh Labour in the National Assembly – latterly, in coalition with Plaid Cymru – to the extent that this programme breaks with the market-driven politics of New Labour in England and promotes a more progressive, egalitarian alternative. This support is not uncritical: we clearly identify the limitations of the Welsh Labour (and now the *One Wales*) agenda, as we see them. Moreover, our criticism goes beyond the content of Assembly Government policy, addressing also the political culture of the Welsh labour movement: the lack of democracy, transparency and accountability in the party and unions alike. We are also unafraid of acknowledging our differences with those in our party who defend the 'New Labour' project and with the 'Labour-unionists', who resist the extension of democratic devolution.

The themes of this book are those which prompted the establishment of Welsh Labour Grassroots (WLG), the centre-left activists' network within the Welsh Labour party, to which we belong. In the five years since its foundation, WLG has gone from strength to strength, building its membership base and extending its political influence. We see ourselves as critical friends of the Welsh Labour leadership, irreconcilable opponents of New Labour, supporters of greater devolution, and advocates of a vibrant, participatory democracy within the Labour party, the wider labour movement and Welsh society in general.[1]

The views expressed on many of the issues discussed here are, however, primarily those of the two authors and not necessarily of WLG as a whole and some of our arguments would be controversial even among our close comrades. We would like to express particular gratitude to Paul Flynn MP for writing the foreword and to Meic Birtwistle and Julian

7

Tudor Hart for their detailed and very helpful comments on earlier drafts. They are not, of course, responsible for any remaining errors of fact or interpretation, or for our sins of omission. Nor, indeed, are any of the following, for whose advice, assistance and/or encouragement we are also grateful: Clive Boutle, Ben Curtis, Jane Davidson, David Davies, John Lewis, Philip Marchant, Shirley Newnham, Richard Price, Jonathan Scourfield, all our friends and comrades in WLG and in the labour and socialist movement generally, and – last but most important – our families, especially Brigid and Siân.

Finally, we would also like to thank Graham Bash, Jenny Fisher and their editorial colleagues at *Labour Briefing* magazine for giving us the opportunity to test out some of the analysis here in a series of articles over the last few years.

Nick Davies and Darren Williams
South Wales, March 2009

Chapter 1

Introduction: New Labour and Welsh Labour

We are living through extraordinary times. In the autumn of 2008, it became clear that the world economy was facing its most serious systemic crisis since the great depression of the 1930s. Soon, all the nostrums of free market capitalism were being cast aside, as governments around the world – including even George W. Bush's 'neo-con' Republican administration – discovered the necessity of state intervention to rescue their economies from the chaos to which they had been reduced by the unregulated financial markets. Gordon Brown won kudos for his calm and statesmanlike response to the crisis, providing a much-needed boost to his opinion poll ratings after several months of faux pas and disastrous council and by-election results had suggested that a Tory general election victory was all but inevitable. At the time of writing, it would be futile to speculate either about the likely length and depth of the recession or about its ultimate impact on the political fortunes of the Labour party. Brown may eventually be judged not on his attempts to resolve the crisis but on his contribution to the free-market policies that brought the crisis about. Indeed, the frequent ups and downs in the government's fortunes, throughout the Brown premierships and before, threaten a loss of perspective about the scope and origins of the problem with the New Labour project. Many governing parties suffer the 'mid-term blues' after a few policy mistakes; many, too, see their fortunes affected in unpredictable ways by changes in the economic situation, over which they may have only limited control. What

9

the Labour party has experienced through much of the Blair-Brown period, however, is a deep-seated political crisis.

Long before recent economic and political problems, the attitude of Labour's members, supporters and voters to their party's continuing ascendancy was, to put it mildly, somewhat ambivalent. Notwithstanding New Labour's unprecedented electoral success and its many undoubtedly progressive policies – from Surestart to civil partnerships to the national minimum wage – the wild euphoria that greeted the expulsion of the Tories from Downing Street in May 1997, after eighteen terrible years, has long departed. This is not just a matter of the party having become accustomed to being in office. Under the Blair and Brown premierships, the people of Britain have experienced a very different kind of Labour government from those headed by Harold Wilson and James Callaghan in the 1960s and 1970s. For all their faults – and there were many – those governments did at least make some effort to make Britain more equal. Under New Labour, however, all talk of redistributive taxation or extending public ownership (at least, as something other than a crisis measure) has been airily dismissed. The representatives of big business have been warmly embraced as paragons of civic virtue, the trade unions treated with, at best, polite tolerance; at worst, weary exasperation – if not outright hostility. Private companies have been encouraged to get into the 'business' of providing public services and where this is not possible, their methods are emulated by public bodies. NHS patients, welfare claimants, passengers on public transport and service-users of all kinds are now 'customers', free to exercise their consumer choice – whether they want to or not. There is apparently no corner of the public sector so essential, integral or successful that it cannot be remodelled, slimmed down and subjected to the rigours of the marketplace.

Most disturbingly of all, we have seen a Labour prime minister establish himself as the principal international ally of what is probably not just the most right-wing US administration in living memory, but the most corrupt and lawless one as well. In defiance of majority world opinion – whether expressed in the United Nations or on the streets of every major city, in the biggest demonstrations ever held – the British government took part in a war of conquest and plunder in Iraq, the dangerous and unpredictable consequences of which will no doubt continue to be felt all round the world for years to come. By June 2007, when Blair finally resigned as prime minister and Labour leader – his disastrous foreign policy and police investigations into the sale of honours having made him a liability – New Labour had managed to alienate almost every section of the coalition that had brought it to power: the trade unions, public sector workers, pensioners, students, peace activists, environmental campaigners and the black and minority ethnic communities.

A legacy of disaffection

Many of those who previously saw themselves as 'lifelong Labour people' have felt increasingly alienated from 'their' party. Membership is now around a third of the 1997 figure, many local parties rarely meet and electoral turnout in 'solid' Labour areas has slumped to an all-time low. Some of those who have left the party have attempted to set up alternatives: the Socialist Labour Party, the Scottish Socialist Party, the Socialist Alliance and Respect. These have rarely, however, made much impact on Britain's unyielding political terrain. Charismatic, but flawed, leaders like Arthur Scargill and George Galloway have often provoked as much hostility as admiration, while the first-past-the-post electoral system provides little space for newcomers. In any case, most disillusioned Labourites do not want a new party; they want their old one back. Labour was set up in 1900 to provide a political voice for the working class and the working class is not ready to let go of it just yet. The left within the party – weakened, diminished and outmanoeuvred during the arduous 1990s – has subsequently regrouped and has won a few victories at conferences and internal elections. Increasingly, the veterans of the 'Bennite' movement have found themselves on the same side as former adversaries like Roy Hattersley and Frank Dobson, who have come to regret their initial indulgence of New Labour. At the top levels of the party, however, there have been no dissenting voices. As Labour leader, Blair – like Thatcher before him – always insisted that there was no alternative to his policies.

During Blair's long-drawn-out departure, every effort was made to ensure that the transition to a new leadership did not provide the occasion for a genuinely open discussion of policies and ideas. Despite a vigorous campaign by activists throughout the labour movement and beyond, Labour MPs decided that party and affiliated union members would not have the opportunity to vote for John McDonnell, who would have offered a genuine alternative to the prevailing orthodoxy. Instead, the focus of attention was displaced onto the far less significant matter of who would be the best sidekick for Gordon Brown. It seems that Labour party members could have any policies they liked, so long as they were New Labour. Anyone mistaking the change in tone under Gordon Brown for a change in substance was soon disappointed. One of the architects of New Labour, Brown has continued his enthusiasm for privatisation and deregulation and drafted into his cabinet open enemies of the labour movement such as the former CBI boss, Digby Jones. Even the right of the party conference to hold the leadership to account, tolerated under Blair but ignored in practice, has now been swept away.

Devolution, however, allowed for a degree of policy diversity. As Mayor of London, Ken Livingstone pursued progressive policies in many areas which would probably not have been followed by a New Labour incumbent, but possessed limited powers and was defeated in his attempt to prevent tube privatisation. Scotland's Labour-led government departed from the Westminster script in a few important cases – reversing the internal market in health, scrapping up-front student tuition fees[1] and introducing free personal care for older people – but these initiatives owed less to Scottish Labour, which made no general break with New Labour's programme, than to its Liberal Democrat coalition partners. Only Wales has seen the presentation of a coherent alternative policy agenda.

'Clear Red Water'
On 11 December 2002, six months before he was due to face the electorate, the Welsh first minister, Rhodri Morgan, gave a speech at Swansea University in which he set out, for the first time, the political philosophy behind his governmental programme. It was a philosophy far more recognisable than that of Tony Blair to those who had grown up under Attlee or Wilson. He talked unashamedly about being a socialist, about the limits of market-based politics and about the 'powerful glue of social solidarity'. He explained that a series of initiatives whereby particular public services in Wales had been made free at the point of delivery represented a deliberate, ongoing programme of de-commodification. And, in a memorable phrase, he said that policies like these were evidence of 'clear red water' between Wales and Westminster.[2]

The significance accorded this speech grew when Welsh Labour made a comparatively strong showing in the May 2003 Assembly elections, winning back seats it had lost to Plaid Cymru four years earlier and securing an effective working majority. In reality, Welsh Labour had won fewer actual votes than in 1999 but, on a reduced turnout, it had lost less ground than Plaid Cymru. Moreover, its performance compared well with the battering Labour received in the simultaneous

English local elections, under the shadow of the Iraq war. Many centre-left commentators held up the Welsh results as evidence that Labour could still win when it distanced itself from the right-wing domestic and international policies of Tony Blair and appealed to the progressive traditions of the labour movement. Subsequently, Welsh Labour has continued to pursue a policy agenda that diverges considerably from that of Westminster, particularly in health, education and the provision of public services in general.

The party activists who established Welsh Labour Grassroots (WLG) in 2003 saw the 'clear red water' speech, and the policies it described, as having created a significant opening for the left and centre-left within the party in Wales. Not only was there the increasingly reactionary agenda of Tony Blair to fight against; there was also now a progressive alternative with which one could engage positively, making the case for a more thoroughgoing socialist agenda. Rhodri Morgan and his ministers have however, been generally more muted in their public acknowledgement of their differences with the Labour leadership in London, usually explaining policy differences in purely pragmatic terms, related to the distinct culture or geography of Wales. Only in November 2006, with Assembly elections once again only six months away, did Morgan develop the 'clear red water' theme (in a speech discussed in chapter ten below), distancing Welsh Labour even more emphatically from the agenda followed in Westminster and setting out the contents of a specifically Welsh socialist project. While his own left-wing were cheered by this, the party's poor showing in the subsequent elections pushed the enthusiasts for the 'clear red water' onto the defensive.

Defending – and extending – the Welsh agenda

Although now somewhat overshadowed by the even more dramatic defeats of 2008, the May 2007 Assembly election results represented a historic setback for Welsh Labour, giving the party its lowest share of the vote in Wales since 1918 and leaving it five seats short of an overall majority in the Senedd. While there were undoubtedly some specifically Welsh factors at work, such as hospital reconfiguration, anecdotal evidence from canvassers strongly suggests that most defectors from Labour were casting their vote against the Westminster government, and the prime minister in particular. Thus – ironically – a resolutely non-Blairite administration was being punished by the electorate for the sins of Blairism, more than for any shortcomings in its own policies or performance. To some extent, this is unsurprising, given the far higher media profile accorded UK politics compared to Welsh issues, but it is a problem that has to be addressed if Wales is ever to break from the Westminster political cycle.

In the elections' aftermath, some within Welsh Labour sought to blame the 'clear red water' agenda for the party's electoral woes, arguing that it should offer policies more in line with those in England, and thereby appeal to more 'aspirational' voters in key marginals like Cardiff North. Subsequent local and by-election setbacks have, however, underlined the point that New Labour policies like foundation hospitals and city academies are by no means a guarantee of electoral success, even if they were right in principle. 'Appealing to the aspirational' is short-hand for a retreat to the (increasingly narrow) electoral 'middle-ground', seeking the votes of the assertive middle class and thereby abandoning policies based on far nobler aspirations like alleviating some of the worst poverty in Western Europe. It has, unfortunately, become a recurrent feature of Labour's political culture to respond to adversity by searching for short-cuts – rather than make the case for the policies we consider necessary to make a real difference.[3]

Rather than aping the New Labour project – which, at the time of writing, is looking more tarnished with each passing day – Welsh Labour should, we believe, be promoting its own policies within the British labour movement as a practical example of how a progressive administration can use its powers to make a positive difference. The defence of the political record in Wales will also be an important feature of the election to replace Rhodri Morgan on his forthcoming retirement. A revival of the debate that followed the Assembly elections still seems likely, despite the ever-decreasing credibility of arguments based on the electoral popularity of New Labour policies. Prospective Welsh leadership candidates will have to overcome the diffidence hitherto shown by most Labour AMs in discussing the ideological character of their policies and contrasting them with their English counterparts. A big part of our aim in writing this book has been to drive home the significance of the divergence in Labour governmental agendas under democratic devolution. Political debate about policy options cannot be restricted to the intelligentsia and the professional 'commentariat', however. In our view, Welsh Labour's 'clear red water' agenda can ultimately succeed only if it is based on the committed, determined support of activists within the Welsh labour movement and progressive civil society. Two immediate practical conclusions flow from this:

14

- First, such support has to be informed by a clear understanding of the progressive goals that these policies are seeking to achieve and how they differ from the agenda of New Labour; this in turn means an open, honest, accessible debate, engaging every level of the Welsh Labour party, the labour movement and ultimately Welsh civil society;

- Second, the outcome of such debates has to be expressed through democratic decision-making, freed from the bureaucratic obstructions that currently exist. Only through a lively, democratic political culture can Welsh Labour resist the control-freakery of New Labour and fight off any attempts to pull its leadership into line.

Beyond short-term politics

Our approach to politics is geared not to the electoral cycle but towards a long-term project aimed at the creation of a fairer, more equal society. Winning elections is never more than a means to an end; what really matters is our capacity to make a positive and lasting difference to people's lives. Notwithstanding the poor electoral showing that led to the present 'red-green' coalition in Cardiff, there are enormous opportunities represented by its radical programme – incorporating all of Welsh Labour's manifesto commitments – and its secure overall majority. It is because it presents such favourable conditions for effecting progressive change that WLG supported the establishment of the coalition, controversial as it was among many party members. And it is in large part for the same reason that we support the further development of the devolution project – including the plans for a referendum on primary powers – which are essential to enable Welsh Labour to put its policies into practice, without fear of a Westminster veto. As the electoral system we have in Wales might throw up an absolute majority only once every two or three elections, it is also necessary for Welsh Labour to abandon tribal 'party patriotism' and seek out allies among progressive forces, in order to be able to implement that agenda.

In this book, we attempt to develop these arguments in more detail, putting the current political situation in historical context and sketching some policy proposals for the left. Chapter two briefly recapitulates the major challenges facing the Assembly on its establishment in 1999. In chapter three, we evoke the radical inheritance of the Welsh labour movement. In chapter four we consider the project of democratic devolution from the unsuccessful referendum in 1979 to the victory eighteen years later and its aftermath, the devolution settlement and the new

Government of Wales Act. Chapter five examines at the Assembly's agenda for public services, looking at Welsh Labour's approach in the first two terms and the current *One Wales* programme. Chapter six deals with the economic infrastructure and the environment of Wales. In chapter seven, we consider the political implications of the diverse national community of Wales. In chapter eight we argue for a more open and accountable political culture within Welsh Labour. In chapter nine we identify the political forces most likely to aid or to obstruct us in the pursuit of democratic socialist policies. Chapter ten critically evaluates Welsh Labour's political perspectives, as set out by Rhodri Morgan, and goes on to situate Welsh politics within the broader global context and the battle for a more equitable and sustainable world order. Finally, the conclusion draws together the main themes of the book and underlines what is at stake in the future.

Chapter 2

The condition of Wales in 1999

As this book deals principally with what the Assembly has done, and what more it could do, to address Wales' many problems, it is worth reminding ourselves of the scale of the challenge that the new institution faced when it came into being on 12 May 1999.

A post-industrial economy
Economically, Wales was adjusting to the consequences of a long process of industrial decline, which had been accelerated in the 1980s and 1990s by recession and Thatcherism. The demise of heavy industry in Wales was as dramatic as had been its birth – both brought on by tectonic shifts in the world economy. Welsh iron had played a central part in the early and rapid industrialisation that confirmed Britain's international ascendancy during the nineteenth century; later, Welsh coal had proven vital to the maintenance of the imperial economy. These strategic assets ensured the intensive development of the coalfields and nearby towns and the establishment of a modern road and rail infrastructure serving these areas, while the rural hinterland was left to languish in undeveloped privation. The advantages conferred by Welsh industry's early start proved short-lived: outdated production techniques, international competition, the rise of alternative energy sources and an unfavourable exchange rate led in the interwar years to the collapse of the coal industry and the consequent devastation of the Welsh economy and society. The partial recovery prompted by the demands of a war economy after 1939 was consolidated by the post-war boom and state intervention to rationalise and diversify Welsh industry. Optimism about an economic

17

renaissance, with new industries and major infrastructural projects like the M4 and the Severn Bridge, began to peter out in the early 1970s, however, as the world recession of 1974–75 ushered in a long period of slow or negative growth, provoking distributional conflict between capital and labour and reducing the tax revenues available for public spending. Governments introduced swingeing budget cuts and sought to clamp down on workers' pay demands.

The Thatcher government, like the Reagan administration in the United States, took a particularly draconian approach, allowing 'uneconomical' firms go to the wall and generating high levels of unemployment in order to create a pool of surplus labour that would undermine union power and lower the wage bill. The state sector saw savage cutbacks and widespread privatisation. The resistance of key sections of the labour movement – in Wales, especially, the steelworkers and miners – was broken and a new economic regime, in which the free play of market forces was unhindered by 'restrictive practices', was established. By 1999, Welsh coal mining had been virtually obliterated by a government programme of pit closures – leaving Tower Colliery, bought-out by its workforce, as the only deep coal mine in Wales – while steel had undergone a massive contraction under public ownership, prior to its sell-off in 1988. Manufacturing industry in general had been devastated by the 1980–81 recession, causing massive economic hardship and social dislocation. Having fatally undermined the foundations of a way of life in the industrialised parts of Wales, the Tories had sought to recreate the country as a giant business park-cum-tourist resort. Thus, a recovery, of sorts, had been under way since the late 1980s, as Wales became a favoured location for foreign direct investment (FDI) in industries like electronics and electrical engineering, promoted by the Welsh Office and the Welsh Development Agency (WDA), while its mountains and coastline were heavily marketed by the Wales Tourist Board (WTB).

The quality of the new employment thus created was a matter of concern, however, with a predominance of low wage, low skill jobs in 'branch plant' factories and the lower end of the service sector. The new industries (whether under foreign or domestic ownership) were also generally less unionised than the old, required fewer skills and were less secure (for example, the hopes vested in the much-vaunted LG development in Newport began to recede after the South-East Asian financial crisis of 1998). Much was being made of the 'flourishing' small and medium enterprise (SME) sector, especially in 'hi-tech' industries and services, but the Welsh economy was increasingly reliant on state employment in health, education, social services and public administration, which by 1999 accounted for a higher proportion of the workforce than in any other UK region: 48 per cent of women and 23 per cent of men.[1] Moreover, while the official unemployment rate in Wales – twice the overall UK rate during the 1980s – had decreased to around the UK level, this disguised a major problem of 'hidden unemployment', with thousands claiming incapacity benefits rather than continue searching for non-existent jobs.

Poverty and social exclusion

There had been significant levels of poverty and deprivation in many parts of Wales even before the Thatcher era – testimony to the limits of the Keynesian welfare state and its regional policy – but eighteen years of Tory rule had enormously magnified these problems. While the 'green shoots' of the new economy emerged alongside the M4 and A55 corridors, large swathes of the country had been reduced to a wasteland. From Rhyl to the Rhondda, once-proud working class communities had been laid low by the 'restructuring' of the Welsh economy in the interests of capital and the withdrawal of the state from many of its previous functions aimed at promoting social cohesion. The closure of pits and factories in towns and villages lacking alternative sources of employment, the rollback of the welfare state, the depletion of the social housing stock (thanks largely to the mass sell-off of council houses), the underfunding of health services and the decay of social amenities – all contributed to a 'spiral of deprivation' described with passionate indignation by David Adamson:

> A generation of Welsh people are being born into social disadvantage which will ensure that they will underperform at school, be unemployed or work in marginalized and low-wage employment, will live in some of the poorest housing in Europe and be prone to disease and ill-health. If I were writing about the 1930s these claims would cause little surprise; writing in the 1990s, they are a national scandal.[2]

The spatial concentration of unemployment, poverty and deprivation turned isolated council estates into ghettoes, plagued by drug addiction and rising crime (the latter exacerbated by the Thatcherite promotion of possessive individualism in place of the collectivist values that had sustained communities through previous adversity). Rubbing salt into the wounds they had themselves inflicted, the Tories and their propagan-

19

dists in the media blamed the victims, excoriating a 'feckless' underclass of delinquents, dole scroungers and single mothers. As Adamson pointed out, the 'increase in lone-parent families is a symptom and not a cause of decay in working-class communities', as the unavailability of work and affordable housing 'effectively abolished traditional routes into adulthood', with significant consequences for the social behaviour of young working-class men.[3]

Amid the increasing social polarisation of the 1980s and 1990s, some parts of Wales – especially in the easternmost areas of the country – experienced growing prosperity, while at the other extreme, many communities endured the consequences of cumulative neglect and marginalisation. The challenge facing the Assembly in 1999, then, was not just to address the myriad manifestations of poverty – from low educational attainment to the prevalence of coronary heart disease – but to re-create the conditions for some sense of social solidarity and shared citizenship within the 'new Wales'.

The democratic deficit

The demand for an elected Assembly in the 1990s was fuelled not only by Wales' growing social and economic problems but also by a lack of democratic accountability that had become something of a scandal in its own right. With so little political representation in Wales, either at parliamentary or municipal level,[4] the Tories increasingly relied on a proliferation of quangos to run the country.[5] Administrative devolution prior to 1979 had already left Wales with a greater concentration of these bodies than any other part of the UK but the Tories doubled their number over the next twelve years, so that by 1991 there were 80 Welsh quangos, employing 57,311 people, with a combined budget of £1.8 billion. There were some 1,400 appointments in the gift of the Secretary of State and these were filled from a list of volunteers and nominees, rather than by open public advertisement and selection. Many of the plum jobs went to leading Conservatives, such as the former Welsh Office minister, Ian Grist, who lost his parliamentary seat in the 1992 general election, only to be made chief executive of South Glamorgan Health Authority.[6] Such blatant abuse of already objectionable patronage powers, together with high-profile malpractice on the part of the 'flagship' Welsh Development Agency (WDA) led to widespread calls for reform and a promise by Ron Davies, as Shadow Welsh Secretary, to carry out a 'bonfire of the quangos' once in office. This promise was fulfilled to only a limited extent after 1997, with a slight reduction in the number of

20

bodies and a partially more open approach to appointment – although some key positions were still filled without public advertisement.

If the establishment of the Assembly was to signal a genuine rebirth of democracy in Wales, then there was an urgent need to make a clean break with the remote and technocratic mode of governance that had characterised 'administrative devolution'. Popular scepticism about the capacity of *democratic* devolution to live up to its promise is evidenced by the fact that barely more than a quarter of the electorate had voted 'yes' on 18 September 1997. The Assembly had to demonstrate that decision-making would now be more transparent and accountable, that public services in Wales would become more accessible and responsive.

Nor was the democratic deficit in Wales evident only at the centre: Welsh local government had also acquired a reputation for conservatism, corruption and nepotism – not least in Labour's valleys strongholds, where decades of almost uninterrupted control by the party had fed a complacent, self-serving culture (a sad comedown from the heroic role Labour councils had played in the interwar depression, protecting their communities from starvation, and in helping to construct the post-war welfare state). A fresh spate of scandals over fraud and financial mal-practice had hit several of the new unitary authorities in the late 1990s and, as Kevin Morgan and Geoff Mungham point out:

> It was a rich coincidence that on the very day the Assembly opened for business the former leader of Blaenau Gwent, Bernard Assinder, was in court pleading guilty to fraud, provoking calls for the Assembly to launch 'a radical crackdown on town hall mismanagement'.[7]

Even those councils with a stronger commitment to serving their communities had been deprived of much of their power to effect positive change by the Tories, who had constrained their financial autonomy and transferred powers to central government and quangos.

Welsh democracy was also deficient in its capacity to represent the people of Wales. Only four women had sat for Welsh constituencies at Westminster between 1929 and 1997, and not more than two at any one time. As of 1997, there were four Welsh women MPs – an advance which could not have come about without Labour's introduction of all-women shortlists in three of the constituencies in question (provoking a furious backlash from reactionary elements within the party). At local government level, less than a fifth of all councillors were women. Only a handful of Welsh councillors, and not a single MP, were from ethnic minorities and councillors were more likely to be over 75 than under 45. The 1999 Assembly election, among other things, marked a huge step forward in the representation of women, who accounted for 24 of the 60 seats (again, largely due to positive action by Labour – this time in the form of 'twinning' constituencies to guarantee a woman candidate in half of them), but there were still no black or brown faces among the 60. One of the Assembly's most pressing priorities, then, was to rehabilitate public faith in the capacity of government and political action to effect positive change.

A new national mood
While the Assembly inherited major problems, it was also the potential beneficiary of a historic opportunity, in the shape of a major resurgence of national pride and self-confidence in Wales. A strong sense of Welsh identity, nurtured by the endurance of the Welsh language, had survived the country's political incorporation into the English realm in 1536 and had been rekindled in the eighteenth century by the development of modern nationalist ideas, influenced by the French and American revolutions.[8] The subsequent shift in Wales' relationship to the British state, from peripheral backwater to industrial engine-room, accompanied by a massive and sustained influx of labour – especially from England – began to weaken the distinctiveness of Welsh identity, at least in the country's most populous and developed areas. Even when Wales' prosperity began to falter, the collective aspirations of the most advanced sections of Welsh society (pre-eminently, the working class) were invested in the project of using the British state to effect progressive change, first through the Liberal party and then through Labour. Only in the 1960s, as the limits of Britain's post-war settlement became more evident, did Welsh national sentiment, expressed in political, cultural and linguistic terms, begin to find mass support. This movement seemed, however, to have run into the ground in 1979 when Wales voted 'no' in the first Assembly referendum. Still reeling from this defeat and from the subsequent Thatcherite onslaught, Gwyn Alf Williams in 1985 described the Welsh as 'a naked people under an acid rain',[9] yet in the years that followed, they were to display a remarkable resilience.

Perhaps the most striking manifestation of this was the turnaround in the fortunes of the Welsh language, as the rapid post-war decline in its use was arrested: the 1991 census showed a decrease of only 1.4 per cent over the previous ten years, compared to falls of 8.2 per cent, 17.3 per cent and 6.3 per cent over the preceding three decades, and significant increases in the number of children speaking Welsh, especially in the hitherto most Anglicised parts of the country. This trend had been bolstered by an increase in the number of Welsh-medium schools, a proliferation of Welsh-language publications and the establishment of S4C. This positive picture was mitigated somewhat by the continuing attenuation of the language in its traditional heartlands, as economic decline drove out native Welsh speakers, whose place was taken by monoglot English incomers, but overall there were grounds for optimism.[10] In addition, Welsh rock and pop music were, by 1999, enjoying an unprecedented popularity, with bands like Catatonia and the Manic Street Preachers topping the charts, prompting media references to 'cool Cymru' and descriptions of Newport as the 'new Seattle', and Welsh film and theatre were also experiencing a creative and popular resurgence.

The vote in favour of an Assembly in 1997, despite the wafer-thin margin, can itself be seen as a reflection of the growing mood of national assertiveness – especially when set against the debacle of eighteen years earlier. Moreover, the outcome of the first elections – a major upset for Labour, a huge boost for Plaid Cymru – demonstrated that devolved politics in Wales could not be assumed to follow a pre-set pattern. Largely, it represented a protest vote against New Labour, disillusionment with whose policies was becoming widespread, two years into the Blair Government. But it also reflected a degree of resentment at the attempt by New Labour to manage Welsh politics from Westminster, by imposing 'a safe pair of hands', Alun Michael, on the Welsh party, instead of the popular preference, Rhodri Morgan (of which, more below). And more generally, it showed that voters were willing to behave differently in Welsh elections, as compared to Westminster elections. It indicated, perhaps, an appreciation that democratic devolution provided an opportunity to find distinctive Welsh solutions to Welsh problems. The question was, what sort of social and political programme was best able to take advantage of that opportunity? In our view, it could only be a socialist one, based primarily on the labour movement. We therefore need to turn next to an examination of the Welsh labour movement and of its fitness to discharge this historic commission.

Chapter 3

The Welsh labour movement, from insurrection to pacification

The prospects for a viable socialist politics in Wales today owe a great deal to the legacy of radicalism bequeathed to us by the working-class and popular movements that have arisen in modern Welsh history. Over the course of a century during which industrial capitalism was at its most voracious, working people waged passionate struggles against injustice and exploitation. Bonds of solidarity were forged, which enabled communities to survive the most desperate adversity. Popular resistance against injustice was increasingly wedded to the vision of a more just society. Leaders emerged – from John Frost to Noah Ablett and Nye Bevan – who embodied and articulated the ideas and principles of the working-class communities from which they came.

These heroic traditions, however, represent only part of the story. The Welsh labour movement has always been a coalition within which more radical and more conservative elements have co-existed. Even in the early days of the Chartist movement, there was a wide spectrum of political views and preferred strategies; later, there was conflict within the trade unions between those like William Abraham ('Mabon'), who consistently sought compromise with the employers and those like Noah Ablett and AJ Cook who believed that class conflict was necessary and unavoidable if workers were to secure real improvements. In particular: from the point at which the labour movement began to secure real influence – around the time of the First World War – there was an increasing tendency for sections of the leadership to abandon the militant perspectives with which they had started out, to place respectability above radicalism and to counsel patience to their supporters, exhorting them to put their faith in gradual, piecemeal improvement secured through negotiation and compromise. The grassroots radicalism represented by the Chartists and the militants of the 'Fed' has, therefore, always been in tension with a more cautious, conservative outlook, which has been the dominant trend in the labour movement from the second half of the twentieth century.

Radicalism becomes more palatable, of course, with historical distance. Official and semi-official Labour histories are happy to lay claim to the heroic militancy of Wales' 'frontier years' but see this as the appropriate political response to circumstances that have long since been superseded, with the enhanced political rights, and greater economic security won by the working class after 1945. These accounts represent the more 'respectable' labour politics of the post-1945 period as having continued and conserved the earlier radical tradition. The battles for the welfare state and against fascism were, they suggest, the last popular mobilisations necessary. Whatever problems remain, they can be dealt more sedately by the political professionals. Yet, looking at the devastation inflicted on Wales by de-industrialisation and the vicious class warfare waged by the Tories, it is difficult to accept such a view. The Assembly government has taken significant steps to address Wales' most pressing social and economic problems but the task is immense, even without the limits imposed by the free market orthodoxy espoused by Thatcher and upheld by New Labour. It is our view that the past struggles of the Welsh working class need to be reclaimed and revived by the socialists of today – not entombed within museums. We share the concerns of the late, great Professor Gwyn Alf Williams, who wrote that the

Celebration of a Heroic Past … seems rarely to be brought to bear on vulgarly contemporary problems except in terms of a merely rhetorical style which absolves its fortunate possessors from the necessity of thought. This is not to encapsulate a past, it is to sterilize it. It is not to cultivate an historical consciousness; it is to eliminate it.[1]

Revolt on the industrial frontier

The first appearance of the Welsh working class as a political force followed closely on the rapid industrial development of parts of the country in the late eighteenth and early nineteenth centuries. In 1750, Wales was still an overwhelmingly agricultural nation, with the majority of the population scraping a living that was barely above subsistence level. There was some limited small-scale industry: coal and tinplate in the south and north-east, lead and copper in the west and flannel in Mid Wales. Iron was smelted, generally with charcoal, at a few scattered forges, mostly employing only a handful of workers. In the final decades of the eighteenth century, however, the development of a range of new industrial techniques, and the increased demand for iron and coal as a result of the wars with the American colonies and with France, created profitable investment opportunities for merchant capital. There was an explosion of the iron industry on the South Wales coalfield, which grew from fifteen furnaces with an annual output of 12,500 tonnes in 1788, to 122 furnaces producing 454,000 tonnes by 1839.[2] The industrialising areas of Glamorgan and Monmouthshire sucked in thousands of people from rural Wales, and from England and Ireland, turning peasants into proletarians and villages like Merthyr Tydfil into major towns. While the profits of industry created new dynasties like the Crawshays and Guests, who supplanted the landed gentry at the apex of Welsh society, the new working class was crowded into squalid housing, subjected to the vagaries of a fluctuating labour market and exposed to the evils of child labour and the truck system (whereby wages were paid in kind in over-priced company shops).

Early examples of industrial militancy bore a close resemblance to the kinds of popular unrest that Wales had frequently witnessed in pre-industrial times: 'natural justice' actions, which sought to right wrongs through mass mobilisation. The years, 1793–1801, during the wars with France, saw an upsurge in bread riots, as corn being held back for export or sale at an exorbitant price was seized and distributed by mobs of starving people.[3] In October 1816, a strike by ironworkers in Merthyr and Tredegar over rising bread prices and falling wages sparked several months of industrial unrest that spread throughout the South Wales coalfield and led to troops being brought in to prevent workers engaging in 'collective bargaining by riot'. Further strikes broke out in later years as employers cut wages in response to fluctuations in the iron trade. In both 1822 and 1830, Monmouthshire colliers and ironstone miners took effective direct action to prevent the movement of coal, winning some concessions from the employers as a result. The impressive co-ordination and discipline demonstrated during these strikes came not from any formal trade union body – since unions were outlawed under the Combination Acts until 1824 and remained heavily constrained even after that date – but from a secretive movement known as the 'Scotch Cattle'. Drawing on pre-industrial traditions of ritualised vigilante activity, the Cattle enforced workers' unity and resisted employers through nocturnal displays of force and intimidation. The Scotch Cattle's activities were primarily directed at the most immediate economic interests of their class – maintaining wage rates and protecting the secrets of their trade – but such concerns increasingly led to wider, and often overtly political conclusions, as is demonstrated by the fact that at least one of the Scotch Cattle's warning notes, dating from April 1832 – during the time of the crisis over the Parliamentary Reform Bill – carried the slogan, 'Reform'.

In Merthyr in May-June 1831, economic grievances and popular support for parliamentary reform gave rise to an insurrection which saw the red flag of revolution flown for the first time. Insurgent workers held the town for four days, while a panicking ruling class deployed troops to restore order and defend private property. Twenty-eight people identified as leaders of the rising were put on trial; four were transported to Australia, one – Richard Lewis, known as 'Dic Penderyn' – was executed on 13 August, as an example (which he became – but not in the way that the ruling class had intended). As Gwyn Alf Williams wrote, 'In Merthyr Tydfil in 1831 the prehistory of the Welsh working class comes to an end. Its history begins.'[4] He has demonstrated that radical ideas, inspired by the French Revolution, were circulating in the months before the rising. These found expression, to some extent, within the campaign for parliamentary reform but this was seen not simply as an end in itself but as a means of securing social and economic justice. While employers like William Crawshay of Cyfarthfa favoured an extension of the franchise, their actions at the workplace denied them any authority as leaders of a mass movement and the upsurge of popular militancy developed an independent working-class character. Within a month of the rising, the first Welsh branches of a colliers' union, affiliated to the National Association for the Protection of Labour, were formed.

The conviction that current grievances could best be redressed through fundamental political change came to fruition with the Chartist movement, which spread across much of Britain during the 1830s and

1840s, demanding real democracy. Chartism flourished in the South Wales coalfield, with dozens of lodges of the Working Men's Association established in the space of a few months in 1838–39.[5] While the movement embraced a wide spectrum of opinion, from relatively modest reformers to committed revolutionaries, it was the latter who took the lead early on in Wales, embracing the vision of a workers' republic. It was in Wales, too, that Chartism saw its most spectacular upsurge, with the abortive challenge to the state undertaken by some 5,000 Monmouthshire colliers and ironworkers who marched on Newport in November 1839, only to be dispersed when fired on by troops, leaving some two dozen dead. Their leaders, John Frost, Zephaniah Williams and William Lloyd Jones, were given death sentences, later commuted to transportation to Australia and, while Chartism survived in Wales into the 1860s, the revolutionary ambition of 1839 was increasingly dissipated.

The vision of a better society, in which working people would exercise democratic control over their own lives, lay dormant during the third quarter of the nineteenth century – the period of 'Mid-Victorian Prosperity'. Coal had supplanted iron as the dominant industry in the Welsh economy around the middle of the nineteenth century and for the next hundred years it was to make a vital contribution to the expansion of the British Empire. Renewed agitation for parliamentary reform, but under 'respectable', middle-class leadership, yielded an extension of the franchise in 1867 that gave the vote to a layer of skilled workers and a further extension in 1884 diffused democratic rights more widely again. These developments helped to bring the working class into an alliance that included progressive employers and the Nonconformist chapels, which cemented the hegemony of the Gladstonian Liberal party over Wales. While the Liberals held almost every constituency in Wales, industrial conflict sharpened and persuaded workers that they needed a voice of their own in Parliament. Initially, this took the form of a pressure group within Liberalism and it was as a 'Lib-Lab' that Wales' first working-class MP, William Abraham ('Mabon') – the pre-eminent leader of the South Wales miners – was elected for the Rhondda in 1885.

Mabon rose to prominence at a time when his policy of compromise with the employers – typified by the Sliding Scale, whereby wages were tied to the price of coal – seemed to provide an acceptable standard of living for the miners he represented. In the mid-1890s, however, a decline in trade led to repeated wage-reductions, prompting a bitter six-month strike and lock-out across the South Wales coalfield in April-

September 1898, which ended in defeat for the miners. This produced increasing demands for a more assertive approach, underpinned by tighter organisation, and thus led to the formation, out of the seven existing district unions, of the South Wales Miners' Federation (the SWMF, or 'Fed'), and its affiliation to the Mineworkers' Federation of Great Britain (MFGB). By 1906, Mabon – now SWMF president – had been joined in Parliament by the union's general secretary, Thomas Richards, and its vice-president, William Brace. Along with other MPs sponsored by the MFGB, they initially continued to take the Liberal whip; only in 1909 did the MFGB decide to affiliate to Labour. Even when Keir Hardie was elected for Merthyr Boroughs in 1900 – one of the first two MPs for the Labour Representation Committee (renamed the Labour party in 1906) – he did so with the tacit cooperation of the Liberals. The principal factor that convinced the miners and several other unions of the need for a working-class party was the Taff Vale Judgement of 1901, which gave employers the right to claim damages from unions to compensate them for lost revenue resulting from industrial action.

The growth of a mass movement

By this time, the gospel of socialism was being enthusiastically spread by a growing band of activists in the South Wales valleys and in parts of North Wales, challenging Liberal and 'Lib-Lab' hegemony. They addressed their message to a labour movement whose militancy had been reawakened by the 'new unionism', which began to displace the conciliatory and elitist craft unions from the late 1880s, recruiting unskilled and semi-skilled workers and challenging the employers. The Independent Labour Party (ILP) recruited strongly during the coal strike of 1898 and, while this proved to be a false start, by 1910 the ILP had more than 100 branches and two thousand members in South Wales and sixteen branches in North Wales. In places like Aberdare, where it held seven of the 20 seats on the Urban District Council, it formed something of an 'alternative society', as recent labour historians have shown:

> With its own institute, the party offered weekly meetings, regular concerts, an ILP Band of Hope, its own football team, annual teas, a children's Christmas party, education classes, numerous committee meetings and the chance to see famous figures such as Victor Grayson, the 'victor of Colne Valley' at the Market Hall. The ILP in Merthyr even had its own

tobacconist and newsagent, whilst the Swansea Socialist Society ran a shop and boot club.[6]

Trades and Labour Councils, which were spreading rapidly across Wales at this time, often took the lead in running Labour candidates in local and parliamentary elections, sometimes after local Liberal Associations had refused to adopt working-class candidates. Liberal hegemony was slow in receding, at least at a parliamentary level, although Labour gains in local government came more quickly in some areas: Abertillery had a Labour mayor as early as 1904 and a Labour majority on its Urban District Council by 1912; and the ILP provided the first two mayors of Merthyr Tydfil Borough Council.

The ideas of Liberalism, still cherished by leaders like Mabon, were also challenged on the industrial front, after the policy of conciliation with the employers was utterly discredited by the Cambrian Combine coal dispute of 1910–11, which saw running battles between rioting strikers and the army and police. In 1912, an 'Unofficial Reform Committee' of the SWMF, which included Noah Ablett, produced an influential book called *The Miners' Next Step*. This demanded that 'The old policy of identity of interest between employers and ourselves be abolished, and a new policy of open hostility be installed' and called for the union to be transformed into a revolutionary organisation, which could overthrow the coalowners and take direct control of the industry. While the ultimate aims of *The Miners' Next Step* remained unfulfilled, a new leadership took the 'Fed' in a more militant direction and many of the book's ideas were adopted by the Communist party – established in 1920 – which was to enjoy steadily increasing influence on the South Wales coalfield.

The catastrophe of the First World War transformed the political landscape in Wales – as it did everywhere – finally ending Liberal domination to the benefit of Labour (although, ironically, it was the Labour leadership's active support for the war effort that, for many, granted it the 'respectability' that assisted its electoral breakthrough). From 1919, Labour began to win control of an increasing number of county, borough and district councils, establishing its dominance of local government throughout the South Wales coalfield by the end of the 1920s. In the 1922 general election, the party won a plurality of seats in Wales for the first time – an achievement it has maintained in every subsequent election (indeed, since 1945 it has consistently won an absolute majority of Welsh seats). Two years later, In January 1924, the first (minority)

Labour government was formed under Ramsay MacDonald, who then represented the constituency of Aberavon. Although this was not to prove the instant breakthrough that the party had hoped for, in Wales, at least, it was able to maintain and steadily consolidate its base through all the vicissitudes of the interwar years. Even in 1931, when the Labour vote collapsed across Britain after MacDonald split the party by forming a Tory-dominated 'National' coalition, Labour's vote in Wales actually *increased* from 41 per cent to 47 per cent and Wales accounted for a third of all the Labour MPs returned.

These were years of heightened class conflict, especially across the South Wales coalfield – but also in the North Wales slate industry, where the quarrymen fought a bitter three-year lockout. The ferocious struggle that had beset the coal industry before 1914 resumed soon after the war, when the Government refused to act on the Sankey Commission's recommendation that the industry be nationalised. It reached a climax in 1926 with the General Strike and subsequent lock-out; afterwards, the coal-owners did their best to drive home their advantage and smash the 'Fed'. They sponsored the establishment of a rival 'non-political' (i.e. scab) union, the SWMIU, sparking a battle for the loyalty of the work-force that lasted more than a decade. Meanwhile, the Depression brought the scourge of long-term mass unemployment to Wales: the unemployment rate remained between a quarter and a third of the working population until the Second World War. Around half a million people – a fifth of the population – left Wales and it was only in 1961 that the Welsh population returned to its 1921 level.

But these years also saw evidence of a remarkable resilience and a willingness to fight, as whole communities were mobilised in a struggle with the employers and the state, their unions – especially the 'Fed' – in the vanguard. In February 1935, some 300,000 people in the South Wales valleys marched and demonstrated against draconian changes to the already degrading Means Test for unemployment assistance, in a campaign that forced an immediate Government climbdown. The following year, Franco's rebellion in Spain prompted the international solidarity effort that saw hundreds of Welsh miners join the fight against fascism. The Communist Party, which had established a firm base in the Rhondda and many other parts of Wales, frequently played a leading role in these events, as did the ILP, which by this stage had disaffiliated from the Labour party. Individual Labour activists were also often involved but the party leadership often held aloof, both in order to establish its respectability and because it sought to counter the influence of the CP over its own supporters. The CP's call for a 'Popular Front' against fascism was rejected by the Labour leadership and many of those who continued to make common cause with the Communists were expelled.

Throughout these years, the Welsh working class was at the leading edge of the struggle for a better society. The Second World War, however, precipitated a more generalised popular radicalism, fuelled by a determination to build a new society that would not fall prey, once again, to depression, fascism and world war. People throughout Wales – and across Britain – invested their hopes in the prospect of a majority Labour government beginning the construction of a socialist society. The landslide election victory in July 1945 seemed to promise that the New Jerusalem was indeed at hand and Wales was prominently represented in the new government, with Nye Bevan as Minister of Health and Jim Griffiths as Minister of National Insurance.

The New Jerusalem?

The achievements of the 1945 government represent the high-water mark of Labour in office; they are the standard against which all subsequent policies have been judged. The National Health Service (NHS) and the National Insurance system were established and much of the fuel and power and transport industries were nationalised, along with iron and steel and the Bank of England. There was a massive expansion of both education and housing and the Tories' 1927 restrictions on trade union rights were reversed. There is a danger, however, of mythologising this government; it is necessary to take into account the circumstances which allowed it to do what it did, and to consider how much more it might have achieved. The war had established a precedent of state intervention in the economy, making it easier for this to continue when hostilities had ceased. There was little resistance to most of the nationalisations – these were failing industries, even on their own terms, and the former owners received compensation that was extremely generous. Although there was certainly a degree of ideological inspiration in the government's choices – and some nationalisations of profitable private concerns (particularly iron and steel) were pursued against the opposition of the capitalists – in general, these policies should be seen as the reconstruction and strengthening of capitalism, rather than the first steps towards socialism. By 1948, almost all the major measures had been taken and the last three years can be seen as a missed opportunity (worse, in some respects – the Government took part in the Korean War, with only a tiny minority of backbench MPs – including Merthyr's S.O. Davies – offering consistent opposition).

Nevertheless, there were major achievements, which proved enormously beneficial to the working class in Labour's industrial heartlands – not least Wales – which had been devastated by the Depression. The nationalisation of the coal industry, which took effect on 1 January 1947, represented the fulfilment of the dream of many generations of Welsh miners, who had long sought the expropriation of the rapacious coal-owners, allowing the industry to be run in the interests of the community as a whole, with the active involvement of the workforce. Nationalisation in practice proved not to be the quite the revolutionary act that many had hoped for, however. The compensation left the former owners better off than if they had retained their assets and lumbered the industry with huge debts that were later held up as an example of the inherent unprofitability of public ownership. Senior executive and managerial positions were given to men associated with private industry and finance – in Wales, mainly to managers from the hated Powell Duffryn Group – who set about running the industry, unsurprisingly, according to strictly business criteria. Any idea of introducing workers' control or industrial democracy was rejected as 'impracticable'. Instead, nationalisation followed the so-called 'Morrisonian' model (after Herbert Morrison): heavily centralised and bureaucratic.

The top-down organisation of the new nationalised industries reflected the organisation of British and Welsh society after 1945. The Attlee governments had established a new settlement in the social, political and economic governance of the country – one which Conservative governments left largely undisturbed until after 1979. It was certainly a more humane and equitable state of affairs than the one which had preceded it but the corollary of the introduction of social reform by central government was the political demobilisation of the organised working class. Any ambitions for the construction of a socialist society were now to be channelled through parliamentary and electoral means. The ordinary workers had to trust the leaders and not take matters in to their own hands. By way of illustration, there is the case of Ness Edwards, one of the outstanding leaders of the Welsh labour movement. He was schooled in Marxism at the Central Labour College and influenced by the politics of *The Miners' Next Step*; in the 1920s he wrote the first political history of the Welsh working class; he was a miner's agent who played a key role in the battle against scab unionism in the 1930s; he became a Labour councillor and, from 1939 until his death in 1968, was

MP for Caerphilly. Yet, in the 1950s, he attacked miners for taking strike action – under a Tory government – on the grounds that they were undermining a nationalised industry.[7]

In the 1950s and 1960s, even while Labour remained out of office in Westminster for thirteen years, the upper echelons of the Welsh labour movement increasingly took on the character of a new establishment. The party consolidated its control of the municipal strongholds that it had begun to capture in the interwar period and never held fewer than 27 of Wales' 36 parliamentary seats. As the academic, Ian McAllister, has pointed out, however, prolonged electoral dominance provides little incentive to maintain efficient party organisation, except as a ladder to public office for the select few. Many CLPs – including some of those in staunch Labour areas – allowed their membership levels and political culture to stagnate. After 1963, the party ceased publishing individual membership figures for Wales, after repeated exhortations from national officials had failed to redress falling recruitment levels.[8] The party and trade union leadership in Wales became increasingly ossified and conservative; even when, during the 1950s, a Welshman – Aneurin Bevan – was the party's most inspirational figure and the undisputed leader of the parliamentary left, there was not a single Welsh MP among the remainder of the 'Bevanite' group (although the Merthyr MP, S.O. Davies, was to the group's left). As Gwyn Alf Williams wrote:

> The Labour hegemony in Wales had hardened into an oligarchy. Social democracy had become a recognised career structure in the life-cycle of able and ambitious Welsh people. … [T]he party was degenerating into a vote-winning machine which came to political life only during elections; inbetween times it appeared to many to be simply a caucus of power-brokers.[9]

In 1966, Labour had its best-ever election performance in Wales, winning 32 of the 36 seats and 61 per cent of the vote. Yet discontent with the party's regime in Wales was about to make itself felt in a series of shock by-election results, as Plaid Cymru captured Carmarthen and came an uncomfortably close second in both Rhondda West and Caerphilly – right in Labour's 'heartland'. The death in 1972 of S.O. Davies – who had retained his seat as an independent two years earlier, after being deselected by Labour – symbolised the decline of the Welsh radical tradition of the first half of the twentieth century. The bulk of Welsh Labour MPs were increasingly visionless placemen (and they were, indeed, all men[10]) content to rely on huge majorities and a relatively conservative trade union machine.

The Labour and trade union structures had become part of the establishment in Wales, at a time when young people, in particular, were increasingly challenging the status quo and throwing themselves into campaigns that broke free of established party politics: the movements for women's liberation, for gay rights, for defence of the environment; the campaigns against nuclear weapons and in solidarity with the victims of oppression and war around the world. In Wales, too, the Welsh Language Society (Cymdeithas yr Iaith Gymraeg) mobilised thousands of young people in a passionate defence of the right to use Welsh, carrying out a long-running programme of non-violent direct action that saw hundreds jailed.

From the late 1960s, this upsurge in radicalism began to filter through to the Labour party, to an extent, as the party saw an influx of activists from white-collar jobs which had become increasingly proletarianised, and especially from the rapidly-expanding state sector. Many had been radicalised through student politics – in particular, the campaigns against apartheid and the Vietnam War. It was principally from this quarter that the demand came for democratisation of the party, as embodied in the Campaign for Labour Party Democracy (CLPD), established in 1973 in response to disillusionment with the Wilson governments of 1964–70. This movement was always strongest in the big cities, however, and made less of an impression in Wales (outside Cardiff) than in other parts of Britain. It was to reach its apogee after the decline and defeat of the Callaghan government, with Tony Benn's 1981 deputy leadership bid – a contest in which most Welsh MPs voted for Benn's right-wing opponent, Denis Healey.

The limits of Labourism

By the time that Labour left office in May 1979, the party had ruled Britain for exactly half of the 34 years since the end of the Second World War and had maintained its ascendancy over Welsh parliamentary politics throughout the whole of that period. Notwithstanding a few recent upsets, it had dominated local government in South Wales and the more industrialised parts of North Wales since the 1920s. The policy agenda inaugurated by the Attlee Government had sought to banish Beveridge's 'five giants' of idleness, ignorance, disease, squalor and want and to organise the country's 'material resources ... in the service of the British people.' The party formed by the working class to pursue its interests had set out to address the injustices against which the Welsh workers had periodically revolted over the course of the previous century. While revolutionaries from the Chartists to the syndicalists of the 'Fed' had sought to advance their aims by direct action, Labour had secured mass support for its strategy of patient electoral advance towards the policy-making citadels of the British state.

By 1979, life for the majority of people in Wales was certainly more comfortable and secure than it had been in the pre-war period. The welfare state had provided a safety net that precluded any return of the outright destitution experienced in the 1920s and 1930s. The state now routinely intervened in the economy, both by the use of Keynesian demand management to moderate the effects of the trade cycle and through the deployment of a battery of regional policy measures to promote economic regeneration in Wales. But all this did not add up to the Welsh working class having secured control over their lives, even at one remove, through the Labour party. Inequality still blighted Wales in 1979 – both relative to England and internally, with areas of severe poverty. Average household income was lower in Wales than in any region except Northern Ireland and Wales was more heavily dependent on social security than any other part of the UK. Around a third of the Welsh population suffered inadequate housing. More than a quarter of all school-leavers had no qualifications at all – a far higher proportion than in any other part of Britain. The death rate (the number of deaths within a given period, as a proportion of the overall population) was 10 per cent higher than for England and Wales combined – a disparity that had remained unchanged since before the foundation of the NHS – and the disparity in mortality rates between different social classes within Wales had actually increased. Deaths through industrial accidents were much higher and expenditure on sickness, injury, invalidity and disablement benefits was much higher than in any English region.[11] On every measure, the patterns of poverty and inequality reflected the uneven development of the Welsh economy.

Industrialisation had taken place in Wales in a partial and uneven way, in response to the requirements of a capitalist economy that needed its raw materials and its labour; the motive force was profit: investment and disinvestment alike were driven by the enrichment of a few, not by any consideration of the interests of the people as a whole. This did not fundamentally change after nationalisation: the industries were run according to essentially the same criteria as they had been under private ownership. Thus, when the markets for coal and steel determined that production was no longer profitable on the same scale as hitherto, pits and steelworks were closed. This applied as much to Labour, as to Tory governments: the first Wilson period (1964–70) saw the greatest contraction of the coal industry between nationalisation and the Thatcher years, with 34 collieries shut in South Wales – reducing the workforce by 47 per cent – and three of the six North Wales pits also shut. As Ben Curtis has argued, these measures were a response to short-term market conditions, based on a 'cheap energy' policy that exaggerated both the 'obsolescence' of coal and the potential of alternative fuel sources and stored up greater problems for the future.[12]

Alongside this 'rationalisation', state involvement in the post-war restructuring of the Welsh economy also took more positive forms, with measures to promote the growth of manufacturing and services to offset the reduction of jobs in coal and steel. Nationalised concerns and government offices were sited in Wales, the transport infrastructure was expanded and incentives were provided to attract private investment. These policies, however, produced new patterns of inequality. In South Wales, most of the new investment was concentrated in the towns of the valley mouths or the coastal plain, rather than in the same areas from which mining jobs, in particular, had been lost. This contributed to the decline of these older industrial areas, as those who were able to relocate – mostly younger people – did so. The new employment was generally less skilled than the work that had disappeared and it largely took the form of a massive growth in female employment, rather than the re-employment of redundant miners. Similarly, in rural Wales, the state promoted the establishment of new industrial plant to compensate for jobs lost through the 'rationalisation' of agriculture and the decline of the slate industry. However, much of this new plant came from capital-intensive sectors like the oil, nuclear and water industries, offering relatively little long-term employment opportunity after the construction phase and often bringing environmental problems. New factories often represented satellite extensions of a core enterprise located outside Wales and saw management and skilled workers being brought into the area, leaving only low-paid, low-skill work for the local population. Likewise, state promotion of tourism gave rise to mainly seasonal, low-paid employment, while also putting additional pressure on thinly-stretched local services.[13]

At best, then, state intervention in the Welsh economy after the Second World War did no more than ameliorate the workings of capitalism, rather than challenge its basic logic. Still less did it establish a new structure of power in Welsh society, in which working people were able to exercise any meaningful degree of collective authority. While it was incomparably more benevolent than what was to come after 1979, the Labour version of welfare capitalism had a paternalist, almost authoritarian character. Workers and communities which had once taken their destiny in their own hands were encouraged to rely on 'their' representatives in the political establishment to ensure that the state provided for them. They had not built durable institutions of their own, other than the trade unions, and the latter were thrown on the defensive by the restructuring of the Welsh economy that took place from the 1950s. Notwithstanding the determined resistance offered by the miners' strikes of 1972 and 1974, the unions' general response was to put their faith in Labour's intermittent stewardship of the British state to protect the interests of their members and communities. By the late 1970s, however, that state could – or would – no longer deliver the goods. Meanwhile, the working class had been quietly disarmed and was left exposed when the Thatcherite onslaught began after 1979. As Wales was subjected to the full impact of the 'free market', there was increasing support for some degree of democratic devolution, if only as a bulwark against the further destruction of the country's social fabric.

Chapter 4

Democratic devolution: the long and winding road

With the National Assembly now well into its third term, it is already becoming easy to forget the tortuous journey by which democratic devolution arrived in Wales. In the referendum held on St David's Day in 1979, Welsh voters rejected the proposal of an elected Assembly by a majority of four to one. Even in the north-west of Wales, the 'yes' vote was only 22 per cent. In Gwent it was a pitiful seven per cent. Among those mobilising the anti-devolution forces was the ambitious young Labour MP for Bedwellty, Neil Kinnock, who fulminated:

> We do not need an Assembly to prove our nationality or our pride. That is a matter of hearts and minds, not bricks, committees and bureaucrats.[1]

Kinnock was expressing views that had been commonplace within a significant section of the labour movement – and especially its leadership – for many years.

Such views had not, however, consistently enjoyed widespread currency in the movement; nor would they always continue to do so. Similarly, national sentiment of a politically assertive kind had continuously ebbed and flowed among the Welsh populace since the defeat of Owain Glyn Dŵr's military challenge to the English crown in the early fifteenth century. At times, prevailing opinion in Wales had been reconciled to a subordinate position in the English (later, *British*) state – as when the ascent to the throne of Henry Tudor brought Welsh nobles

39

unprecedented status and influence in the English court. Between 1536 and 1543, Wales was formally absorbed into the legal and governmental systems of England and the Welsh language was stripped of any official status. In the Civil War of the 1640s, Wales was, for the most part, a royalist stronghold. 150 years later, however – as the industrial revolution began to transform Welsh society – modern, *bourgeois* nationalist ideas, inspired by the French and American revolutions, began to take root in Wales. A high-water-mark was reached in the 1890s, not to be surpassed for 70 or 80 years, with the rise of Cymru Fydd (Young Wales), the political expression of a national community united by religious Nonconformity, political Liberalism and the Welsh language. The principal aim was not political devolution but disestablishment of the Anglican Church in Wales, eventually achieved in 1920.

The embrace of British labourism

Cymru Fydd was comparatively weak in industrial South Wales, where different concerns and priorities were coming to the fore. Nevertheless, the claims of Wales were still important to the Labour party in its early years: the party was committed to Welsh devolution and Keir Hardie was one of its most passionate advocates. Yet, when Labour formed its first majority government in the 1940s, the party leadership refused even to introduce a Secretary of State for Wales, despite the latter having been unanimously endorsed by the conference of the South Wales Regional Council of Labour. The most the Government was prepared to concede was a toothless, nominated advisory body, the Council for Wales & Monmouthshire. When the Parliament for Wales Campaign was launched in 1950, it could count only five Welsh Labour MPs among its supporters. One of these – Merthyr's S.O. Davies – sought to introduce a parliament by means of a private member's bill in 1955 but this was heavily defeated, its supporters harassed and vilified by the Labour establishment.[2] In 1959 the party finally committed itself to introduce a Secretary of State, which it duly did on being elected five years later – in the person, initially, of Jim Griffiths. This did not, however, settle the matter of Wales' relationship to the UK. During the 1960s, there was a revival of Welsh nationalism – which saw the emergence of Plaid Cymru as a serious political force – to a large extent, as a reaction against Labour's conservatism on the national question. By the late 1960s, in response to the growing challenge of Scottish and Welsh nationalism, the Government felt obliged to reopen the whole question of the British constitution, setting up the Kilbrandon Commission. The group set up by Welsh Labour to provide evidence to the Commission recommended a 72-member legislative assembly; this was opposed, however, by a majority of the party's Welsh MPs, who continued to hold out against legislative devolution throughout the 1970s as the policy found increasing support at successive party conferences, as well as from the (recently-established) Wales TUC and all the major unions. While most Welsh Labour MPs ultimately supported party policy, however reluctantly, when the referendum took place, a vociferous minority – including Leo Abse and Donald Anderson, as well as Kinnock – mounted an effective opposition campaign and undoubtedly spoke for a large section of the labour movement and Welsh society.

The 1979 devolution proposals were the classic example of a compromise that pleased no one, exciting little enthusiasm even among those who campaigned for a 'yes' vote. Yet the ferocity with which the likes of Kinnock denounced devolution and the level of support that the 'no' camp won within the labour movement can clearly not be attributed to general indifference or mild disdain. Two major factors help to explain Labour antipathy towards devolution. The first relates to political identity: by the middle of the twentieth century, national and class consciousness had significantly diverged. The emergent Welsh working class movement in the 'frontier years' of the nineteenth century had been united by a common language – Welsh – that also divided workers from their (mostly English) employers. This labour movement was defeated – by military force at Newport in 1839, and afterwards by slow attrition. When its successor emerged towards the end of the nineteenth century, it was much more integrated into the British labour movement, both politically and industrially. The new working-class political culture that developed reflected the fact that a new urban-industrial society had been created in Glamorgan and Monmouthshire, with English increasingly the *lingua franca* of its nationally and ethnically diverse workforce. This in turn contributed to a widening cultural divide between industrialised South Wales and the more conservative rural parts of the country to the north and west, where the Welsh language and the sense of Welsh nationhood remained strong. For militant South Walian socialists like Nye Bevan and Ness Edwards, their loyalty was to the working class, and that class could best achieve its objectives by building the maximum unity, across national boundaries. In this scheme of things, the idea that Welsh nationhood might retain any political saliency was seen as divisive and anachronistic.[3] Conversely, most of the unashamed Welsh patriots in the party who supported devolution – at least in Parliament – were from the rural north and west of Wales and had political views that would not have been out of place in the Liberal party 50 years before. S.O. Davies was unusual in combining class-conscious militancy with a passionate commitment to Welsh self-government.

The second factor is the attitude of the Welsh Labour political leadership to the British state. Whereas the earliest leaders of the Welsh working class saw the state as the instrument of the employers and their allies, the growing electoral success of the Labour party – and particularly its experience running both local and central government during the 1920s – promoted the idea that state institutions could be used by the labour movement to secure its political objectives. For the more militant Labour leaders, like Nye Bevan, this did not imply any watering-down of their goals: the class-struggle would simply be played out in Parliament, as it was in the workplace and in society at large. Others, however, became more fully incorporated into the world of Westminster politics, accepting its prevailing standards and values. Their very presence in the House of Commons reassured them that parliamentary politics could address the aspirations of the workers, rendering other forms of political struggle redundant. All that was necessary was to 'play the game' and use the structures and processes of government – however cumbersome they might appear – to secure benefits for their constituency at home. The latter, meanwhile, had to wait patiently for their leaders to deliver the goods; to do otherwise would jeopardise Labour's respectability and undermine the legitimacy of its goals.

To this way of thinking, the establishment of a Welsh Parliament or Assembly would have been, at best, an unnecessary distraction; at worst, it might have dissipated the beneficial influence over policy-making that had carefully been established by Wales' Labour MPs (to put it a little less charitably, it might have diminished their own status and authority). For many Welsh MPs, Wales hardly existed as a political entity: their work took place either in their own constituencies or in Westminster and there was nothing in between. (By way of illustration: the average number of Welsh Labour MPs – out of a total of 27 or more – who attended the party's annual Welsh conference between 1950 and 1964 was six.[4])

The impact of Thatcherism

This attitude is more comprehensible in the context of the long postwar boom, which saw virtual full employment and provided the economic basis for an expansive, interventionist state. The chaotic and destructive impulses of capitalism, which had caused such misery between the wars, appeared to many to have been reined in by rational planning and intervention. Policies implemented from London were protecting the security and wellbeing of the Welsh people; a Welsh government would have lacked the leverage necessary to subject the capitalist economy to social control.

Such complacency about the benevolent character of the constitutional *status quo* was shattered by what happened after Margaret Thatcher entered Downing Street, only two months after the Welsh people had rejected devolution. The Tories' slash-and-burn attack on the British economy devastated Wales. Between June 1980 and June 1982 alone, the official working population fell by 106,000. There were heavy losses in chemicals, engineering, manufacturing and textiles but the hardest hit industry was steel, which had already lost 20,000 jobs in Wales during the 1970s. In December 1979, with a pay dispute already under way, management announced swingeing 'rationalisation' plans that threatened half of the remaining Welsh steel jobs, and which also had serious implications for the beleaguered coal industry. Plans by the unions in Wales to broaden the pay strike to encompass the defence of jobs, and to bring in the miners and transport workers, were scuppered by a lack of support from the TUC and individual unions' British leaderships and by the willingness of British Steel to offer substantial redundancy payments. The cuts went ahead and by 1983 the Welsh steel industry employed barely 19,000 workers, compared to nearly 66,000 ten years earlier. By this time, the total working population in Wales was a mere 882,000, down from 1,022,000 in 1979.[5] At the same time, public spending was massively cut back and much of the state sector privatised.

In tandem with the attacks on jobs and services was the assault on trade union rights, as the Tory government introduced a series of laws reducing workers' ability to defend themselves. The decisive moment in the trial of strength between the classes proved to be the defeat of the miners in the great strike of 1984–85, which cleared the way for the obliteration of the once-mighty Welsh mining industry by the early 1990s. Before the strike there were some 22,000 miners in Wales; ten years later, there was less than a tenth of that number. As the industrial heart of the Welsh economy was torn away, the country was blighted with mass unemployment. A lost generation of young people grew up never knowing regular work. Tens of thousands of former manual workers were thrown on the scrap heap in middle age. Wales was forced to endure some of the worst poverty in Western Europe, manifested, for example, as sub-standard housing, low educational attainment and chronic ill-health.

A national response

In many respects, the experience of Wales under the Thatcher and Major governments was little different from other parts of Britain, such as Merseyside or the North-East of England. The whole British economy underwent a painful restructuring which, in regional terms, primarily benefited the south-east of England. What was different in Wales, as in Scotland, was that there was a specifically *national* response to this process. A revival in national sentiment in Wales had already begun in the 1960s, in reaction to the conservatism and complacency of the Labour-dominated establishment and to national slights like the drowning of the Welsh-speaking community of Tryweryn in Merioneth to provide a reservoir for Liverpool. With the decline and 'rationalisation' of Wales' heavy industry under way, and widespread disappointment with the Wilson and Callaghan governments, there was diminishing faith in the idea that policies drawn up in London could deliver prosperity and social justice to the people of Wales. Welsh economic development, based as it was on centrally-run nationalised industries, tourism and low-wage, low-skill 'screwdriver assembly plants', and concentrated along the M4 and A55 corridors, appeared to be primarily for the benefit of England, or of multinational capital.

This lack of confidence in English solutions to Wales' economic problems dovetailed with the political demands of a resurgent Welsh nationalism, exemplified by the establishment of the Welsh Language society, Cymdeithas yr Iaith Gymraeg and the rise of Plaid Cymru as an electoral force. More than 40 years after the establishment of the Welsh Nationalist Party (as it was originally called), Gwynfor Evans captured the party's first parliamentary seat in the Carmarthen by-election of June 1966, and Plaid came close to winning both Rhondda West and Caerphilly over the next two years. By October 1974, the party had three MPs, having won 166,000 votes – nearly 11 per cent of the total Welsh poll – in that month's elections. Two years later, it took control of Merthyr and Rhymney councils, demonstrating that it could win in the south as well as the north and west.

A false start

Well beyond the nationalist movement, support for Welsh autonomy was growing rapidly by the early 1970s. In the trade union movement, this gave rise to the establishment, after a long struggle, of the Wales TUC in 1974. In the Labour party, as we have seen, it was reflected by the steadily increasing support for a Welsh Assembly. The lost devolution vote of 1979 has to be seen, then, as something of a false start. While support for self-government was already on the rise, it was not yet strong enough to overcome the cumulative influence of centralism, conservatism and cultural alienation from the idea of Welsh nationhood. It took the experience of Thatcherism to produce sufficient recognition that Wales needed a democratic and accountable political regime of its own.

Although the 1979 general election gave the Tories them their best result in Wales for 50 years – 32 per cent of the Welsh vote and 11 seats – this revival was to prove short-lived: by 1992 they had been driven back to the coasts and borders and five years later Wales became, in parliamentary terms, a Tory-free zone. Throughout eighteen years of Tory rule, Wales consistently voted overwhelmingly for the non-Tory parties and returned a majority of Labour MPs. This reflected the country's radical and egalitarian political traditions but also the lack of a real social foundation in Wales for Thatcherism, which was based economically on finance capital and the service sector and on the property-owning, share-holding floating voter. Yet, despite the minority status of Welsh Conservatism, the absence of any all-Wales tier of government left the country unprotected against the onslaught of 'free-market' policies. The problem was summed up by a famous piece of graffiti on a railway bridge in Ron Davies' Caerphilly constituency: 'We voted Labour – we got Thatcher'.

The lesson was driven home by the increasing contempt shown by the Tories for the Welsh people in the way that they governed Wales. This was evident in the choice of politicians chosen to serve as Welsh Secretary, as 'one-nation' patricians like Peter Walker gave way to free-market zealots like John Redwood. And it was even clearer in the government's growing reliance on the 'quango state': doubling the number of unaccountable public bodies by which Wales was administered, stuffing them with time-servers qualified only by their loyalty to the Conservative party and allowing them to run amok with public money, culminating in the discovery in December 1992 of gross financial malpractice by the 'flagship' (WDA).[6] In the face of such misrule from the centre, the case for democratic self-government in Wales became ever more appealing.

Devolution back on the agenda

The growing popular support for democratic devolution bore fruit only gradually in Wales, and in the shadow of a much stronger campaign in Scotland, fuelled by mass unemployment, the use of North Sea oil revenues to featherbed the south of England through two recessions, the treatment of Scotland as a testing ground for the hated poll tax and the electoral success of the Scottish National Party. Scottish national consciousness had always been more developed than that in Wales, reflecting Scotland's existence as an independent state as recently as 1707, and the retention of a number of trappings of statehood, particularly its own legal and education systems. Thus, there was a lively and robust campaign for devolution involving every layer of Scottish society. Labour's proposals for the Scottish Parliament were developed jointly with the Liberal Democrats, the trade unions, the churches and a number of community organisations, through a 'constitutional convention'.

In Wales, however, Labour rejected a Wales TUC conference resolution in support of a Welsh constitutional convention and produced a cautious and tentative set of proposals for an Assembly – initially in the context of plans for local government reform. While Scotland was, by 1995, promised a full parliament with primary legislative and tax-raising powers, elected by proportional representation and providing for gender balance, the proposed Welsh Assembly was only to inherit the administrative powers of the Welsh Office, along with the block grant allocated to Wales by Westminster. The efforts of Labour's most dedicated devolutionists – who formed the pressure group, Welsh Labour Action – together with the personal commitment of Ron Davies, who was to become Welsh Secretary in 1997, secured important concessions: the commitment to introduce some form of electoral proportionality and to 'twin' constituencies for candidate selection purposes, thus ensuring a female candidate in 50 per cent of seats. Scottish-style parliamentary powers were not, however, to be forthcoming.

The campaign for a 'yes' vote was led by a progressive alliance that temporarily brought together Labour, Plaid, the Liberal Democrats and the unions, in a joint effort to convince the people of Wales of the benefits of self-government, in however limited a form. The outcome of the referendum, on 18 September 1997 was nail-bitingly close, however. The margin in favour was 0.6 per cent, or 6,721 votes, on a turnout of only 50 per cent. It was up to the pro-Assembly forces to do their best to win over the sceptics and ensure that the Assembly could deliver real, material benefits to the people of Wales.

Government by remote control

However, such hopes received a body blow in October 1998 when Ron Davies was forced to resign, shortly after piloting the Government of Wales Act through Parliament, following the 'Clapham Common' incident. He was replaced as Welsh Secretary by Alun Michael, a Blair loyalist, who subsequently became Labour's candidate for leader of the Assembly, following a ham-fisted operation by the New Labour bunker and its Cardiff satellite, in defiance of majority opinion within the Welsh labour movement. Michael had shown no interest in devolution since 1979 and had not sought to be a candidate; the selection process had to be reopened for his benefit. He was placed as Labour's number one candidate on the Mid and West Wales regional list – the party's best chance of a 'top-up' seat under the additional member system. The timing and other arrangements for the leadership election, including the composition of the electoral college, helped to ensure Michael's victory.[7] Two-thirds of party members, and all those unions that conducted a full ballot, voted for Rhodri Morgan, always a consistent supporter of devolution. Above all, it was the leadership of the TGWU, AEEU and GMB – none of whom balloted their members – who delivered the vote for Michael. This process brought the Labour party in Wales into disrepute and left the party membership bitter and demoralised.

Almost as soon as it arrived, then, Welsh devolution became a victim of New Labour manipulation. The election of Michael was one of the first indications that, despite the huge majority at Westminster, there was to be no let-up in New Labour's attack on party democracy and its abuse of the political process. At the time, the differences between Morgan and Michael were arguably as much about style as politics. While Rhodri was no Blairite, he was not exactly on the far left of the party either. He was, however, independently-minded and strongly committed to the meaningful devolution of power and responsibility to Wales; it seems that this in itself was enough to put him 'off-message'. Within Wales, key party and union officials cooperated with the operation, not necessarily through loyalty to Blair but also because of their own suspicions of Morgan – whom they saw, according to one account , as 'eccentric', 'not dependable' and 'not one of us'.[8] Thus, Old Labour and New Labour were united in control-freakery.

The conflict between the need for devolution better to serve the interests of the people of Wales, and the priorities of the New Labour project, particularly the lack of political accountability and democracy, were to become a recurring theme of the Assembly's early years.

From constitutional devolution to policy devolution

With the 'reliable' Alun Michael duly installed, Labour fought the 1999 election on a manifesto distinguished only by its vacuity. Conversely, Plaid Cymru fought on an essentially 'Old Labour' platform, promising to restore the link between pensions and earnings and to reinstate the student grant. Labour's response was a particularly wretched document entitled *The A to Z of Nationalist Madness*. But as Paul Flynn MP commented in *Tribune*, 'the people of Wales found this insanity irresistible', turning to Plaid in huge numbers and giving it an 80 per cent increase over its 1997 vote. Labour lost supposedly impregnable seats like Rhondda, Islwyn and Llanelli. Many of the party's 'core' voters clearly thought they had nothing to lose in voting for a Plaid programme which seemed more authentically 'Labour' than the official version. With Labour three seats short of an overall majority, the three opposition parties exploited their opportunity to obstruct Michael's minority administration, exacerbating the uncertainty about the scope of the Assembly's powers and the gathering intrigue against Michael within his own group. When, in February 2000, he resigned to forestall a no confidence vote in the Assembly chamber, his Labour colleagues declined to renominate him, and he was succeeded by Rhodri Morgan – a humiliating defeat for Blair's attempts to run Wales by remote control.

After six months in office, Morgan caused widespread consternation within his party when he signed a 'partnership' agreement with the Liberal Democrats, bringing two of their six AMs into the cabinet. Concerns were occasioned both by the lack of consultation about the deal and by the prospect of Welsh Labour becoming exclusively dependent on a party politically to its right (simultaneously freezing out Plaid Cymru – then probably to Labour's left on most issues). Nevertheless, fears that Liberal Democrat influence would push Assembly government policy to the right proved to be unfounded. For one thing, the cabinet reshuffle also gave Rhodri another opportunity to promote his own allies at the expense of remaining Alun Michael supporters. In addition, the Lib Dems' main preoccupations were with questions of democracy; they had no particular ideological axe to grind on social and economic policy, and consequently allowed Labour to do largely as it chose. The stability afforded by the coalition thus allowed Welsh Labour to begin to enact a series of measures that gradually took on the character of a distinctive Welsh Labour programme. Thus, three years after the referendum and more than eighteen months after the elections, devolution began to develop some practical content.

The new Welsh policy agenda

It was only on 11 December 2002, when Rhodri Morgan gave his land-mark 'clear red water' speech at Swansea University, that the idea of a distinct, coherent Welsh Labour policy agenda was explicitly stated.[9] Most of the policies to which he referred on that occasion had been under way for some time – particularly in education, where Jane Davidson was busily championing comprehensives and early years learning, rejecting league tables and SATs tests (first at age seven, and later, in their entirety), introducing the Assembly Learning Grant and free nursery places for three-year-olds. Similarly, in health policy, under Jane Hutt, there was an emphasis on public health, a rejection of foundation hospitals and of the English policy of allowing private diagnostic and treatment centres to cream off the most lucrative NHS work, and charges for prescriptions had been abolished for the under-25s (as they would later be for everyone else). A number of other services had also been made free at the point of delivery, including bus travel for pensioners and the disabled and admission to museums and galleries. As finance minister, Edwina Hart had indicated that the Assembly government would avoid using PFI wherever possible. The novelty of the 'clear red water' speech was that, whereas these policies had previously been offered as piecemeal, pragmatic measures, they were now presented as part of an overall strategy of de-commodification. Morgan claimed for the Assembly government's programme 'ideological underpinnings' in the best tradition of the labour and socialist movement. The overall strategy was 'the creation of a new set of citizenship rights ... which are as far as possible, free at the point of use, universal and unconditional', and which would be built on if Labour won a second term of office. For the first time, the Welsh Labour leadership was publicly distancing itself from New Labour in Westminster.

Undoubtedly, the invocation of 'clear red water' – which soon became the accepted shorthand for the distinct Welsh agenda – was motivated partly by electoral considerations, at a time when many of New Labour's policies were becoming unpopular and war in Iraq was on the horizon. Rhodri's intervention almost certainly assisted Welsh Labour in the May 2003 Assembly elections – although the electoral dividend was not as great as generally believed. While the Rhondda, Islwyn, Llanelli and Conwy were recovered, giving Labour an effective working majority of one, the party's overall vote – on a reduced turnout – was lower than in 1999 in absolute (but not percentage) terms. Plaid's vote, however, was down in both absolute and percentage terms, although still higher than in every election before 1999.[10]

But, while the 'clear red water' was evident in areas like education and health, it was less apparent in those fields of governance where the Assembly's powers were more limited. This variance had been thrown into sharp relief by the major crises that had arisen since 1999 – namely Foot-and-Mouth and the 'down-sizing' of the Welsh steel industry. In the former case, the Assembly Government found its capacity to act constrained by the residual authority of Westminster, while in the latter it lacked any significant power to intervene and was forced to look to the UK Government to rescue the situation. Edwina Hart, as minister for regeneration and social justice, publicly voiced her support for the 'fourth option' in council housing – the right, denied by the privatising ideologues of New Labour, for local authorities to borrow funds to renew housing stock themselves, rather than transfer them to a housing association or 'mutual' – but, with typical candour, admitted that she could not turn this support into action because housing finance remained under the control of the Treasury.

A process or an event?

The limitations of the devolution settlement, and their capacity to inhibit the Assembly in addressing the real and pressing needs of the people of Wales, were thus becoming clear – although they remained unacknowledged by the ministerial team in Cardiff Bay. Blair's imposition of 'his man' as Welsh leader, and its later undoing, had suggested that the main obstacles to genuine autonomy for Wales were political, rather than constitutional. With Michael's removal having apparently freed Welsh Labour ministers to conduct a distinct policy agenda geared to the needs of Wales – rather than simply implement policies dreamt up in London – they increasingly turned their attention to the substance of that agenda and away from the structures of devolved government. In his 'clear red water' speech, Rhodri Morgan went so far as to dismiss any remaining preoccupation with the *form* of devolution as 'political anorakism'. Yet, however little he affected to care about such matters in 2002, the devolution settlement had already been found wanting on several occasions. There was confusion about the respective jurisdictions of Cardiff Bay and Westminster, even on the part of Assembly ministers. Moreover, whenever there was a question over the Assembly's powers – to make pay arrangements for teachers, to prohibit GM crops, to take charge of the response to Foot-and-Mouth – it was always resolved in favour of Westminster. Rhodri's attitude, by the final stages of the

Assembly's first term, was that it was better to concentrate on the considerable policy areas where his administration *did* have the power to make a real difference, than to concern itself disproportionately about what it still could not do.

This attitude was understandable to a degree, not least because an obvious response to any demand for further powers would have been to seek evidence that the Assembly was making the best use of those powers it already had. Nevertheless, for socialists, the weakness of the devolution settlement was always more than a question of constitutional niceties. However successful the Assembly government's policies might prove to be, they were ultimately dependent on the good will of Westminster. Even when dealing with clearly devolved policy areas, the Assembly often had to ask the UK government to pass Wales-only legislation through Parliament: for example, to facilitate the reorganisation of the NHS or to establish the office of Children's Commissioner for Wales. What protection did the existing settlement afford to any progressive policy agenda, therefore, when there remained the possibility of a future Tory government in London, with no incentive to cooperate with a Labour administration in Cardiff Bay?

It was, however, the Liberal Democrats – rather than the socialist left – who kept these issues on the agenda after the mid-point of the Assembly's first term: part of the price of their participation in the 'partnership government' between October 2000 and May 2003 was the establishment of a commission into the powers and electoral arrangements of the Assembly. This was duly established under the Labour peer, Lord (Ivor) Richard in July 2002; it quietly went about its work while most people's attention was focused on more pressing matters, like the Iraq war, and it was only in the period immediately before its report was published on 31 March 2004 that much public attention was paid to the issues it had considered.

The Richard Commission was certainly thorough: it held 115 evidence sessions, three seminars and nine public meetings, issued two consultation papers and received over 300 written submissions. It visited Westminster, the Scottish Parliament and the Speaker of the Northern Ireland Assembly as well as monitoring the Welsh Assembly in action. Its report runs to 263 pages, even without the appendices. Its proposals were sober and measured, yet they would, if adopted, have represented a significant enhancement of the Assembly's powers and a deepening of its democratic legitimacy. It recommended that by 2011 the Assembly be granted full law-making powers in each of the currently-devolved policy areas, that its membership be increased to 80, to enable it cope with the increased responsibility and that the single transferable vote (STV) be adopted, as the most appropriate method of electing such an enlarged Assembly. Tax-raising powers were considered desirable, although not essential.

These proposals were presented dispassionately, as prospective solutions to the practical problems encountered in the first few years of democratic devolution and were immediately welcomed by a wide spectrum of opinion – including the Welsh Labour leadership. Within the party, however, some remained deeply suspicious of *any* proposal to advance the devolution project. They included a large number of Welsh Labour MPs, nineteen of whom signed an open letter to Peter Hain in January 2004 – some two months before the Richard Commission published its report – arguing that any substantial extension of the Assembly's powers should be subject to a further referendum. The motivation seems unlikely to have been a commitment to plebiscitary democracy as a matter of principle, but rather a desire to place obstacles in the path of primary powers. A significant consideration was no doubt the fact that any extension of the Assembly's remit would have seen a corresponding reduction in the role – and perhaps even the numbers – of Welsh MPs.

The reassertion of Westminster control

The views expressed in the MPs' open letter were echoed by Hain himself when the Richard report was published: while affirming the need for widespread consultation on Richard's conclusions before Labour reached any decision, he added that 'a referendum would be required on a Scottish model' and that 'any reforms agreed must be consistent with maintaining the existing number of Welsh parliamentary constituencies.'[11] The message could hardly have been clearer: Westminster comes first and the Assembly could expect no extra powers that might disturb the status quo. Regrettably, Rhodri Morgan – himself a long-standing supporter of primary powers – soon began talking about the impracticability of the Richard scheme and the need to look to extend the Assembly's powers in a way that would not involve a risky and time-consuming referendum.

While the *One Wales* commitment to hold a referendum by 2011 makes the point somewhat academic, the need to do this at all seems somewhat questionable – although Britain's lack of a written constitution makes it hard to say for sure. The only referenda carried out in mainland Britain have been on the country's continued membership of the European Economic Community (1975) and the two attempts (in 1979 and 1997) to introduce Scottish and Welsh devolution. Custom and practice dictates – it might therefore be concluded – that a referendum is required when a significant change in governance in proposed. Yet the *principle* of Welsh devolution had surely been established by the 1997 referendum result: to introduce primary law-making powers would simply have extended the implementation of that principle.[12] Similarly, once Britain's entry into the EEC had received popular consent (two years belatedly), there was no move to seek a further mandate for the transfer of additional sovereignty represented by the Single European Act (1987) or the Maastricht Treaty (1992). In reality, it seems that the 'need' for another Assembly referendum was invoked by Labour's 'devo-sceptics' simply as a convenient means of obstructing any progress towards greater Welsh autonomy. The other argument put forward for holding a new referendum has been that the development of the Assembly cannot run too far ahead of public opinion. This assumes, however, that popular attitudes to devolution have changed little since 1999. In fact, public opinion is more fluid than that, if polls are a reliable guide: the latter have consistently suggested that the Assembly's popularity has increased and that there is some appetite for it to accumulate additional powers. For example: a poll conducted by Aberystwyth University's Institute of Welsh Politics in June-July 2008 found that 39 per cent of those questioned wanted the Assembly to have full law-making and taxation powers within the UK, while a further ten per cent sought complete independence; 31 per cent favoured the retention of the status quo, while only 15 per cent wanted the Assembly abolished.[13] While hardly conclusive as to the likely outcome of a referendum on primary powers, such polls do indicate the significant progress made over the last decade.

Welsh Labour responded to the Richard proposals by conducting a hasty consultation lasting three months – for two months of which most party activists would have been somewhat preoccupied by the local and European election campaigns. The outcome was a flimsy document entitled 'Better Governance of Wales', containing only eight pages of substantive text. The suggestion that the Richard Commission's work had not been taken seriously was strengthened by the peremptory manner in which its recommendations were dealt with. The proposal to introduce STV, for example, was rejected in a single sentence, with no reason given, whereas two paragraphs were devoted to the so-called

'Clwyd West Question'. This was the phenomenon of 'failed constituency candidates ... rejected by the electorate of a single constituency and yet elected to the Assembly via their party list' – a means of 'back-door' entry into the Assembly from which all three defeated opposition candidates in Clwyd West had benefited. This was supposedly 'confusing and frustrating' for the electorate.[14] Labour's outrage seems, however, decidedly hypocritical in view of the fact that every one of its own constituency candidates had also been placed on a top-up list in the previous year's elections. Nevertheless, the 'correction' of this anomaly was one of three legislative proposals set out in 'Better Governance for Wales', rubber-stamped by a special Welsh Labour conference, embodied in a white paper (also called *Better Governance for Wales*) and finally incorporated in the Government of Wales Act 2006.

A missed opportunity

Of the other two measures embodied in the 2006 Act, one was even less momentous than the resolution of the 'Clwyd West Question': namely, the introduction of a legal separation between the National Assembly as a whole and its executive arm. This was a sensible amendment to the provisions of the 1998 Act, which had made the Assembly a unified 'corporate body'; its practical impact was limited, however, since a *de facto* separation between executive and legislature had long since developed, strengthened by the re-branding of the executive as the 'Welsh Assembly Government' in 2001.

The core of the 2006 Act – which came into force at the beginning of the Assembly's third term – was its provision for the extension of the Assembly's legislative competence. Adopting a proposal considered by the Richard Commission and recommended as a stop-gap measure, it gives the Assembly the power to write its own legislation – known as Assembly 'Measures' – in devolved areas, but only within parameters explicitly approved by both Houses of Parliament on each occasion. This is accomplished either by creating 'framework powers' covering Wales within the scope of a relevant UK bill, or through a device called an Order in Council or a Legislative Competence Order (LCO), which can be put forward either by the Assembly government or by a back-bench AM, subject to a ballot.[15] The process whereby an LCO is considered and agreed, facilitating the passage of a Measure, is complex and drawn-out, involving pre-legislative scrutiny in both Westminster and Cardiff Bay. Thus, while the 2006 Act supposedly allows the Assembly to take over the detailed drafting of primary legislation affecting Wales, it remains beholden to MPs to grant the necessary authority. The fact that, for each legislative proposal, Parliament is required only to approve a general principle – rather than to provide clause-by-clause scrutiny – provides no protection against politically-motivated obstruction, since the Assembly has to give a detailed explanation of its intentions, enabling MPs to exercise great wariness in dispensing their approval.[16]

The limitations of the new system soon become evident. An LCO on 'environmental protection and waste management' put forward by Jane Davidson as sustainability minister, sought to give the Assembly the power to combat climate change and was intended to facilitate measures such as a ban on single-use plastic carrier bags. It was laid in the Assembly in June 2007 and quickly completed pre-legislative scrutiny by the relevant Assembly committee but subsequently disappeared without trace, having apparently been vetoed by Whitehall, supposedly on the grounds that it was 'too widely drawn'. According to the *Western Mail*, an 'Assembly source' speculated – very plausibly – that the real reason was pressure from 'the business lobby'.[17] Another LCO, on 'social welfare and other fields', had sought – among other things – the power to introduce a ban on the physical punishment of children in Wales, after Westminster ministers had declined to introduce their own legislation to this end. The UK government refused to grant the request, however, on the grounds that it was a 'criminal justice' matter and therefore beyond the scope of the present devolution settlement, within which the Assembly can draw down powers. The LCO was finally approved in a much-modified form.

Finally, and most ominously, an LCO on affordable housing, which sought to restrict the right to buy council houses in areas of extreme housing pressure, has been the victim of sabotage by the House of Commons Welsh Affairs Committee. The Committee argued that, despite the Assembly government's intention to introduce no more than temporary and geographically-limited suspensions, the power it was seeking could facilitate a permanent, Wales-wide ban on the right to buy and this had to be explicitly ruled out by the LCO before it could be approved. There have been strong suspicions that these objections were motivated by political opposition to the intent behind the Assembly policy, rather than considerations of legislative propriety. In any case, the outcome has been a 'compromise', whereby the Assembly is to be granted the powers originally sought in the LCO but their use will be subject to a veto by the Secretary of State for Wales – whoever that may be at the time. This humiliating denouement demonstrates the superficiality of most Labour MPs' commitment to devolution, as well as calling into question the supposed democratic advance represented by the 2006 Act.

Notwithstanding the technical objections proffered in each case, these examples show that the Assembly's ability to use its new powers to secure real benefits – for the environment, for children, for people denied affordable housing – is already under threat. Any proposition that appears even slightly radical risks being vetoed by Westminster politicians or civil servants. And this under a UK government with which, we are constantly told, the Assembly administration enjoys an excellent working relationship. In the all-too-likely event of another Tory government in the near future, the obstacles would surely multiply considerably. The remedy is clear: only when it can directly exercise primary powers will the Assembly genuinely have the scope to give effect to its political decisions.

Deepening devolution

Whether or not the Assembly should have access to effective law-making powers is a question not simply of convenience but of principle. The fullest expression of democracy entails that people have the greatest possible say in the decisions that affect them; this means bringing the locus of power as close as possible to the citizen. Moreover, a majority of the people of Wales clearly consider that they belong to a distinct nation, with a shared history and culture and discrete interests. It should, therefore, be for the people of Wales themselves – not the British parliament – to determine their governmental arrangements. The Assembly is the manifestation – however imperfect – of the general will of the people of Wales; rather than Westminster deciding how much power it should cede to Cardiff, then, it should be Cardiff that decides how much power it takes. While the current Assembly seems unlikely to assert itself to quite this extent, the commitment in One Wales to move towards an early referendum on primary powers, and the establishment of the All-Wales Convention to prepare the ground for this, represent a major step forward, raising the prospect that the present, unsatisfactory status quo may prove relatively short-lived. The repeated attempts by Peter Hain, Paul Murphy and others to play down the referendum, or to postpone it to the indefinite future, must be rejected: it is incumbent on socialists and democrats to lead the way in building a campaign for such a referendum, and in making the arguments for a 'yes' vote. Moreover, a referendum should also include the introduction of tax-raising powers: real autonomy would mean release from the financial blackmail that a

Westminster government is presently able to impose. Assembly government could therefore introduce a more pr(
regime than in the rest of the UK, setting an example for other a̶d̶m̶i̶n̶i̶s̶
trations to follow.

'Devo-sceptics', including many in the labour movement, have tried to rally opposition to deeper devolution by presenting it as a 'slippery slope' to an independent Wales; in doing so, they can point to the renewed advocacy of separatism by leading figures within Plaid Cymru, such as Leanne Wood, Adam Price and Helen Mary Jones, who have been emboldened by the SNP government's commitment to a referendum on Scottish independence.[18] We remain unmoved by the panic that such talk seems to induce in many Labour party members. First of all, Welsh independence is not remotely on the agenda for the foreseeable future, principally because there is not widespread popular sentiment in favour of it. What *has* happened – as numerous opinion polls testify – is that the generally positive experience of democratic devolution since 1999 has strengthened the view that the Assembly should accumulate greater power; the people of Wales have not generally concluded, however, that formal separation from the UK must be the conclusion of this process. They may, of course, come to that view in the future. In that eventuality, we should not dogmatically insist on preserving 'the Union'; socialists and progressives should have no timeless allegiance to any particular state – especially one as centralised, elitist and encrusted with feudal detritus as the UK. On the other hand, Plaid undoubtedly invests too much significance in the achievement of formal national 'sovereignty' – a rather questionable concept in an increasingly 'open' world economy. Realpolitik, as well as principled internationalism, would dictate that a newly 'independent' Wales, if it ever came about, should immediately re-forge a union of a more voluntary and mutually beneficial kind with all the nations of the British-Irish Isles – and, indeed, with other countries in Europe and beyond.

Returning from such speculative considerations to more immediate concerns, it should be recognised that a further referendum victory can only be secured by consistent evidence that the Assembly is already making a positive difference to people's lives and that an extension of its responsibility would enable it to consolidate its achievements. It is time, therefore, to examine the Assembly's record to date in more detail.

Chapter 5

Public services:
Third Way v. the Welsh Way

In this chapter and the next we will be critically examining Welsh Labour policies, considering how far they differ from those pursued by New Labour in Westminster, and how these deviations from Blairite orthodoxy could be consolidated, as part of a thoroughgoing socialist agenda for Wales.

How Labour learned to love the market

Notwithstanding some significant tactical adjustments in response to the present economic downturn, New Labour's policies for the economy and public services have generally remained within the framework of 'neo-liberalism'. That is, they are based on a belief in the fundamental desirability of a free market in goods and services. Supposedly, it is through the operation of the market that people are able to enjoy the greatest freedom, as producers and consumers alike, and market forces are the most efficient means of allocating goods and services to those who want them. Neo-liberals generally acknowledge that the free play of market forces can occasionally have some socially undesirable consequences; the state therefore has a role in ameliorating these effects – recent government economic rescue measures being an obvious case in point – as well as in providing certain vital goods or services, where it is not commercially viable for these to be supplied via the market. In general, however, government is seen as having no legitimate business in seeking to replace private enterprise as the provider of goods and services, or in declaring any area of human interaction 'out of bounds' for the market.

These ideas were, of course, enthusiastically promoted by the Tories from the 1970s – just as they were adopted by market 'visionaries' around the world, from Reagan to Pinochet to Deng Xiaoping. They represent, however, a clear divergence from the historic philosophy and economic programme of the Labour party. It was originally the compulsion of changed economic circumstances – the end of the long post-war boom and the onset of a global recession – that drove Labour, somewhat hesitantly, to adopt neo-liberal policy priorities in Government from December 1976, when Chancellor Denis Healey agreed to implement swingeing cuts as the condition of an IMF loan. The party reverted to Keynesian type once back in opposition but began shifting ground more permanently from the late 1980s. New Labour, like other social-democratic parties, has increasingly made a virtue of (perceived) necessity and now sings the praises of the market with the zeal of the convert, declaring that its previous approach – 'the old tax-and-spend policies' – is simply not practicable in a globalised, deregulated world. 'In a fast changing global economy,' the party's 2005 manifesto tells us, 'government cannot postpone or prevent change.'[1] The world economy is treated here as something as remote from human control as the weather – thereby ignoring the role of governments in establishing and enforcing free markets. Such an attitude dismisses the validity of any alternative view; for New Labour, as for the Tories, fundamental economic questions have been taken out of the realm of politics altogether. Policy goals that might require some interference with the workings of the market are now anathema; any idea of equality of outcome has long been abandoned in favour of the more modest goal of 'social inclusion' – meaning little more than the provision of a safety net for the worst off.

In New Labour's brave new world, the public sector is subject to the rigours of the market place, its services treated as commodities, and service-users as consumers. Rather than the market being adapted to human need, people have to adapt to the market. The idea that this is the most modern and rational approach to managing human affairs has recently come under unprecedented attack, as the chaotic consequences of unregulated markets have increasingly threatened the livelihoods of millions and the stability of the system itself. In Britain, the government's resort to massive borrowing to finance the bail-out of the financial sector and its measures to boost aggregate demand, along with the longer-term prospect of extremely modest tax increases for the better-off, have prompted the claim that neo-liberal economics have now been vanquished by a resurgent Keynesianism.

The reality is less edifying, however: analysis of the Chancellor's November 2008 pre-budget report has revealed plans to cut public spending after 2011 by £37 billion – more than ten times the expected yield from progressive tax increases.[2] In other words, it is the majority who will bear the overwhelming burden of recession through cuts in services, with the rich expected to make only a minimal additional sacrifice. This underlines the point that the choice between alternative policy options is governed not by a commitment to any internally-consistent doctrine of economic management but by the pragmatic adoption of whatever approach might facilitate the continued functioning of the capitalist economy, in as undisturbed a manner as possible. Whatever the pretensions of its intellectual apologists, neo-liberalism has always been fundamentally about the accumulation and retention of wealth and power by the dominant class, through means such as privatisation, deregulation, regressive fiscal measures and anti-union laws, on the pretext that these policies are more 'efficient'.[3] New Labour agreed at the outset to govern within this basic context, and the recent turn towards greater state intervention represents only a tactical modification, not a paradigm shift. Indeed, Lord Mandelson acknowledged as much in a speech to the Institute of Directors on 26 November, when he said:

> It is the times that have changed, not New Labour. The New Labour principle still stands: we will only tax out of need, not out of envy or spite.[4]

By 'envy or spite', he means, of course, a commitment to equality and social justice.

Thatcherism with a human face?

Of course, the New Labour programme is not simply a continuation of Thatcherism. Many of its more progressive policies would have been almost inconceivable under a Tory government: Scottish and Welsh devolution, for example, or civil partnerships. There has also been some attempt (albeit not entirely consistent) to protect the worst off from the most perilous aspects of the 'free market' economy, through initiatives like the national minimum wage, the 'Fairness at Work' legislation, the introduction of tax credits and policies like Surestart, which seek to eliminate child poverty. In addition, New Labour has made the improvement of public services a central priority and has invested

record sums (as we are repeatedly reminded) to this en
that have accompanied this investment are often satur;
eral dogma. Money has gone into schools but, far fror
for the enrichment of the pupil, or of society as a wh
for the benefit of employers – hence the dull, spoon-fe
the national curriculum. Again, massive investment has undoubtedly
gone into the National Health Service but the marketisation of health
care services means that NHS trusts that cannot balance their books are
closing wards and laying off staff.

Having renounced any meaningful attempt to manage the economy,
New Labour tries instead to micromanage people. Whether as service
users or providers, people are driven to distraction by targets, tests,
league tables, and all the other paraphernalia of competition. The message emanating from government seems almost designed to induce confusion, stress and demoralisation. On one hand, the government
trumpets that public services are the best they have ever been, yet on the
other, 'failing' schools and hospitals are constantly being exposed to
public humiliation.

An alternative Labour agenda

New Labour's advocacy of progress through competition seems particularly inappropriate in Wales, where the workings of the market economy have already left a legacy of poverty, unemployment, poor housing,
and ill-health, and where a child born in the Cardiff North constituency
can be expected to live five years longer than a child born only an hour's
journey away. Welsh Labour's policies recognise this reality and are
more closely attuned to the sense of community solidarity that is still
valued by so many in Wales than to the neo-liberal credo of individual
self-advancement. This is nowhere more evident than in the development and provision of public services. The principles underlying the
Welsh approach were first publicly acknowledged by Rhodri Morgan in
2002, most famously in his 'clear red water' speech. They have been
elaborated most clearly, however, by the first minister's special advisor,
Professor Mark Drakeford, in an article in the Institute of Welsh Affairs'
magazine, *Agenda*.[5]

According to Drakeford, Welsh Labour's approach towards public
services begins from the position that government can be a force for
good, taking shared values and turning them into practical policies – a
clear break with the neo-liberal notion that government does best when
it governs least. Unlike New Labour, Welsh Labour has a preference for

61

...rsal, rather than means-tested services. For example, free school
eakfasts (a policy now being followed in England) are provided for *all*
pupils, not just those marked out, in a way that demeans them, as needy.
As Drakeford argues, 'services which are reserved for poor people very
quickly become poor services'; conversely, universal public services can
be the 'glue which binds together a complex modern society'. But this is
also a *progressive* universalism: it provides additional support on top of
the basic received by everyone, targeting those who need it most, as in
the 'Flying Start' policy, discussed below. Welsh Labour also prefers to
conceive of the government engaging with the individual as *citizen*,
rather than as *consumer* – implying a cooperative, rather than a competitive or commercial, relationship. Consumerism is rejected as a model of
provision: services can be made more responsive to people, not by
improving individual 'choice', but by providing a greater 'voice', which
people can exercise collectively. Democratic accountability of service
providers to service users allows for collective solutions, which can
improve the service across the board. This involves creating 'high trust'
relationships between providers and users – a practical rebuff to the
Thatcherite and Blairite assumption that the interests of the two must
necessarily be in conflict. The portrayal by New Labour ideologues of
the public sector unions as having interests somehow divorced from
those who use the services provided by their members is not simply a
crude divide-and-rule tactic; it suggests a worrying incomprehension of
the motives that drive people to work in the public sector. The most
important and ambitious principle expounded by Drakeford is the commitment to equality of *outcome*, rather than just equality of opportunity,
and the pursuit for Wales of the better health, lower crime, greater
social cohesion and enhanced economic success enjoyed by more equal
societies.

These principles were incorporated into a practical policy agenda
with the publication in October 2004 of *Making the Connections:
Delivering Better Public Services for Wales*. This key document explicitly
rejects the 'competitive model' for improving public services as one that
breaks up organisations into free-standing businesses that must prosper
or perish and empowers managers but not service users. Instead, it seeks
to deliver efficiency gains through the creation of a more cohesive and
integrated Welsh public service (starting with the merger of three major
quangos into the Assembly government[6]) and to empower citizens to
help 'design, develop and deliver' the services they use. Throughout, the
emphasis is on making services efficient through partnership and col-

laboration, and more responsive through democratic accountability and popular participation. The contrast with New Labour's approach is underlined by the fact that, a couple of months before *Making the Connections*, Gordon Brown had, on the basis of the Gershon Review, announced swingeing cuts in the civil and public services, including the cutting of 104,000 posts, and the setting of 'efficiency' targets for every major Whitehall department. By contrast, *Making the Connections* devotes one of its six chapters to 'engaging the workforce', sets no targets for job cuts (although it anticipates some overall reduction in public sector staffing, as a result of economies of scale) and gives individual organisations the responsibility to 'decide their own efficiency measures'.

As a framework of principles and priorities, *Making the Connections* is resolutely progressive. Its impact on public service delivery in Wales will ultimately depend, however, on the specific programmes that flow from it. In organisational terms, the agenda has been strongly influenced by the Beecham review of local service delivery, whose report (*Delivering Beyond Boundaries*) recommended much greater pooling of resources by organisations contributing to the provision of common or related services. The Assembly government's principal response to this has been a commitment to establish 'local service boards' (based on the existing community strategy partnerships), which are intended to facilitate 'a more effective network of public services in Wales ... without creating new bureaucracies and processes'.[7] The commitment to engender a more fluid approach to public service, driven by community and user need, rather than organisational imperative, is commendable. But how easily this can be secured by introducing what is effectively a new tier of administration – along with all manner of overlapping partnerships and joint working arrangements – is an open question. The difficulty of getting from the present situation to the desired outcome of a thoroughly 'joined-up' Welsh public service brings to mind the old chestnut, 'If I was going to Tipperary, I wouldn't start from here'. One can only hope that, in its enthusiasm for 'new ways of working', the Assembly government does not lose sight of the 'citizen-centred' priority of *Making the Connections*; it is certainly hard to imagine most citizens getting to grips with the complexities of the proposed system.

The journey from the discreet, but unmistakable, radicalism of *Making the Connections* to the technocratic outcome represented by the establishment of local service boards provides an instructive example. In seeking the advice of a review team consisting of a local government leader, an NHS chief and a university vice-chancellor, the Assembly government ensured that the progressive ambitions of the original document would be translated into the politically-neutral language of organisational change. The generally wise, if uninspiring, counsel of Beecham was then further interpreted by Assembly officials to produce organisational 'solutions'. There is a perpetual danger that the radical edge of the best Welsh Labour policies will be blunted in the course of their implementation by the intervention of the state apparatus. The principles set out by Mark Drakeford encompass a burning desire for profound social change, transforming the lives of the most deprived and marginalised. Yet the details of policy delivery are entrusted to officials schooled in the arts of cautious, deliberate administrative adjustment, ensuring that anything remotely radical or ambitious passes through a series of filters that serve, all too frequently, to mitigate its impact. Such in-built conservatism characterises (but is not unique to) the institutions of the British state. The presence in Cathays Park of a cadre of senior officials who have emerged from this background, and who regard themselves as the guardians of good governance, moderating the intemperate demands of the politicians, is itself a potential problem. Their elite status is reflected in their salary structure: the *Western Mail* recently revealed that the 30 highest-paid Assembly government civil servants collectively earn at least £3.3 billion; six of them are better-paid than the first minister and all of them earn more than the rest of the cabinet.[8] It is widely known that the Assembly ministers most determined to implement bold and sweeping reforms have faced subtle but concerted obstruction from their own officials. There is a clear case here for the establishment of an autonomous Welsh public service, freed from the Whitehall embrace, which could develop less hierarchical structures and a culture conducive to the energetic prosecution of democratically-sanctioned policies.

Recent developments have suggested that the progressive principles underpinning the *Making the Connections* agenda might be under threat not just from unsympathetic officialdom but from within the political leadership of Welsh Labour itself. In his November 2008 response to the report of the Assembly finance committee's inquiry into public-private partnerships (PPP), Andrew Davies, minister for finance and public service delivery, promised 'to create a PPP Unit in the Assembly Government' that will 'help the public and private sectors to identify, promote and coordinate the delivery of PPP opportunities.'[9] This move – while foreshadowed by some earlier pronouncements by Davies – represents a troubling departure from the established policy of both the present Assembly coalition and its predecessors.[10] Davies' preference for a more 'pragmatic' approach toward private sector involvement in public services has recently been echoed by other prominent figures in Welsh Labour, such as the deputy regeneration minister, Leighton Andrews, the former Welsh Secretary, Peter Hain, and Eluned Morgan MEP. With Andrew Davies a possible election candidate in the leadership election consequent upon Rhodri Morgan's long-anticipated retirement, the political future looks increasingly uncertain. To understand what is at stake, it is necessary to examine the Assembly government's record in the key areas of public service policy. It is to this that we now turn.

Welsh health policy: reclaiming Bevan's legacy

The establishment of the National Health Service (NHS) in 1948 is still widely seen as Labour's greatest ever achievement and the Service is held in particularly high regard in Wales – fittingly, for an institution founded by a Welshman: Aneurin Bevan. Popular support for the principle of universal, comprehensive health care, free at the point of delivery, was consolidated during the 40-odd years after its creation when the structure of the NHS was left fundamentally intact and there has been outrage in response to the attempts to 'reform' it since the 1980s. It speaks volumes about the distance travelled by the Labour leadership in recent years that the marketisation policies pursued by the Tories before 1997 have been continued and deepened under New Labour. To appreciate fully the significance of Welsh Labour's divergence from the Blairite health agenda, it is necessary to consider the impact of NHS 'reforms' over the last 25 years or so.

The dismantling of the NHS since the 1980s

Such was the degree of public support for the founding principles of the NHS that the Thatcher government would have found it politically difficult to introduce sweeping changes all at once, even had this been the intention from the outset, which is by no means clear.[11] During the 1980s, it was the Tories' under-funding of the NHS that excited most concern, rather than their structural reforms, the impact of which was cumulative and only fully apparent in retrospect. The management structure was redesigned on the basis of a report by the Sainsbury's chief executive, Sir Roy Griffiths, shifting power away from clinicians towards a new stratum of general or senior managers, whose numbers in England grew from 1,000 in 1986 to 16,000 in 1991 and then to 26,000 in 1995.[12] Privatisation began on the fringes of the service, with non-clinical functions such as cleaning, catering and laundry contracted out to the private sector, resulting in poorer pay and conditions for the staff in question, and a deteriorating service to patients and 'core' staff. The coverage of the NHS was also cut back: free eye tests were ended in 1989, thousands of dentists were driven out of the NHS by under-funding and responsibility for long term care of the elderly was transferred to local councils, which were given financial incentives to place elderly 'clients' in private care homes.[13]

Only in 1991 did the Tories effect their most significant 'reform' of NHS structures, in the face of overwhelming opposition; this was the introduction of the 'internal market', under which hospitals were allowed to opt out of district health authority (DHA) control and form self-governing NHS hospital trusts, with administrative and financial autonomy. The role of the DHAs was reduced to 'purchasing' health services for their populations, from 'providers' in the shape of the new trusts and – increasingly, in later years – the private sector. Successive waves of government-promoted opt-outs had largely completed the 'purchaser-provider' split by 1997. At the same time, groups of GPs with lists of at least 5,000 patients were given the opportunity (and financial inducements) to become GP fundholders, receiving a top slice of the DHA allocation for purchasing a range of non-emergency services for their patients. By 1996, around half of the GPs in England were part of the fundholding scheme, and the inducements to participation had begun to create a two-tier service in primary care, with non-fundholders and their patients losing out in the allocation of resources.

The internal market regime imposed on hospitals the obligation to generate enough income to break even, mainly through securing contracts for particular services from 'purchasers'. This meant that each operation or other form of care had to be costed and invoiced. The provision of health care was no longer determined by planning to meet the needs of a particular population but by which combination of services would secure sufficient revenue. When Labour was elected in 1997, its first health secretary, Frank Dobson (who was personally committed to the founding principles of the NHS but constrained by the pro-market inclinations of the New Labour clique) declared the end of both the internal market and GP fundholding. The changes he introduced were, however, to prove superficial and short-lived. 'Purchasing' was re-branded as 'commissioning' and the elaborate system of transactions simplified and stabilised but the retention of the purchaser-provider split facilitated the renewed marketisation of the NHS under Dobson's successor, Alan Milburn. Similarly, the reorganisation in England of all GPs and community health staff into 'Primary Care Groups' (PCGs), which advised health authorities on commissioning, provided the basis for their reconstitution from 2001 as 'Primary Care Trusts' (PCTs), which duly assumed direct responsibility for commissioning. The PCTs, in turn, have now begun to delegate commissioning to GP practices – thereby effectively completing the Tories' fundholding 'reforms'.

Markets and 'choice'

New Labour went a step further than the Tories towards dismantling the NHS as a unified service, with the introduction in 2003 of foundation trusts. These are hospitals, PCTs or other NHS bodies that have been freed from the control of the Department of Health and its strategic health authorities; they own their own assets and can set their own pay rates, determine their own priorities and generally behave like commercial businesses. While there are some residual limits to their freedom – they are, for example, prevented from charging fees to NHS patients – they can evade these constraints by entering into joint ventures with private companies, which are free to do as they please. With no obligation to cooperate with other NHS bodies in the overall public interest, foundation trusts will increasingly compete for the best staff and other resources, abandon less 'cost-effective' types of care, build up financial surpluses that could be usefully deployed elsewhere and contribute to increasing inequalities between the levels of service available in different areas or to people with different health needs.

Another means by which NHS hospitals are being transformed into commercial businesses is the system of 'payment by results', which was introduced within foundation trusts in 2004, rolled out to cover 80 per cent of all hospital work two years later, and which will eventually apply to all NHS services. This involves contracts between commissioners and providers that specify the type and volume of services that will be provided, with only those actually delivered being paid for. Since the price for each procedure is set by the NHS' national 'tariff', providers able to deliver services at a lower cost are able to make a surplus, which they can retain, while those unable to cover their costs are forced to make cuts in order to retain work. This is supposed to be an incentive to greater efficiency but fails to take into account the fact that some hospitals have higher costs than others for historical reasons that cannot easily be addressed. Payment by results denies hospitals a guaranteed level of funding, sufficient to plan services to meet the needs of the local population; moreover, it encourages them to focus on patients with relatively straightforward conditions, who can be treated more quickly, at the expense of those with more complex needs.

These problems have been exacerbated by the introduction of the 'choose and book' system, which represents the culmination of the government's conception of NHS patients as consumers making choices in a market. From December 2005, all patients needing elective care had to be offered a 'menu' of four or five choices of provider, including at least one from outside the NHS; as of April 2008, they are able to choose any provider which meets the standards set by the Healthcare Commission and can provide the care at the price set by the national tariff. All this forces hospitals to compete for patients in order to survive, wasting public money on advertising their services. In place of a planned and integrated health system, within which resources can be deployed where they are most needed, there is now a chaotic assemblage of largely independent 'businesses', tied together by financial transactions, ruthlessly competing in the new NHS 'marketplace'. It is little wonder that one in three trusts was facing financial deficits in 2006–07 and meltdown was avoided only by cutting more than 22,000 posts, according to the RCN.[14]

Making offerings to the vultures

Not content with reinventing the NHS in the image of the private sector, New Labour has also, since 2000, doggedly sought to involve private companies in the provision of core NHS services – reversing the approach of Frank Dobson, who had instructed trust chief executives to make use of private hospitals only as a last resort. Under a concordat with the Independent Healthcare Association (IHA) signed in October 2000, the Government committed itself to 'planning the use of private and voluntary care providers, not only at times of pressure but also on a more proactive longer term basis'[15] but this deal was scrapped four years later due to the exorbitant rates charged by UK private health firms for operating on NHS patients.

Instead, the Government turned to the international healthcare industry, inviting private providers to run a network of new independent sector treatment centres (ISTCs), which would help to drive down waiting times by tackling part of the NHS' backlog of routine elective surgery and diagnostic tests. Examination of these centres' record, however, dispels the Government's claims about their supposed augmentation of NHS capacity. After initially being required to provide their own staffing resources (albeit with exemptions for staff seconded by PCTs), the companies running treatment centres have subsequently been given almost free rein to poach NHS personnel. Moreover, the first wave of providers were given five-year contracts that provided a fixed income on the basis of a guaranteed supply of patients – even though the specified volume of operations has often exceeded the actual overflow from the NHS. Sometimes this has meant patients being treated privately when the capacity existed to treat them on the NHS; in other cases, firms have been paid the agreed sum despite much of the contracted activity having failed to take place – for example, one company was paid £13.4 million for £10.1 million worth of operations.[16] Consequently, more recent contracts have incorporated the principle of payment by results. Nevertheless, private providers have continued to receive a rate of payment in excess of the standard NHS charges. This is supposedly necessary to accommodate ISTCs' higher 'start-up costs'; while commissioners pay only the price set by the national tariff, the difference is covered by the Department of Health from a central budget – a direct public subsidy to the private sector. The extra cost per operation, compared with the NHS, has averaged 11.2 per cent, even by the Government's own reckoning; it has been argued that the true figure is closer to 30 per cent when ISTCs' less complex case-mix is borne in mind.[17]

Stewart Player and Colin Leys, in a detailed analysis of the ISTC programme, demonstrate that it has not increased elective capacity at all: the volume of procedures carried out has been considerably smaller than claimed by the Government and tiny in comparison to those done by the NHS. Given that the diversion of NHS patients to ISTCs has, in several cases, resulted in a loss of income – under payment by results – to NHS hospitals (and in-house treatment centres) that could have provided the treatment themselves, and given the higher unit cost of privately-performed procedures, the net result of the programme has been to *diminish* the volume of work that would have been achievable with the same resources. Player and Leys argue convincingly that the real aim of the programme was always to stimulate the creation of an NHS marketplace, providing domestic and foreign healthcare companies with an incentive to restructure their businesses in response to the lucrative new opportunities that would increasingly be made available.[18]

No sooner were private companies ensconced in NHS secondary care than the Government began bringing them into primary care as well. The 2004 General Medical Services (GMS) contract allowed GP practices to opt out of providing 'non-essential' services such as vaccination and cervical screening, as well as 'out-of-hours' services generally, and enabled PCTs to purchase these services from 'alternative providers'. The Government set aside ten per cent of the primary care budget for deals with the private sector and by 2006 multinational corporations were being allowed to compete to run entire GP practices. Even the commissioning of primary care is being offered up to the private sector, both through allowing companies to bid for the management functions of PCTs and through GP practice-based commissioning, which is being rolled out at the same time as practices themselves are beginning to be privatised. Increasingly, there is the danger that private commissioners will be able to refer patients to providers owned by the same, or an associated company. The whole range of decisions about healthcare provision will be based not on patient need but on commercial considerations.

New Labour's ideological attachment to the private sector has also been demonstrated by its stubborn adherence to the private finance initiative (PFI) or public-private partnerships (PPP) as the basis of any new hospital construction, despite damning evidence of the initiative's fundamental flaws. Originally dreamt up by the Tories in the early 1990s as a means of financing new public buildings without recourse to taxation, PFI involves consortia of construction firms, facilities management companies and banks raising money to build and operate public buildings (hospitals, in this case) which they then lease to NHS trusts for a period of 25–30 years (sometimes longer). The one supposed advantage of PFI – that the cost to the taxpayer is spread over many years – is more than offset by its many problems, ably identified by Allyson Pollock, among others, viz:

- it is more expensive than conventional funding because the cost of borrowing is higher for private companies than it would be for the Government and this is passed onto the trust;
- this extra cost has usually been accommodated by reducing bed numbers (by 30 per cent, in the first wave of PFI hospitals), by cutting staff and limiting services, regardless of local need;
- trusts are contractually tied, for decades into the future, to a fixed set of facilities that may prove increasingly inadequate to changing needs;
- at the end of the contract, the premises still belong to the private consortium, not the NHS.[19]

Labour denounced PFI when it was first developed by the Major government: as late as October 1996, health spokesperson Chris Smith attacked the decision to build a PFI hospital at Dartford and Gravesham as an example of the Tories' privatisation agenda. Yet the 1997 Labour manifesto promised to 'reinvigorate' PFI – criticising the Tories only for mismanaging the scheme. As the official NHS historian, Charles Webster, has pointed out, Gordon Brown's commitment to stay within Tory spending limits for the first two years of a Labour government meant that embracing PFI was the only way to avoid cutting back on capital investment in the NHS.[20] As greater experience of PFI has made its shortcomings more obvious, New Labour has clung remorselessly to the policy, presenting distorted 'evidence' of its success[21] and denigrating critics like Pollock.[22] The Government has now gone a step further, with the building, under a PFI scheme, of an NHS hospital in Hampshire that will be run entirely by a private company, Partnership Health Group (a subsidiary of Care UK) – including its emergency care. This development presages the realisation of a vision of healthcare provision long cherished by the private sector, whereby the NHS will become little more than a 'brand' attached to services provided by a multiplicity of independent suppliers, with the state acting primarily as an insurer.

The Welsh way in health

Devolution has resulted in the development of four different healthcare systems within the UK; this was the verdict of NHS Confederation chief executive, Gill Morgan in January 2008, shortly before her appointment as Permanent Secretary to the Welsh Assembly Government.[23] For Scotland, Wales and Northern Ireland, this divergence has entailed a rejection of the market-based approach to 'reform' imposed by the UK Government on England. While developments in Scotland and Northern Ireland principally reflect a greater pragmatism than is allowed by New Labour's dogmatic attachment to the market, the Welsh approach increasingly demonstrates a determination to restore Nye Bevan's socialist vision to the NHS.

The Assembly government has effectively renounced PFI (seven new community hospitals have been, or will be, built through conventional funding methods), rejected foundation trusts and made use of the private sector only as a last resort, to plug gaps in NHS capacity. In his 'clear red water' speech, Rhodri Morgan ridiculed the idea of the user of public services as 'some sort of serial shopper' and suggested that foundation trusts would 'end not with patients choosing hospitals but with hospitals choosing patients'. In the same speech he described the policy of making services free at the point of delivery as the 'introduction of a new set of citizenship rights'; this has now taken its most significant form with the phasing out of prescription charges between 2002 and 2007. The 'clear red water' applies in workforce matters too: as long ago as 2002, Welsh Labour broadened the definition of the 'clinical team' to embrace ancillary staff such as porters, cooks, and cleaners, thus protecting them from transfer to the private sector in the event of a PFI contract – although, in fact, no further PFI hospitals have been commissioned in Wales since this date – and has now ended the contracting-out of hospital cleaning.[24] And in March 2008, the Assembly health minister, Edwina Hart, announced the abolition of car parking charges at NHS hospitals in Wales, which she described as a 'stealth tax on the sick' – prompting a somewhat petulant response by the English health minister, Ben Bradshaw, who suggested that the UK government was spending its money more wisely on 'patient care'.

While Welsh Labour has prevented the emergence of full-blown market relations, however, the seeds of their future development have remained in place, until now, in the division between commissioning and service provision. When the Assembly government embarked on its first major reorganisation of the NHS in Wales, it did not – unlike the Scottish Executive – take this opportunity to end the organisational basis of the internal market, in the form of the commissioner-provider split. Instead, it abolished the five Welsh health authorities, transferring their commissioning powers to 22 local health boards (LHBs), coterminous with the local authorities. With the exception of Powys, where the LHB has integrated the two functions, the bodies charged with planning services to meet the health needs of their population were therefore obliged to contract with largely autonomous business-style organisations – NHS trusts – to secure the provision of those services. The devolution of the commissioning function to 22 bodies had the commendable aim of strengthening local accountability – always one of the weaker aspects of the original NHS structure – with representation from primary and community care, public health, local government and the voluntary sector, as well as 'lay' members. In practice, however, the sheer number of LHBs is widely considered to have contributed to the fragmentation of service planning and left these bodies in a comparatively weak position vis-à-vis the trusts from which they were commissioning services.

Despite the Assembly government's attempt to create a public service culture characterised by integration and partnership, the NHS trusts have sustained an ethos that prizes independence, responds to 'market signals' and expects 'efficiency' to be rewarded with increased resources. This has posed a constant threat to the Assembly's attempts to ensure that resources are allocated, and services configured, in response to the health needs of the people of Wales as a whole. By the time of the 2007 Assembly elections, there were indications that Welsh Labour planned to resolve this situation, its manifesto promising to 'reform the way NHS Trusts are managed so as to end for good the Tory model of competition for patients and resources and improve Trust accountability to local communities'.[25] With the establishment of the Labour-Plaid coalition, an even more emphatic commitment was incorporated in the *One Wales* agreement: 'We will move purposefully to end the internal market'.[26] Edwina Hart's appointment as health minister ensured that little time was wasted in putting this pledge into effect: after first securing a series of trust mergers, she published a consultation document that proposed a full-scale overhaul of the NHS in Wales, reducing the number of LHBs to eight (with boundaries equivalent to those of the newly-merged trusts); changing the LHBs' function to the development of primary and community care services; and creating a new national NHS board to plan and fund services on an all-Wales basis. On the basis of the consultation responses to these proposals, the minister has decided – subject to a further consultation – to go a step further than originally envisaged and merge the functions of trusts and LHBs 'to create single local health organisations that would be responsible for delivering all healthcare services within a geographical area' – burying the internal market once and for all. In her comments on this decision, she talks about putting 'an NHS structure in place to last us for the next 20 to 30 years.'[27] The clear intent here is not just to re-establish an NHS structure in Wales that might enable the service to live up to its founding principles, but to make this, as far as possible, irreversible. In December 2008, further proposals were issued for consultation, which would see seven new, unified LHBs established on a shadow basis as early as 1 June 2009, becoming fully operational four months later.[28]

Public health

The avoidance of New Labour's market mania would be cause enough for praise but Welsh Labour has a coherent and positive health agenda of its own, which only begins by setting aside market-based 'solutions'. That agenda is underpinned by an approach to health and wellbeing that is recognisably socialist in inspiration – and therefore fundamentally different from the approach favoured by UK governments for almost 30 years. The first point to make about that policy is that it is thoroughly holistic: health is seen in relation to the full range of social, economic and environmental factors, not simply as a universal, undifferentiated attribute that can be maintained or restored by various discrete treatments. Consequently, Welsh Labour places far greater emphasis than New Labour in England on the prevention of illness through an active public health policy, rather than simply focusing on trying to ameliorate disease and infirmity that has already been allowed to develop. Thus, Health Challenge Wales has been launched to promote healthier, more active lifestyles and there have been important initiatives like free school breakfasts and free swimming pool access for older people, and for children during school holiday periods, as well as the ban on smoking in enclosed public places.

Closely related to this is Welsh Labour's explicit recognition of the link between inequality and ill-health and its determination to address this as far as possible within the limits of the Assembly's powers – a far cry from Tony Blair's apparent unconcern about the widening gap between rich and poor. A growing body of research demonstrates that inequality is *in itself* injurious to health, giving rise to significant variations in life expectancy even within and between wealthy societies – not just because of the less healthy lifestyles of the poor, but because of the 'psycho-social' implications of feeling forever devalued.[29] Thus the Assembly government's health policy – in the words of Cabinet special advisor, Mark Drakeford – 'embod[ies] a radical shift from the politics of equality of opportunity to the far more fundamental politics of equality of outcome.'[30] The respected academic, Peter Townsend, was commissioned to develop a needs-based formula for the allocation of funding to local authorities, to ensure that resources were targeted at the areas of greatest deprivation. A Health Inequalities Fund has been established, with an annual budget of £5 million, to support community-based schemes that aim to tackle the risk factors for coronary heart disease in disadvantaged areas.

Thus far, the Assembly government's approach to public health has been somewhat weakened by its diffusion among a large number of separate strategies and initiatives. In September 2008, however, Edwina Hart announced the formation of a unified public health organisation (UPHO), in accordance with the recommendations of an independent review; a consultation was to follow early in 2009.

Accountability

Welsh health policy also puts a strong emphasis on local accountability: the establishment of the 22 LHBs as the principal commissioning bodies – for all the difficulties with this policy – was intended to democratise health provision, bringing a broad-based local perspective to the planning and allocation of services. With the planned merger of LHBs and trusts and the transfer of service planning 'upwards' to a new national NHS board, the challenge for the Assembly government will be – to quote its 2005 health strategy document, *Designed for Life* – 'to strike a balance between local planning and delivery and a broad all-Wales strategic framework.'[31] *Designed for Life* affirms Welsh Labour's commitment to citizen 'voice' – and pointedly spells out its precedence over consumer 'choice': 'We will aim to empower the community to have its voice heard and heeded, rather than simply being given a choice of treatment location.'[32]

The April 2008 consultation paper on NHS reorganisation acknowledges that, '[w]ith fewer organisations, patient and public engagement will have to be secured in new ways' and asks how the new bodies' governance arrangements can ensure that the views of local populations – whether 'small communities, housing estates, or population groups' – are reflected in the deliberations of the National Board.[33] The December consultation proposes the establishment of stakeholder reference groups (SRGs) with up to 25 members apiece, which would 'sit alongside' each new LHB, 'provid[ing] advice to the LHB Board on any issues it considers important to citizens'. It is suggested that SRGs could include representatives from:

* Community Groups;
* Young People;
* Provider Bodies;
* Fire Service/Police Service;
* Community Councils;
* Black and Minority Ethnic groups.[34]

This is a welcome proposal; with the decision to merge LHBs and trusts, it becomes even more important that robust structures of local accountability are built into the system. Accountability within the NHS has always tended to be 'upwards', ultimately to the Department of Health and the Secretary of State, to the near-total exclusion of any local, grassroots influence over decision-making; the NHS in Wales now has an opportunity to address this.

SRGs will, however, have only advisory powers; one means of further strengthening accountability that should be considered would be making some of the positions within the new LHBs subject to election. This policy may be applied to Scotland's health boards, under legislation recently introduced in the Scottish Parliament by the SNP Government (although the idea was first proposed by the Labour MSP, Bill Butler, in 2006). The proposals, which would initially be implemented on a pilot basis, would see a majority of health board positions filled by a combination of direct election for four-yearly terms and nomination by local authorities from among their own elected members.[35] Another means of involving patients and the public in the workings of the NHS in Wales is through the community health councils (CHCs), which were abolished in England in 2003 but retained in Wales and function as independent local health watchdogs, monitoring NHS performance and providing a patient advocacy service for pursuing complaints. It is reassuring to note that the recent consultation saw a 'general consensus' in favour of strengthening CHCs' scrutiny role and that the further consultation that is due to take place will incorporate proposals on their number and future role. It is also vital that the views of health workers are represented in the decision-making process. Since 2001, union representatives have sat on the boards of NHS trusts and the December 2008 consultation paper proposes that this arrangement be carried over to the new unified LHBs. It is important that unions are given sufficient seats on boards to provide them with an effective voice and that their role, with its attendant rights and responsibilities, is made clear at the outset.

'What matters is what works'

The progressive thrust of Assembly government health policy has not been sufficient to secure consistent public acclaim. In part, this reflects a failing on the part of ministers and their spokespeople: the ideas underlying specific policy initiatives have rarely been stated explicitly; where they have been articulated at all, it has been in the context of more discursive comments on Welsh Labour's philosophy by Rhodri Morgan or his key advisors. This somewhat diffident approach, combined with the hostility or indifference of the media, has left many Welsh people with a jaundiced view of the NHS in Wales, influenced disproportionately by reports of (real or perceived) service failures – in particular, the problem of long waiting times, where progress has been evident only comparatively recently. The situation has improved somewhat with Edwina Hart's appointment as health minister, as her resolute action has been matched by a refreshing political clarity in the presentation of policy. Socialists in Wales still have a major job to do, however, in explaining and arguing for Welsh Labour's under-appreciated health policy as a progressive alternative to its equivalent across the Severn Bridge.

It is almost inevitable that a policy oriented towards the long term will appear less impressive in the here-and-now. For some time, the uproar over Wales' persistently lengthy waiting times – compared unfavourably with their steady reduction in England – drowned out any discussion of Wales' more positive long-term policies. In the run-up to the 2005 general election, there was vocal criticism even from within the Labour party, as certain MPs in marginal seats expressed concern that the negative publicity over waiting times was making their electoral demise more likely. A more considered critique came from Chris Bryant, probably the Welsh MP who is ideologically closest to New Labour. In a pamphlet on 'progressive reform', he argued that the

> refusal or reluctance to use measures such as diagnostic and treatment centres or private-sector capacity in sufficient measure as to increase surgery capacity at speed seems like an ideologically driven decision that reduces the health opportunities of the poorest in the Rhondda... To reject policy ideas that do seem to have delivered improvements in England and to do so purely so as to establish clear red water would be irresponsible and wrong.[36]

As the different approaches have been put to the test, however, it has increasingly been the Westminster government's methods that have appeared more 'ideologically driven' – not least in its persistence with measures such as ISTCs, in the face of evidence that they represent questionable value for public money, to put it mildly. In Wales, significant progress has been made since the time – barely four years ago – when the numbers waiting more than eighteen months for both outpatient and inpatient appointments could be counted in the thousands. It was announced in April 2008 that outpatient and inpatient waits of more than 22 weeks had been virtually eliminated and there is now a commitment to reduce the entire 'patient journey' from primary care referral to treatment, including any waiting for diagnostic tests, to no more than 26 weeks by the end of 2009.[37] Critics of the Assembly government's progress point out that it is still lagging behind England, where the target is a maximum eighteen-week overall wait by the end of 2008. Research published recently in the *Health Service Journal* casts doubt, however, on the extent to which England may have out-performed Wales in this respect. The research was prompted by a Civitas report suggesting that the UK government's waiting times initiative had significantly reduced the longest waiting times in England but had relatively little impact on median waits; it had basically 'tighten[ed] up the distribution of waits to produce a much shorter "tail" '. An examination of median and ninetieth percentile waiting times in England and Wales for a sample of four representative procedures over the previous five years concluded that 'waits in both countries are decreasing at a very similar rate'. The author reflected:

> This raises a big question about the strategy to reduce waiting in England. Wales has not made a large-scale investment but has focused on systemic tools such as demand and capacity planning. Did England need to spend so much, and did it really need to develop a plurality of providers, in order to achieve its waiting time gains?[38]

It is to be hoped that the progress made in Wales will increasingly be recognised. It should also be noted, however, that the concentration on waiting time statistics is out of proportion to the significance of what is being measured: neither primary care, nor emergency admissions, nor follow-up outpatient or inpatient appointments are covered by the figures and most patient experience of the NHS does not involve ever being on a waiting list (although this is not to dismiss the inconvenience and discomfort of those who do have to wait).

Nevertheless, public dissatisfaction with aspects of the NHS in Wales lingers. During the 2007 Assembly elections, hospital reconfiguration, insofar as it entailed cutbacks to local services, undoubtedly cost Welsh Labour votes, especially in West Wales; the subsequent commitment in *One Wales* to undertake thorough consultation over any contentious proposals will hopefully facilitate a greater consensus over some of the difficult decisions that need to be made. Cross-border differences with England will no doubt continue to cause sporadic discontent, as long as the comparison is unfavourable to Wales. The 'postcode lottery' in relation to the availability of particular drugs will, however, be overcome – within Wales, at any rate – when service planning is taken on by the proposed all-Wales board.

Ultimately, though, socialists must focus on the 'big picture' and assess the capacity of Welsh Labour's health policy to meet its progressive, egalitarian objectives. The declarations of *One Wales* could hardly be clearer with regard to health policy, especially on privatisation:

> We firmly reject the privatisation of NHS services or the organisation of such services on market models. We will guarantee public ownership, public funding and public control of this vital public service.[39]

Nevertheless, there remain some vestiges of privatisation, which sit uneasily with these overall policy aims – not least, the private sector's encroachment on NHS primary care in the form of contracts to run GP out-of-hours services. This issue is not specifically addressed in *One Wales* but Edwina Hart has recently made it clear that she intends to bring these services in-house at the earliest opportunity. There have also been some voices pushing for the introduction of the 'payment by results' framework, which would be a highly destabilising measure and should therefore be strenuously opposed. A longer-term, and somewhat more benign, anomaly is the continuing status of GPs as independent contractors – a remnant of the compromises that Bevan had to accept in establishing the NHS. The Assembly government has favoured the introduction of salaried GPs, albeit mainly as a way of plugging gaps in primary care provision caused by retiring GPs; it should be strongly encouraged to expand the salaried model wherever possible.

In the long term, as Julian Tudor Hart has argued, it is not sufficient simply to defend the founding principles of the NHS from the incursions of the marketeers; those principles must be realised more fully than they ever were before the neo-liberal attack on the service began in the 1980s. As part of this, the barriers between health professionals and patients need to be broken down, with the former acknowledging and embracing scientific doubt and the latter becoming more proactive in taking responsibility for their own health. Working together in partnership, health professionals and patients could not only produce steady improvements in health but also contribute towards the construction of a cooperative socialist society.[40]

Education for equality

From an early stage, education policy began to be seen as the flagship of both Welsh Labour's progressive agenda and the devolution project itself. While the New Labour government in Westminster pursued a 'reform' programme that has provoked ever-greater controversy, the Assembly government's record in education and lifelong learning presented an appealing contrast. Its clear alternative vision, and the evident determination to realise that vision, have become the most widely-recognised evidence of the positive impact of devolution, with even sections of the British media acknowledging that Assembly policies were working in Wales – and might even prove better for England than New Labour's approach, if they were implemented there.[41] Wales' distinct policies have contributed to significant improvement in Welsh educational performance but there remain serious gaps in attainment both within Wales and between Wales and other parts of the UK. Given the Assembly's inheritance of severe poverty and inequality, and the limited powers it has to combat these problems, it would be surprising if it were otherwise. Yet the Assembly's policies are both evidence-based and founded on a commitment to social justice – something that cannot be said for the deeply ideological, market-driven agenda pursued by New Labour, which has now given rise to the nightmarish project of academies and trust schools run by corporate hucksters and religious fundamentalists.

The 'quasi-market'

As with health policy, New Labour has largely adopted and extended the education programme of the Tories, which the party strongly criticised while in opposition. The central thrust of this is the commodification of learning, as an early speech by then education secretary, David Blunkett, made clear:

> We must move from an education system which caters for the producers to one which puts the needs of the consumers – pupils and their parents – at the heart of its approach.[42]

The crucial turning-point, as with the NHS internal market, had come during Thatcher's third term, with the 1988 Education Act's creation of a 'quasi-market', through the introduction of a number of inter-related mechanisms. First, 'open enrolment' allowed parents to exercise their 'consumer choice' between schools, rather than have their child automatically attend the designated school serving the local area.[43] Second, there was significant devolution of budgetary and administrative responsibility from local education authorities (LEAs) to schools themselves – encouraging them to behave as competing businesses – along with the option of schools seceding from LEA control altogether, to take up 'grant-maintained' (GM) status (to their considerable financial advantage). Finally, the establishment of the national curriculum and standardised testing allowed for the compilation of league tables based on test results, thus providing 'market signals' to enable the parent-consumers to select the 'producer' (school) most likely to provide them with a satisfactory commodity (the educated child). In keeping with the market principle of diversity of provision, the Tories also introduced the assisted places scheme, which provided state funding to enable pupils from lower-income families to attend independent schools; city technology colleges (CTCs), established with private sponsorship and free from LEA control, which were intended to compete for pupils with established schools in areas where existing provision was considered inadequate; and a network of 'specialist schools', given additional resources to sustain their proven excellence in a designated field such as foreign languages, sport or the arts.

The Tories also began the reintroduction of pupil selection by schools, rolling back the comprehensive education revolution of the 1960s and 1970s. In reality, this was an inevitable concomitant of 'open enrolment', since an excess of demand over supply for places in the more popular schools gives those schools the discretion to choose which pupils to admit. CTCs were allowed to set written examinations for potential pupils and interview their parents; many GM schools used the freedom to set their own admissions criteria in order to introduce selection by general ability; and, from 1993, all secondary schools were permitted to select up to ten per cent of their pupils on the basis of aptitude in a subject area regarded as the school's particular strength.[44]

'Diversity and choice'
While New Labour scrapped some Tory policies, such as the assisted places scheme and nursery vouchers, there has been more continuity than change overall, especially in the areas of selection, school diversity and the downgrading of LEAs. David Blunkett's pre-election promise to end selection by ability in nominally comprehensive schools was abandoned when Labour came to legislate: individual schools' pre-1997 selection practices were allowed to continue – provided that the degree of selection did not increase – but a code of practice on admissions was instituted, along with an adjudicator, to whom parents could direct challenges to schools' policies. Moreover, the right of specialist schools to select up to ten per cent of their pupils by aptitude was enshrined in law. Nor was there any real attempt to deal with the remaining grammar schools: provision was made for local ballots on going comprehensive but the rules under which these were to be conducted made any attempt

to end selection almost impossible.[45] The grant-maintained schools programme was brought to a halt but existing GM schools were given the option of returning to LEA control or becoming 'foundation' schools (which most chose to do) and retaining most of the freedoms they had enjoyed under the Tories. The 2006 Education and Inspections Act saw the effective rebirth of GM status, through the creation of self-governing 'trust' schools, which own their own assets, employ their own staff and set their own admissions policies (subject to a strengthened admissions code); the main innovation is that the trust has to be formed with an external partner – a business, charity or another educational institution. This development continued the attenuation of LEAs: New Labour had already gone further than the Tories in giving all schools 100 per cent financial delegation; as of the 2006 Act, English local authorities effectively ceased to have a distinct educational function, beyond being a 'champion of parents and pupils' with a duty to promote choice, diversity, high standards and the fulfilment of individuals' potential. In higher education too, New Labour has extended the Tories withdrawal of state support to students, first making students pay their own tuition fees and then allowing universities the discretion to 'top up' those fees.

New Labour did initially introduce a fairer school funding regime, reducing the huge advantages previously enjoyed by GM schools, but it has subsequently created new financial disparities, in promoting an increasing variety of school type. The government has massively expanded the specialist schools programme, with schools initially granted specialist status on condition that they raise £100,000 (later reduced to £50,000) in private sponsorship, which would then be match-funded by the government. The declared aspiration that all schools should develop their own specialism at least establishes the possibility that each might ultimately share in the additional resources currently available only to the select few. Until 2005, extra funding was also made available for 'beacon' schools, which had had particularly good inspection reports and were consequently considered suitable to serve as 'centres of excellence' for those around them.

Perhaps the most striking example of the continuity between Tory and New Labour education policies has been the revival of the CTC concept in the guise of the 'city academies' programme. Despite the failure of CTCs to realise the Thatcher government's hopes for a dynamic business role in education, backed by substantial private money, Blunkett re-launched the idea in 2000 and it has since become the centrepiece of New Labour's schools policies. Academies, established with new purpose-built premises, are supposed to provide a fresh start for pupils from 'failing' schools, especially in deprived inner city areas (although the 'city' tag has been dropped as the programme has expanded). Sponsors from the worlds of private business, charity or religion have been invited to provide £2 million toward the capital costs, in return for which they are able to determine the new school's 'ethos', dictate its curriculum, control its recruitment and appoint a majority of its governors. All the legislative and regulatory obligations of normal state schools are set aside in favour of a 'funding agreement', negotiated by the sponsor with the Department. Controversy has also been created by the influence of religion on some academies' curricula. In the two academies (and the one CTC) sponsored by Sir Peter Vardy, a Christian fundamentalist car dealer, creationism has been presented as having equal validity with evolution by natural selection. Similar concerns apply to the two academies controlled by Vardy's friend, business associate and fellow evangelist, Robert Edmiston; other academies are run by more mainstream Christian organisations.

New Labour ministers brush aside concerns about such issues, arguing that what really matters are the educational benefits conferred by academies, yet the record here is far from unambiguous. While some academies have undoubtedly improved on the schools that they have replaced, in other cases, the existing school was certainly not 'failing' and the academy project had to be forced through against the objections of local people who wanted to retain the status quo.[46] Sometimes, hard-pressed comprehensives making sustained, patient progress with children in deprived inner-city areas have been systematically undermined and denigrated in order to make way for a new academy. By November 2005, three years after the first academies opened, two had failed their Ofsted inspections, one of which was put in 'special measures', and a third was 'teetering on the brink of failure'.[47] In 2008, a quarter of the 36 longest-established academies saw their GCSE results decline[48] and, while academies' results generally outstripped those of other secondary schools – in terms of increased numbers of A*-C passes – it should be borne in mind that they have benefited from far higher funding than the average comprehensive; with an equivalent cash injection other schools might have obtained similar results. It should also be remembered that the vast bulk of this extra money has come from the government. The £2 million that sponsors were originally asked to contribute (£1.5 million apiece if they sponsored more than three academies) represents no more than a tenth of the capital costs of each academy. Not only are the sponsorship fees tax-deductible, but in many cases, part of the money has been paid 'in kind', in the form of facilities or staff time made available to academies. And as of October 2006, new academies' capital costs are met entirely from public funds, with sponsors asked instead to make a £2 million contribution to revenue funding, spread over five years. Moreover, 'successful independent schools' interested in sponsoring an academy are now exempted from any requirement to make a financial contribution.

The academy programme underlines the point that in education, as in healthcare, New Labour has surpassed the Tories in its enthusiasm for involving the private sector in the provision of public services. The government has relied, of course, on PFI for its school rebuilding programme, with all the same problems, not least in terms of spiralling costs, that have been seen in the NHS. The impetus that was to lead to academies and trust schools can be detected in the earlier launch of Education Action Zones (EAZs), which, likewise, sought to raise standards in 'struggling areas' by encouraging businesses to provide financial sponsorship and play a strategic role in local school improvement. EAZs were allowed to set aside the national curriculum in order to concentrate on literacy and numeracy, and to set their own salary levels, but the scheme was adjudged a failure and scrapped in 2001, after three years. Nevertheless, the doors remained wide open to the private sector. Big companies were feted for their civic virtue when they hurried to supplement schools' resources with 'gifts' – computers from Tesco, textbooks (laced with advertising) from McDonald's, a football coaching scheme established by Nike, even a literacy scheme sponsored by the *Sun* – despite the obvious brand-promotion opportunities. Since 1999, New Labour has allowed private and third-sector providers to bid to take over some or all of the functions of 'failing' LEAs – yet many of these were soon failing themselves, with WS Atkins pulling out of Southwark halfway through a five-year contract and the government sending in a taskforce to help Serco run education in Bradford, when the firm had already lowered targets to protect its bonuses.[49] The outsourcing of schools' 'back office' operations was also encouraged, with private companies organising 'everything from recruiting teachers to organising payrolls, ordering stationery and IT supplies, and maintaining classrooms'.[50] Soon, companies like Nord Anglia were being entrusted with the management of complete schools, with bonuses offered for improvements in exam results, exclusion rates and parental preference scores.

The effects of the 'choice' agenda

With a major education act placed on the statute book almost every year since it took office, New Labour has certainly made good Tony Blair's promise that its priorities would be 'education, education, education'. Moreover, it has invested significant resources in the sector (although the extent of any real-terms increase over previous spending levels is a matter of dispute). The social and educational outcomes of its policies are more questionable. In England, there are still 164 grammar schools and one fifth of local authorities have selective schools. Some urban areas have private schools, selective state schools (grammars and secondary moderns), semi-selective 'comprehensives' (specialist and/or foundation schools), city technology colleges, academies and faith schools of one sort or another. 'The government's justification for this dog's breakfast is diversity', commented Alan Smithers, Professor of Education at Liverpool University.

> It is supposed to work through parents expressing their preferences. But that depends on where you live. Only some of these schools will be represented in any given area and they will differ in being foundation, community or aided, coeducational or single-sex, and with or without religious affiliation … LEAs … have a duty to ensure that there are enough school places, but have no control over the type of places or the admissions policies of foundation and aided schools. Instead of selection by ability, Labour seems to be espousing selection by mortgage.[51]

The Tory-New Labour 'choice' agenda does not distribute educational opportunity in a neutral or equitable manner: some parents – notably, the assertive middle class – are better-equipped than others to work the system, making use of SATs and league tables to shop around for the 'best' schools. Their choices restrict others' ability to choose – for example, undermining the viability of a local school on which many families may depend by sending their own children to a 'better' school further away. Locked into this system, many schools will exclude pupils whose performance, for whatever reason, may adversely affect their league table position. In the 2006–07 school year, academies were responsible for 2 per cent of all temporary exclusions and 3 per cent of permanent exclusions in England, despite accounting for only 0.3 per cent of state schools.[52] The same mentality results in whole subjects being dropped from the curriculum, or downgraded. The 'diversity' afforded by recent reforms does not extend to what is taught, or how it is taught:

[C]hoice has increased differences between schools in intake and resources, but has done more to encourage them to play safe than to engage in conspicuous innovation in curriculum or pedagogy.[53]

Thus, schools teach in order to maintain or improve the SATs results and the league table, which in turn results in the factory farming of the national curriculum, and the widespread feeling among young people that education is something done *to* them.

The 'choice' agenda has promoted the growth of covert 'social selection'. Schools' increasing freedom to depart from the strictly comprehensive model and to determine their own admissions policies has increased the social segregation of pupils, as more selective schools have introduced admissions criteria that allow them to filter out less academically promising pupils: hence they have far fewer pupils eligible for free school meals (the main proxy measure for deprivation), fewer with additional needs and a lower proportion of ethnic minorities.[54] Research by Professor Stephen Gorard suggests that this makes little difference to individuals' attainment, since most of the statistical variation in schools' exam results can be explained by reference to their varying pupil intake, but it can have negative consequences for pupils' conception of social justice.[55] Even academies, which were supposed to benefit children from deprived backgrounds, have become more socially selective in many cases, with eight of the first fourteen taking fewer pupils on free school meals than the schools that they replaced.[56] With academies and other favoured schools enjoying enhanced resources and prestige and the ability to cherry-pick the most able pupils, other neighbouring schools are left to educate a disproportionate share of the most challenging children, facing only criticism and decline as their exam results inevitably reflect the difficulties of their task and funding is reduced to reflect falling numbers.

Faced with a competitive and inequitable system, it is understandable that many parents in England should strive to secure the 'best' education – as conventionally defined – for their own children, yet all the evidence suggests that most parents simply want access to a good quality local school, without having to negotiate the paraphernalia of the quasi-market and to choose the variety of educational provision most suited to their own child's needs. The 'choice' agenda has been driven by ideology, far more than by any firm evidence base; the rapid expansion of the government's academies programme, for example, has proceeded against the advice of many – including the Commons Education Select

Committee – who suggested evaluating the results to date before going further. There certainly seems little basis for current policy in any examination of best practice elsewhere: while meaningful international comparisons are difficult, the countries that score most highly in the OECD's triennial Programme for International Student Assessment (PISA), which measures skills in mathematics, reading, science and problem-solving, do not share England's growing emphasis on selection, diversity and choice – least of all Finland, which has the best overall record.[57]

What is education for?

Education systems can tell us a lot about the society of which they are a part. In Britain, government education policy has traditionally reflected the needs of employers. They needed the schools to turn out people educated enough to be able to read, write, do calculations, operate machinery and, where appropriate, progress onto apprenticeships or college. Under New Labour, the principle is the same, albeit updated so that young people are trained less for heavy industry and more for call centres and work with information technology. This is reflected in the national curriculum, with its narrow emphasis on English, maths and IT at the expense of other subjects, and its obsession with targets and testing. (Whether it is successful in doing this, even on its own terms, is difficult to say; every so often, a representative of the CBI will appear in the media berating the education system for failing, as they see it, to train young people for the world of work.)

Of course, even when educated under these conditions, people have benefited from the jobs that are available, as anyone who has found work after having been unemployed will testify. It is, however, possible for education to start from a premise other than what is in the interests of employers – namely, the interests of the young people concerned, their families and communities. The comprehensive movement, embraced by the left in the 1950s and 1960s, was founded on the belief that education should not simply be a preparation for the job deemed most suitable, but the basis for as rich and fulfilling a life as possible. Such progressive ideas were under sustained attack from the new right by the early 1970s and were further undermined by James Callaghan in his 1976 Ruskin College speech, in which he questioned whether Britain's education system was sufficiently assisting the country's competitiveness at a time of deepening recession. An instrumentalist view of education has increasingly prevailed since then but Welsh Labour, at least, has

87

sought to restore the idea that education and lifelong learning are important because they serve the cause of social justice, providing a realisation of human potential and a route out of poverty for disadvantaged people and communities. By opening up the opportunities that come with well-paid, fulfilling jobs, education and lifelong learning help to combat the inequality which still defaces Wales, as it does Britain as a whole.

The Welsh alternative: equality, not 'choice'

As education minister between 2000 and 2007, Jane Davidson was happy to acknowledge that Welsh Labour's education policy represented a radical departure, both in philosophy and in substance, from the market-driven, 'choice'-oriented, class-ridden policies which have plagued England under the Tories and New Labour. For example, at the launch in September 2001 of the Assembly government document, *Wales: A Learning Country*, she said:

> [T]here would be real risks in a wholesale shift to extensive and untested measures delivered solely through the private or other sectors without the most careful consideration. *As a matter of policy*, that reliance on the private sector has been ruled out for Wales. So too has the introduction of a programme of specialist schools.[58]

Former Assembly special advisor, David Egan, has argued that, whereas education policy in England can be said to be based on choice, contestability and the consumer, Welsh Labour has at the centre of its policy a different set of 'C's: collaboration, community and the citizen. Whereas New Labour, in the person of Alistair Campbell, famously declared that the age of the 'bog-standard' comprehensive was over, Jane Davidson stated that 'we have a comprehensive system that we are fully proud of, and which has serves Wales very well. I don't believe the private sector has a role in the delivery of education in Wales'.[59] The consumerism underlying Tory and New Labour education policy – which, as we have seen, is (at best) unproven even in England as an approach to raising standards across the board – is particularly inappropriate in Wales, with its legacy of deprivation and economic decline.

In 1979, more than a quarter of all school-leavers in Wales had no qualifications at all – a far higher proportion than in any other part of Britain – due, in part, to the prevalence of conservative teaching methods and a lack of attention to the needs of low achievers. This became even more problematic as the 18-year Tory assault on Wales wiped out manual jobs in extractive and manufacturing industries and 'numeracy, literacy and IT skills were increasingly required for roles in even the lower reaches of the labour market'.[60] Educational failure became increasingly characteristic of the declining industrial areas – especially the South Wales valleys – as lack of economic opportunity lowered aspirations. The Assembly government has attempted to break the cycle of disadvantage and low attainment, concentrating particular attention on the 'long tail' of non-achievers and low-achievers. Thus far, it has had only partial success. In 1992, only 75 per cent of 16 year olds in Wales obtained the equivalent of at least five GCSE passes and only 33 per cent achieved those GCSEs at the higher grades of A*-C. By 2007, these figures had increased to 86 per cent and 54 per cent, respectively – although the number getting five passes had hardly changed since 2000.[61] The proportion of 16 year olds getting no qualifications or 'just a few' is still higher than in any of the English regions.[62] At 19, one in four young people in Wales still does not have the 'basic' level of qualifications defined as five 'good' GCSE passes or GNVQ level two, and one in ten has no qualifications at all; moreover, this figure has shown no sustained improvement in the last ten years.[63] Wales continues to have a large number of unskilled workers who do not participate in any form of adult or continuing education or training. At the end of 2006, 43,200 19–24 year olds in Wales (18 per cent) were still 'Neets' ('not in education, employment or training'), a figure that was higher than in other parts of the UK and had been steadily rising.[64] There is a strong correlation between deprivation and poor educational attainment: among the tenth of schools with the highest proportion of pupils on free school meals, 25 per cent of 16 year olds failed to get five GCSEs in 2007, compared to 14 per cent of all pupils. The former figure had decreased from 37 per cent ten years earlier, narrowing the gap in attainment, but, again, the rate of improvement seems to have stalled around 2000.[65]

With this in mind, education policy in Wales is underpinned by the doctrine of 'progressive universalism', discussed earlier in this chapter – 'universal' because state education is for everyone, and not simply a safety net service for the poor, but 'progressive' because additional support is targeted where it is needed most. This is the idea behind the 'Flying Start' initiative, which funds supportive services for children aged 0–3 in Wales' most disadvantaged communities, providing free, high-quality childcare for two year olds, extra health visiting, basic skills programmes and parenting courses, which currently benefit around 16,000 children. The Assembly government's RAISE (Raising Attainment and

Individual Standards in Education) initiative, aimed at schools where the free school meals eligibility is 20 per cent or more, also targets the link between deprivation and low educational attainment, providing schools with funding to enable them to give extra support to their most disadvantaged pupils. School breakfasts were a recognition that children from some homes cannot hope to keep up with their peers because when they get to school they have nothing inside them. It is unsurprising that the Tories sneered at the idea – on the grounds that children should be at home, having breakfast with their families – but anyone genuinely committed to a more equal society must recognise that early intervention is vital to prevent children from poorer families falling any further behind than need be the case.

Perhaps the Assembly government's most radical initiative in education has been the Foundation Phase for three to seven year olds, which began to be rolled out across Wales in September 2008 after successful piloting over the previous four years. On the basis of evidence from Scandinavia in particular, this programme places child development and learning through play – rather than formal lessons – at the heart of the curriculum. Notwithstanding some concerns about whether sufficient funding is available to maintain the necessary staff-pupil ratios, the Foundation Phase has won overwhelming acclaim from within the education sector. This has an importance beyond the debates among educationalists. The aim, in imitation of those countries where a similar regime is in place, is an improvement in educational attainment right across the board – and, thus, greater equality. Such innovation in teaching methods is complemented by the promotion of community-focused schools, which act as the focus for a range of learning and other activities, far beyond the traditional school day.

Progress and challenges

In age 14–19 education, again, there is a clear contrast with the policies pursued in England. The New Labour government in London has missed a golden opportunity to reform this sector by rejecting the Tomlinson report; it did not want to upset middle England by getting rid of 'gold-standard' 'A' levels. Wales, by contrast, is committed to transforming 14–19 education in stages up to 2015, offering within the Welsh Baccalaureate a more flexible curriculum, a greater range of attainment and more opportunities for vocational and work-based learning. The emphasis is on offering high quality courses for all young people at the expense of the English fixation with 5 GCSEs at grades A*-C, and at the same time ending the outdated and class-ridden division between so-called 'academic' and 'vocational' education. The Learning Pathways policy provides greater scope for learners aged 14–19 in Wales to follow a course of study that best suits their own needs and interests, chosen from a local area curriculum or 'options menu', and the Assembly government is making use of a legislative 'measure' to impose a duty on LEAs to support this choice.

In higher education, Welsh-domiciled students have been shielded from the impact of New Labour's top-up fees: they are required to pay only the basic £1,255 rate for their tuition, with the Assembly government making up the remainder of the £3,145 that universities are now entitled to charge (students not domiciled in Wales still have to pay the full amount, on graduation). Welsh Labour opposed top-up fees from the outset but had, by 2005, reluctantly decided to back down, for purely budgetary reasons, supported by the Rees review of higher education funding; the original ban on top-up fees was restored, however, as a result of a resolution supported by the other three parties (in the case of the Tories, no doubt for purely opportunist reasons). Welsh Labour has also re-introduced a means-tested maintenance grant, in an effort to assist the 20 per cent who are most disadvantaged and least likely to participate in higher education; students whose family income is below £18,370 receive the full Assembly learning grant of £2,835 per year, while those whose household income is between £18,371 and £39,300 qualify for a partial grant.

Right across the board, therefore, Welsh Labour's education policies differ radically from those of New Labour in their substance and in their philosophy. These policies are continuing under the Labour-Plaid coalition, augmented by, among other things, a pilot of Plaid's policy of a laptop for every child. *One Wales* leaves no doubt as to its central ethos, reaffirming that education is a right, not a commodity to be bought and sold. The aim that education and lifelong learning should serve the cause of social justice is as praiseworthy as it is ambitious, but can it succeed? There have, as we have seen, already been measurable improvements in educational attainment in Wales, albeit that the rate of improvement has slowed. The principal obstacles to further progress are the poverty and inequality that constrain people's life chances from birth in so many parts of Wales. The Assembly government's policy-makers – many of them former teachers or social workers – are well aware of this and its interventions have accordingly been tailored to offset the initial disadvantages that can limit young people's capacity to benefit from education. Moreover, every major education policy initiative undertaken in Wales has been informed by research into 'what works' internationally. Most recently, the implementation of the school effectiveness framework seeks to apply evidence as to how effective teaching, school leadership and community support can make a positive impact even with a given level of disadvantage.

No doubt there remain practical issues that should be grasped,[66] but if the Assembly government maintains its present trajectory in education, modifying its approach as necessary in the light of experience, there is every reason to suppose that its policies will continue to assist people to make the best of the available opportunities to overcome poverty – at least, within certain limits. The first of these is the limited funding available to support the various policies being implemented: dependent as it is on Westminster for its budget, the Assembly government has often struggled to provide the necessary resources for its ambitious programme. The RAISE initiative, for example, was possible only because of a one-off funding package allocated by Gordon Brown in his 2006 budget for educational improvement across the UK. At present, the implementation of the foundation phase is being phased in gradually, beginning with 2008–09 reception classes, because there is insufficient funding to make it available to all three to seven year olds at once. Even more fundamentally, the Assembly's scope for success is constrained by the limited extent to which education policies can make up for the divisions and inequities of a deeply unequal society; we will return to this point later in the present chapter.

Housing: how the market created a crisis
As a result of the failure, or refusal, of British governments over the past 30 years to meet the need for social housing, Wales has serious housing problems. According to Shelter Cymru, 7000 people in Wales live on the street, thousands live in poor quality housing in short term private lettings, illness and accidents resulting from poor housing cost the NHS in Wales £50 million per year, there remain 57,700 unfit occupied first homes in Wales and around 36,000 children live in unfit housing.[67] Recorded homelessness gradually decreased between 2005 and 2007, after having risen sharply over the previous two years, but in the 12 months up to March 2008, 12,937 Welsh households still applied to their local authority as homeless, of which only 6,367 were accepted.[68]

The foundations for current problems were laid in the 1980s and 90s by the Tories, who depleted the social housing stock through a number of privatisation measures – in particular, their promotion of the sale of council houses to their tenants at discounted prices. Wales had 308,000 local authority and other publicly-owned dwellings before the introduction of the right to buy scheme in 1980; subsequently, there have been 142,110 sales, accounting for 46 per cent of the original stock.[69] Throughout Britain, only a quarter of the £45 billion capital receipts yielded by council house sales up to 2005 had been put back into improving public housing.[70] New Labour's refusal to interfere with the right to buy has perpetuated the shortage of social housing, contributing to an unsustainable inflationary spiral in housing prices, which prevents millions of people from affording their own home, while those who can face a lifetime of debt.[71] The Welsh Assembly government is currently seeking to introduce a legislative 'measure' that would allow local authorities to suspend the right to buy in areas of housing pressure for up to five years, thus making good a commitment from Welsh Labour's 2007 election manifesto, which was carried through to *One Wales*.[72] This is an important step in the right direction, although it falls short of what is really needed: the complete abolition of the right to buy in Wales. Nevertheless, the Assembly's plans are too radical for the House of Commons Welsh Affairs Select Committee, which – as noted in the previous chapter – has abused its scrutiny role to obstruct the transfer of the necessary powers.

A central issue of contention in the field of housing policy has been New Labour's continuation of the Tory policy of promoting the large-scale voluntary transfer by local authorities of their entire council housing stock, to 'registered social landlords', which have increasingly taken on the character of private businesses. Rather than providers of housing, councils are forced, effectively, to be 'enablers'. The Treasury, in defiance of the votes at three successive Labour conferences in support of the so-called 'fourth option', has consistently refused to allow councils the same right as housing associations, housing mutuals or ALMOs (arm's length management organisations) to borrow to upgrade their housing stock or embark on new construction. In Wales, such upgrades must be carried out by 2012 in order to conform to the Assembly government's own Welsh housing quality standard (equivalent to the decent homes standard in England). This effectively rigs the ballots in favour of stock transfer. This is an attack on housing as a public service: it threatens to undermine security of tenure, affordable rents and – by replacing an elected local authority – democratic accountability. Tenants have been bribed with lavish propaganda campaigns, only after the 'yes' vote realising what they have lost. Local authorities which would prefer not to transfer their housing stock are therefore placed in an invidious position. As housing finance is not devolved, Welsh Labour's hands are tied. There has, at last, now been some tentative movement in UK government policy – beginning in September 2007, when what would have been a fourth Labour conference vote for the fourth option was avoided through the mover's agreement to remit the motion to the national policy forum (in recognition of the abolition of contemporary resolutions, which had just been agreed); housing minister, Yvette Cooper, talked about enabling councils to build new homes. At the August 2008 national policy forum, her successor, Caroline Flint, conceded that councils would be able to borrow to invest in their stock and would be eligible to apply for social housing grants but there remain concerns about the amount of funding being made available and the continuing financial pressure on councils to transfer their stock. In january 2009 Gordon Brown suggested that he might be prepared to allow local authorities to use more of their rent and sale receipts to build new council homes. Assembly government policy, as set out in *One Wales*, is to ensure that tenants are given access to impartial advice and that, in the absence of a 'significant' change of circumstances, ballots on transfer are not repeated within the lifetime of a council. These commitments are designed to prevent tenants being bombarded with promises and scare stories to make them vote for a transfer, and to prevent local authorities re-balloting until they get the result they want.

One Wales also promises to increase the amount of affordable housing stock by 6,500 over four years, and makes commitments to increase funding to support social housing and to require all 'sizeable' (whatever that means) new housing developments to include 'a percentage' of social housing reflecting local need. Any credible housing policy must address the shortage of affordable housing in rural Wales, where rising house prices, and the ability of second homeowners to outbid local people and buy up the available housing stock threatens some communities with extinction. The Assembly government is committed to introducing powers, based on the Housing Act 2004, to enable local authorities to control the conversion of houses into second homes in areas of housing pressure. Rural Wales shares with parts of rural England the problem of being turned into weekend playgrounds for the urban well-heeled. What is particular to Wales is the destructive effect this has on Welsh-speaking communities. *One Wales* promises to allow local authorities to use language impact assessments in areas of housing pressure and contains other measures aimed at increasing the supply of affordable housing, or the land to build it on, in rural areas. All of these promises are worthy of support as far as they go, and should at least contribute to an amelioration of Wales' housing crisis. They deal more with the symptoms rather than the causes, however. The commitment to specifically social housing is welcome, albeit its extent is rather vague. The pledge to provide grants for first-time buyers may have the unintended consequence of feeding the inflationary beast. Welsh Labour should be demanding that housing finance be devolved so it is no longer under the control of the Treasury. Pressure will need to be maintained on the UK government to ensure that the fourth option becomes a reality, while the left in Wales must press for the complete abolition of the right to buy. Increasing the tax burden on second homes, and imposing a tax on the value of land (as distinct from that of the property on it) – both currently beyond the competence of the Assembly – would have curbed the unsustainable, speculative boom in second homes and buying to let and would have released funds to provide affordable housing. Most importantly, the present chronic housing shortage has to be dealt with by a massive programme of social housing.

Moreover, attempts to deal with homelessness and the resulting exclusion are obstructed by current UK legislation, which imposes a duty on local authorities to investigate whether someone is 'intentionally homeless' and allows them not to re-house those deemed to fall into this category. Those who 'make themselves' homeless due to family conflicts, or as a result of their own mistakes in dealing with previous tenancies, many of them young and inexperienced, can thus be condemned to a 'spiral of homelessness and exclusion' – to quote Shelter Cymru, which is demanding that the Assembly government seeks legislative competency to reform the concept of 'intentional homelessness'.[73] At the very least, this category should not be enforced with regard to those aged under 25, and the duty to investigate 'intentional homelessness' should be reduced to the status of a discretionary power only.

An already serious situation has been given more urgency by the collapse of the housing market amid the slide into recession. Thousands of people in Wales trapped in negative equity face the loss not only of their jobs but also of their homes. Wales needs not only a major programme of social housing, but a commitment from the 'nationalised' banks to convert into lets the mortgages of those faced with repossession.

Child poverty: the 'primary political duty'

One of New Labour's most positive policy initiatives was Tony Blair's commitment, in a speech made on 18 March 1999, to 'end child poverty forever' in Britain within 20 years (supplemented shortly afterwards by the intermediate target of halving child poverty by 2010).[74] It is a scandal that, at the start of the 21st century, in the fifth biggest economy in the world, almost one in three children – 3.9 million across the UK – still lives below the widely-recognised poverty line, set at 60 per cent of national median household income after housing costs (on the government's preferred measure, which is calculated before housing costs, the figure is 2.9 million). In Wales, around 29 per cent of children – some 180,000 – still live in poverty; while this represents a decrease from 34 per cent in 2002–3,[75] it is still a disgrace. Moreover, in some wards, the figure is as high as 82 per cent.[76] The persistence of low wages in Wales means that there has been an increase in the number of working families in poverty. Welsh Labour is committed to addressing this as its 'primary political duty': 'no child will be disadvantaged because of the community into which they were born or the relative socio-economic status of their family'.[77]

At the centre of New Labour's programme to combat child poverty are the tax credit system and the Sure Start programme, which adopts a holistic approach, bringing together early years education, health, childcare and family support.[78] The record of these policies to date is somewhat mixed: it is a major achievement that 600,000 children have been lifted out of poverty since 1998–99, but Labour is lagging behind its own schedule, having missed its first target of reducing child poverty by a quarter between 1998/99 and 2004/05. Moreover, the number of children living in poverty in the UK increased by 200,000 in 2006/07 and by a further 100,000 in 2007/08.[79] By its own criteria, the government will have to free a further 1.2 million children from poverty by 2010; when housing costs are taken into account – as all the major poverty organisations argue they should be – that figure rises to 1.7 million. The Campaign to End Child Poverty has argued forcefully that, to meet this target, the government will need to spend £3 billion on benefits and child tax credits, involving substantial extra funding in the 2009 budget. After the coalition mobilised 10,000 people for its 'Keep the Promise' demonstration in London on 4 October 2008, Gordon Brown made some positive noises about meeting its aspirations; subsequently, however, the chancellor's pre-budget report offered little in the way of additional resources. Only the (temporary) VAT reduction and the bringing forward of increases in child tax credits and child benefits will provide any financial assistance to poor families. The commitment to make the abolition of child poverty a legal obligation is welcome but will not, in itself, guarantee success.

The attack on child poverty also seems increasingly at odds with the government's own welfare 'reform' agenda – as embodied, most recently, in the bill introduced in January 2009. The move towards greater conditionality in relation to benefit receipt, with sanctions in the form of benefit cuts for the non-compliant, would be highly questionable at the best of times but seems particularly wrong-headed as the economy heads into recession. All the compulsion in the world cannot push people into jobs that do not exist. And if the reforms are intended to spread the advantages of employment, this is hardly consistent with making people work for their benefits, rather than for a decent wage; nor is it acceptable to push parents into work where there is no affordable childcare available. The efficacy of the government's plans, even on their own terms, will also vary according to the economic wellbeing of a particular area, as Rhodri Morgan has pointed out:

> Whether you are going to actively participate in the labour market to some extent is determined by your perception of whether there are lots of jobs available. That's going to be very different if you live in Mountain Ash than if you live on the outskirts of London.

He also made clear his differences with the UK government over its tendency to stigmatise claimants as 'scroungers' and its readiness to make use of compulsion.[80]

Strategies, plans and targets
Welsh Labour's policy, now incorporated in the *One Wales* agreement, reflects the UK-wide target to halve child poverty by 2010 and eradicate it within another ten years. A series of documents, published since 2005, set out how it proposes to achieve this. The first of these was the child poverty strategy itself, entitled *A Fair Future for Our Children*. This has been followed by an implementation plan and a further document setting out a series of 'targets' and 'milestones' by which success in the eradication of child poverty in Wales may be measured. *A Fair Future* is a considered and comprehensive document, based on a thorough examination of the issues, including consultation with children and young people, as well as with various relevant organisations, and drawing on

the findings of an independent report by academic experts. The strategy examines, in turn, 'three principal dimensions of child poverty'[81] and sets out a series of measures by which each might be tackled. The three dimensions identified are income poverty; 'participation poverty' (i.e. exclusion from social and cultural activities); and 'service poverty' (i.e. difficulties in accessing services). While this approach helps to capture the full experience of poverty, it is striking that there is no acknowledgement of any order of priority or causal relationship between the three dimensions, yet income poverty is clearly more fundamental than the other two, which are largely consequences of financial deprivation. A similar problem pervades the whole document, which lists more than 150 different measures being undertaken, planned or considered by the Assembly government or its 'partners' such as local authorities or UK government departments. Some of these measures relate to issues like bullying or road safety, which – while important in their own right – are related to child poverty in only very indirect or tangential ways. It might be argued that this approach acknowledges that to conquer child poverty in a comprehensive and sustainable manner will require a myriad interventions, reflecting the complexity of the problem. The very breadth of the strategy suggests a lack of clear focus, however, and the presentation of vague aspirations and minor policy 'tweaks' alongside major initiatives does not convey the sense of urgency required to achieve the strategy's objectives within the declared time frame.

The implementation plan, originally presented in April 2006 and revised eight months later, is certainly a far more concise and focused document than the strategy, with only fourteen 'proposals', although, once again, these vary enormously in their scope, specificity, apparent achievability and likely impact. Alongside the very modest (reviews of programmes, development of terms of reference, establishment of minimum standards) there is the rather heroic commitment to go beyond the abolition of child poverty by 2020 and achieve 'social equality for all children in Wales up to the age of five by 2030'. Such an aim is, of course, entirely laudable but it hardly seems appropriate, in a plan for the implementation of a bold policy objective, whose achievement is by no means assured, to declare an even bolder objective, providing little indication as to how it might be attained. The more substantial proposals in the plan include the commitment that all Assembly government initiatives be 'child-proofed', each being assessed to maximise its positive impact on the poorest children in Wales. Similarly, the spending patterns of all mainstream Assembly government programmes are to be 'bent' to ensure that they give particular benefit to the poorest children and their families. There is a proposed 'Dignity for Children' programme, involving holistic, multi-agency intervention individually tailored to the hardest-to-reach children; 'career ladders', to improve the prospects of the lowest-paid public sector workers; promotion of credit unions and financial advice facilities; and expansion of integrated children's centres and 'flying start' schools. These are all practical and positive measures that might collectively make some impact on child poverty in Wales. The fact that they are the cross-cutting responsibility of the Assembly government as a whole is presented as a positive feature (i.e. child poverty as a key consideration for every mainstream programme, rather than a bolt-on extra) but the absence of a single cabinet minister with overall responsibility for the programme, supported by significant ring-fenced financial and staffing resources, gives little cause for optimism that the various discrete initiatives will be driven forward in a sufficiently concerted and determined way.

Another proposal is to measure the Assembly government's progress by means of medium-term milestones and longer-term targets and a document enumerating these duly followed in October 2006. Indicators for 2010 and 2020 are set out under a number of headings, collectively covering the major dimensions of life within which child poverty is manifested, from household income to birth weight and dental decay. This is, again, potentially a valuable exercise – recognising the complexity of child poverty as a phenomenon, and the need to fight it on several fronts at once – but it appears to have been carried out in a somewhat 'tick-box' manner: many of the targets and milestones had previously been published elsewhere, as part of a discrete area of policy delivery, such as education, while others seem to have been set rather arbitrarily;[82] bringing them together in one document acknowledges their mutual relevance but does not necessarily indicate that any serious consideration has been given to the question of how they complement each other. The Assembly government is now, however, being advised on how to achieve its targets by an expert group established in accordance with a *One Wales* commitment. The present coalition is also taking forward most of the proposals in the implementation plan, although some policies are far more advanced than others. The 'Dignity for Children' programme (or something very similar) – regarded as the centrepiece of the whole strategy by Huw Lewis, the then-deputy minister who drew up the implementation plan – seems likely to be entrusted to a new Integrated Family Support Service (IFSS); this will now be informed by the findings of a Save the Children/Bevan Foundation study on helping children in severe poverty in Wales.[83] Work is also under way to introduce an Assembly measure that would, among other things, establish a statutory requirement on public agencies, such as the NHS and local authorities, to publish a child poverty action plan relating to their activities.[84] The Assembly government's programme does seem increasingly focused on a core set of evidence-based initiatives; it remains unclear, however, that these add up to a coherent, integrated strategy.

Poverty and inequality

The greatest limitations of the Assembly government's strategy on child poverty relate not to what is said in its documents but to what is *not* said. While the dimensions and consequences of child poverty are discussed, along with the appropriate methods for its measurement, it is never adequately *defined* as a social phenomenon.[85] Its effects are identified, but not its causes – as if any problem could be abolished without a clear understanding of its origins! This analytical lacuna is not simply a Welsh problem: the whole mainstream discourse about child poverty in the UK over the past ten years has been characterised by evasiveness and question-begging, which in turn reflects the tensions inherent in the New Labour project – between, on one hand, its acceptance of neo-liberal economics with its embrace of possessive individualism and, on the other, a residual commitment to some notion of social justice, requiring government action to 'correct' the outcomes of the market economy. There is a tendency in government speeches and documents to refer to child poverty as if it were something that arises accidentally – not as an inevitable consequence of a society that promotes individual self-enrichment at the expense of social cohesion and panders to the 'tax-averse'.

The fact that government policy is directed toward *child* poverty is itself significant. There are certainly good reasons for focusing on children in this respect: their inability to alter their own material circumstances and consequent reliance on the intervention of others; and the lasting adverse impact of deprivation in early infancy on a person's later development and life-chances. But there is also a more questionable political aspect to this policy orientation, as David Adamson has pointed out: whereas all but the most zealous free-market ideologues accept the need for state intervention to protect 'innocent' children from poverty, no such consensus exists with regard to needy adults; indeed, an enduring legacy of the Thatcher era has been the revival of the Victorian distinction between the 'deserving' and 'undeserving' poor and there is a corresponding presumption that the impoverished may be largely responsible for their own predicament.[86] While the parents of children in poverty are likely to benefit from measures to assist their offspring, it should not be considered acceptable for childless adults to languish in deprivation.

Even more significant is the reluctance to acknowledge explicitly the link between child poverty and inequality. The status of moral imperative accorded to the eradication of child poverty, across the political spectrum, is sustained by campaigners and politicians emphasising the unacceptability of children – vulnerable and dependent as they are – being exposed to greater risk of ill health, sub-standard housing, educational failure and involvement in crime because they are 'poor'. Such pronouncements tend to suggest that poverty is an *absolute* category, yet the headline indicator against which the campaign's success or failure is assessed – the 60 per cent figure – is a measure of *relative* poverty. This, quite rightly, recognises that lives are blighted not only by lack of food, clothing and shelter, but by an inability to experience the standard of living considered 'normal' in any given society. Measures of relative poverty ostensibly do no more than establish a bare minimum standard, below which no one should be allowed to slip, but since the level of material resources indicated by such a minimum may vary significantly, as society overall becomes more or less prosperous, they also represent an implicit acknowledgement that socio-economic inequalities are harmful and objectionable *in themselves*.[87] This is, of course, a core socialist argument, which the left should advance more forcefully – not least since it is increasingly supported by academic research. It has been well-established that the consciousness of 'inferior' social status tends to generate chronic psycho-social stress, which can be injurious to one's health, independently of the effects of any material want. Thus, as noted earlier in this chapter, more equal societies have generally higher life expectancy, lower levels of crime and violence, a greater degree of trust, etc.

Most campaigners and academic experts recognise that the abolition of child poverty would involve making society substantially more equal and that this would require significant redistribution of income and wealth; so do the principal policy-makers within Welsh Labour, who have explicitly embraced the goal of equality of outcome, as we have noted above. Yet New Labour has consistently eschewed any commitment to greater equality – as demonstrated most (in)famously by Tony

Blair's refusal in 2001 to evince any concern about the growing gap between rich and poor.[88] More recently, the business secretary, John Hutton, argued that we should 'celebrate' huge salaries and not 'plac[e] a cap on that success.'[89] It is hard to see such indifference to inequality being compatible with the determination required to fulfil Blair's pledge to end child poverty by 2020. In this context, it is worth quoting at length from an article by the *Guardian* journalist, Polly Toynbee, who has consistently campaigned against child poverty and in favour of greater equality:

> Poverty will never be abolished without more equal incomes and lifestyles. It takes higher taxes to pay for better public services and education from infancy. The way we live has to become fairer in every way, without such sharp social divisions in wealth and opportunity, and with no housing ghettos or school segregation ... No society as grossly unequal as ours has ever cut child poverty significantly: wherever mega wealth is allowed to let rip, there will be severe poverty too ... [B]y 2002 [top directors in FTSE companies] were paid an enormous 75.7 times more than their average employee. It is a statistical and social impossibility to pretend that we can really abolish child poverty in a society shaped like that.[90]

These considerations provide the context for Welsh Labour's own efforts to abolish child poverty and illustrate the huge obstacles confronting its whole agenda of 'progressive universalism': a subordinate, sub-national administration can make only limited headway in its attempts to promote equality of outcome, when it is constrained by the social and economic policies of a national government that does not see inequality as a fundamental problem in its own right. It would be naive to think that, *by themselves*, Welsh Labour's health or education policies could transform Wales into a Celtic version of the Nordic countries, let alone a socialist society. We have already observed that a country's education system is a reflection of the society as a whole and, indeed, the same applies to its health, housing, transport and other public services. Finland's educational system is rightly admired by Welsh Labour but Finland itself is a profoundly egalitarian society.[91] Its schools do not therefore have to operate in the midst of the poverty and deprivation such as persists in some valleys communities, or the rampant inequality of Cardiff and Swansea. They do not exist in an uncivilised, low-tax, neo-liberal environment, nor are they dependent for funding on a much larger, right-wing neighbour.

One Wales talks about developing Wales-specific solutions, and integrating these with programmes currently within the remit of Westminster. The problem, however, is that many Westminster policies, not least its regressive tax, benefit and pension regimes, cut against the grain of what the Assembly government – and, indeed, the UK government itself – are trying to achieve with their child poverty strategies. Although the Cardiff administration can certainly make inroads into the problem, its lack of control over the fiscal regime governing Wales, and its inability to raise its own funding, mean that it has one hand tied behind its back. Even the best intentions are likely to be frustrated by the UK's shortage of affordable housing, the low level at which the national minimum wage is set and, above all, by its profoundly unequal distribution of income and wealth – factors over which the Welsh Assembly government has very little control, short of a major change in the devolution settlement. *A Fair Future* briefly acknowledges the centrality of non-devolved powers to any attempt to raise income and reports that representations have been made to the UK government to raise significantly the level of child benefit. In general, however, the Assembly government refers to Westminster policies only in the context of effective partnership working between the two administrations and avoids – understandably, perhaps – any overt criticism of the inequality fostered by UK fiscal policy. Nevertheless, it must add to the pressure for a more progressive tax and benefit regime, if it wants to defend the best interests of the poorest children and families in Wales, as well as developing a case for devolved tax-raising powers. Within the scope of its own existing powers, the Assembly government needs – as recent studies have argued[92] – to give greater consideration to the relationship between education and child poverty and to make better use of its financial resources to ensure that its interventions make the greatest possible impact.[93] With the recession threatening to erode the gains that have been made in tackling child poverty, there is a need for determined and energetic political leadership on this question, which would be assisted by concentrating overall responsibility in the hands of a single cabinet minister, with the appropriate administrative support.

Chapter 6

Economy and environment

In this chapter, we turn to policy areas for which the Assembly has only partial responsibility: economic development, transport, energy and the environment. Partly because of the 'semi-devolved' status of these portfolios, Welsh Labour has not established so distinctive a policy course as in health or education. In our view, however, there is the scope – indeed, the *necessity* – for a bolder and more radical agenda here too.

The challenge of the Welsh economy

Some of the most upbeat statements in Welsh Labour's 2007 election manifesto were to be found in the section on economic development:

> Today in Wales there are more people in work than ever before and total jobs are up 140,000 since devolution ... Labour has provided several billions in support for Welsh based businesses – securing and creating thousands of jobs and giving companies the stability and support they need ... The strength of the Welsh economy lies in its increasing diversity.'[1]

The subsequent course of events in the world economy could not have been predicted by the manifesto's authors, but even at the time, the cheery tone glossed over the significant structural problems that a socialist government would seek to address. Wales' economy has continued to be marked by the historical legacy of rapid, uneven industrial development, equally rapid decline and a painful restructuring process, all of which has had grave consequences for the wellbeing of its people and the cohesion of its communities.

For most of the last 250 years, the pattern of economic activity in Wales has been determined by its usefulness, or otherwise, as a source of raw materials and cheap labour for manufacturing industry based in England and further afield. Wales' economy and society were first transformed by the iron industry, only for this to be surpassed, during the nineteenth century, by coal, when 'Wales became the mining annex of the world's greatest imperial power'.[2] The country's landscape, demography and social fabric were all subjected to enormous upheaval at a time when the ruling laissez-faire ideology precluded any government action to ensure that growth took place in a balanced and sustainable fashion. Similarly, the abrupt collapse of Wales' industrial prosperity in the 1930s at first provoked little response from the state. Only when the depression prompted some 400,000 people to leave Wales in search of work, did the government begin to abandon the prevailing free market orthodoxy and invest in infrastructural development, like the Treforest Industrial Estate (established in 1937), to attract new work in place of lost mining jobs. After the war, there was finally some concerted effort by government to re-balance the British economy between and within regions; a range of financial incentives and planning controls was deployed to direct industry to areas like South Wales and there was the beginning of a diffusion of state employment, with government offices like the DVLC and the Royal Mint located in Swansea and Llantrisant, respectively.

Only in 1967, however, was the first attempt made at coherent economic planning for the Welsh economy, with the publication of the Welsh Office document, *Wales: The Way Ahead*. This, moreover, greatly underestimated the depth of Wales' structural economic problems and the scale of the task of reconstruction. At a time of optimism about the Welsh economy, with the growth of newer industries like vehicle manufacture and light engineering, and major infrastructural developments like the construction of the M4, the Severn Bridge and the Heads of the Valleys Road, there was little expectation of the scale of the de-industrialisation to come, as British manufacturing succumbed to the pressure of overseas competition. In the 20 years up to 1986, manufacturing employment in Wales fell by 38 per cent, from 331,000 to 125,000.[3] In the latter stages of this period, of course, the process of industrial decline was exacerbated by the 'shock therapy' to which Britain was subjected by the Thatcher government. Unemployment doubled in Wales between 1980 and 1985, from 60,000 to 120,000, and while the figure fell back later in the decade, it rose again to more than 100,000 by 1993.[4]

Not content with promoting the collapse of Wales' main industries, the Tories also reduced the scope for ameliorative measures, by abandoning many of the tools of regional policy that had been employed by previous governments, such as Regional Development Grants and Industrial Development Certificates, and relied instead increasingly heavily on the attraction of Foreign Direct Investment (FDI). Nevertheless, the Tories in Wales – especially during the tenures of Peter Walker and David Hunt as Secretaries of State – made far greater use of the state apparatus to promote economic development than did their colleagues elsewhere in the UK, as reflected by the growth of the Welsh Office budget from £1.2 billion in 1974 to almost £6 billion by the early 1990s. Policies like Walker's Valleys Initiative represented a significant departure from Thatcherite free-market orthodoxy and the Wales TUC – while excluded from any meaningful consultation on policy – was incorporated in trade missions to woo overseas investors.[5]

A 'made in Wales' economic policy

The creation of the Assembly offered an obvious opportunity to develop, in a more thoroughgoing way, a 'made in Wales' – and made *for* Wales – economic policy. The extent to which this has been possible in practice has, however, been subject to the limits of the Assembly's powers in this field of governance. Control over the principal levers of macroeconomic policy – taxation, monetary policy, etc. – remains, of course, with Westminster. Nor is this all: the Government of Wales Act 1998 includes, among those areas within which functions may be transferred, economic development, industry and tourism, as well as such closely related fields as agriculture, training and transport. The functions that actually *have* been transferred, however – as opposed to those that *might* be, in principle – are strictly limited and mostly relate to various grant-giving powers, the promotion of tourism and the business development functions formerly exercised by the WDA.[6] This obviously leaves a great deal with Westminster: for example, the UK Department for Business, Enterprise and Regulatory Reform (successor to the Department of Trade and Industry) retains responsibility for employment issues – including the minimum wage, working hours and individual employment rights – and takes the lead on European Commission matters relating to financial assistance to business.

The Government of Wales Act 2006 ostensibly allows the Assembly to make primary legislation on any matter relating to economic development in Wales – albeit with the express consent of both Houses of

Parliament, as discussed in chapter four above. There is little reason to suppose, however, that the Assembly government will seek to make use of this provision in order to exercise a greater degree of control over the Welsh economy than it has enjoyed since 1999. In November 2002, the then economic development minister, Andrew Davies, told the Richard Commission that he was satisfied with his existing powers and was seeking to extend those powers only in relation to two, relatively minor, issues: the registration of tourist accommodation and the approval of wind farms.[7] In keeping with this view, there are no proposals either in Welsh Labour's manifesto or in *One Wales* for the extension of Assembly authority in economic matters. This reticence seems to proceed – in part, at least – from the lack of a distinctive perspective on economic policy on the part of the Welsh Labour leadership. Thus, in contrast to its health and education policies (for example), the Assembly government's economic policies are essentially the same as those pursued by New Labour in England.[8]

'Modern regional policy' and the 'knowledge economy'

To a large extent, Welsh Labour's economic policy, like that of the Tories before, amounts to making Wales attractive for private investment. The marketing now takes more sophisticated and less objectionable forms than 20 years ago, when Wales was explicitly 'sold' to potential investors abroad on the basis of its low wage levels. Today, the knowledge that China can undercut any competitor on wages means that other countries and regions need to offer something extra and that usually means a more highly skilled workforce and a supportive infrastructure. To this end, there has been substantial investment in training, in order that the people of Wales can participate in the 'knowledge economy' and don't have to 'get out to get on'. Thus, so the thinking runs, a better-educated population can make the transition from an economy based on declining heavy industry to one based on 'high value-added' activities and the burgeoning tertiary sector (finance, services, information technology etc.) and earn a living wage in the process. (Meanwhile, the Tories' anti-union laws – left untouched by New Labour, and beyond the reach of Welsh Labour – help to ensure that investors are not frightened off by a highly unionised, assertive workforce.) At the same time, the Assembly government has launched a wide range of initiatives to 'place Wales at the cutting edge of technological advancement by continuing our financial support for enterprise, innovation and technology.'[9] These include Finance Wales, the Assembly Investment Grant, the SMART Wales

Innovation grant scheme, 'Wales4Innovation', 'Cymru Ar Lein', Technium centres, the Knowledge Bank for Business, International Business Wales and Creative Business Wales. In prospect are National Business Research Centres, a Manufacturing Forum and Skills Academies.

This is all entirely consistent with the approach to economic development being pursued by New Labour in the English regions, which in turn reflects the prevailing wisdom within the European Commission and the other major centres of economic decision-making. As in almost every other area of New Labour policy – and despite recent setbacks – there is an overarching conviction that the market is the most efficient force for social progress and harmony. Thus – to quote one trenchant critique of the policy – there can be 'no ... return to the pre-Thatcher legacy of using redistributive measures to stimulate growth in the Less Favoured Regions' as this 'fostered a culture of dependency in the regions and failed to encourage self-sustaining growth'. Instead, it is incumbent upon '"underperforming regions" to compete their way out of disadvantage through bootstrapping reforms aimed at mobilising endogenous potential'.[10] There is an obvious parallel with New Labour's renunciation of redistributive taxation and public spending to secure greater equality of outcome among individuals. Regions, like people, can expect state intervention only to remove, or at least reduce, certain obstacles that render them unfit to compete. Just as, at a micro level, the contours of accumulated class privilege and disadvantage are disregarded, so, in regional policy, 'There is no understanding of inter-regional relations as a source of inequality or of broken local economic moorings as a result of secular processes of global integration.'[11]

John Lovering has argued that what he calls the 'new regionalism' proceeds in part from the crisis of the Keynesian welfare state from the mid-1970s. In the context of a massive scaling-down of public spending at the level of the nation-state, a new focus on the regional and local scale assisted in lowering public expectations. Public authorities at this level lacked the means to deliver significant resources to drive economic development so they extolled the virtues of the measures that were within their ambit: 'promoting an innovative and entrepreneurial business culture', etc. An unhealthily close relationship developed between policy-makers, officials (in Wales, the WDA in particular) and academics, who melded into a new 'regional service class'. The dominant analyses of, and policy prescriptions for, the Welsh economy therefore concentrated on the 'modern', 'dynamic' sectors (high-tech production and services) and strategies (inward investment, IT innovation, developing supply-chains, etc) and in this way painted a picture of a thriving economy – yet they did so by neglecting huge swathes of economic activity (and inactivity) in Wales and by ignoring inconvenient facts, like the crucial importance of the public sector.[12] The Assembly government has developed a more rounded view of the Welsh economy, acknowledging problems that were overlooked by the 'new regionalism' at its worst, but has nevertheless inherited much of the latter's fixation on 'the knowledge economy' and related ideas.

There are a number of problems with Labour's 'modern regional policy' approach – not least the fact that, following New Labour's creation of nine English regional development agencies in 1998, it is being implemented in all UK regions, whether deprived or already prosperous, and therefore provides no relative advantage to the worse-off (such as Wales) to overcome their historical weaknesses. Nevertheless, the Assembly government could, until recently, point to the apparent results of the strategy as applied in Wales and claim a degree of success. Welsh Labour's 2007 manifesto celebrated the fact that there were 140,000 more jobs in Wales than when the Assembly was established in 1999, and that the rate of job creation in Wales had outstripped that in the UK as a whole. Wales' unemployment rate was 5 per cent lower than that for the UK and lower than at any time during the previous 30 years. Of course, the evident progress made in recent years is now under threat from the economic downturn, which, by October 2008 was hitting Wales harder than anywhere else in the UK, with (ILO) unemployment at 6.6 per cent of the economically active population (up from 5.1 per cent twelve months before), compared to 6.0 per cent for the UK as whole.[13]

Hidden unemployment

Even before the slide into recession, the official figures greatly understated the true numbers of people in Wales who were jobless and wanting to work. In the South Wales valleys – as in other declining industrial areas, mainly in the North of England and central Scotland – there are large numbers of people claiming incapacity benefits: between 10 and 20 per cent of the working age population, compared with 3 to 4 per cent in the South-East of England. Moreover, the total number on these benefits across the UK has nearly quadrupled since 1979. As Steve Fothergill and John Grieve Smith explain:

This remarkable increase in the number of incapacity claimants does not reflect any deterioration in the nation's health, nor an epidemic of malingering by the workshy. It is basically the result of the destruction of jobs in Britain's older industrial areas.[14]

The collapse of industries like coal, steel and shipbuilding has created a huge problem of 'hidden unemployment', which has been highlighted, in particular, by academics at the Centre for Regional Economic and Social Research (CRESR) at Sheffield Hallam University.[15] In August 2006, South Wales accounted for five of the top six local authority areas with the highest proportion of their working age population claiming incapacity benefits; a further two Welsh authorities were also in the first 20.[16]

Claimants in these areas are typically men aged 50–64 who were made redundant after from a long-term job in heavy industry, have been unable to find alternative employment and have now given up trying – although around half say they want a full-time job and only around a quarter could not work at all. Rather than go through the motions of seeking work that is not available to them – as required to qualify for Jobseekers Allowance (JSA) – they have been signed off by their doctors as unfit for work and are therefore able to claim incapacity benefits – which are, in any case, set at a higher rate (after the first twelve months) than JSA and, unlike the latter, are not usually means-tested. The CRESR researchers have estimated the proportion of incapacity claimants who are effectively unemployed – i.e. those who would work if jobs were available – by comparing figures for the declining industrial areas against more affluent areas with a higher demand for labour and taking account of genuine variations in rates of ill-health. By adding the result to 'official' unemployment figures based on the claimant count and ILO measures, they have arrived at 'real unemployment' figures for each local authority area. Among the top 20 local authorities with the highest 'real' unemployment rates in January 2007 were four in South Wales: Blaenau Gwent (15.9 per cent of the working age population); Merthyr Tydfil (15.3 per cent); Neath Port Talbot (13.6 per cent); and Caerphilly (12.9 per cent).[17]

These figures represent a massive waste of potential and an affront to human dignity and ambition; they are another demonstration of the way in which capitalism gorges itself on whatever human resources are available and then carelessly discards what it cannot readily consume. The Westminster Labour government recognises that hidden unemployment is a major problem, yet its deference to the supposedly intractable laws of the market limits the scope of its interventions. Thus, its efforts are geared almost entirely towards labour supply measures – especially welfare 'reform', to push people off benefits and into work – as if the problem were simply a matter of insufficient individual determination to secure employment. The Assembly government also offers assistance to the economically inactive to return to employment, through initiatives like 'Want2Work' – delivered in partnership with Jobcentre Plus and local health boards – which provides a package of advice, support, training and financial incentives. No doubt such measures can and do prove beneficial in many cases but, as Fothergill and Grieve Smith argue, any serious attempt to tackle the problem must include regional development measures to raise the demand for labour in the worst affected areas and create genuine employment opportunities. Many of the relevant policy levers remain, directly or indirectly, in the hands of the UK government, rather than the Assembly. For example, while Regional Selective Assistance (RSA) is distributed by the Assembly, the funds come from Westminster, and the latter determines the basis on which the money can be used. Fothergill and Grieve Smith argue that better use should be made of regional financial incentives to encourage firms to locate in areas like the Welsh Valleys; there should be fewer strings attached and the maximum aid allowed under EU rules should be made available.

Relocation and redistribution

State employment can also be used as a more direct means of increasing the available jobs in areas of high unemployment. Fothergill and Grieve Smith praise the UK government for relocating some 20,000 civil service posts from London and the South-East to other parts of the UK, as recommended by the Lyons Review (2004). This includes several hundred posts transferred to Newport in the Office for National Statistics (ONS) and HM Prison Service. On the face of it, this seems like a positive move, but a number of caveats have to be borne in mind. First of all, any jobs gain for Wales is likely, in many cases, to be at the expense of low-paid civil servants in central London, who face the choice of re-locating their homes and families 150 miles down the M4 or giving up their careers; the initiative has been carried out over the objections of the trade unions and may yet result in compulsory redundancies. Second, Lyons is driven less by any consideration for impoverished areas than by the imperative of saving government money by releasing expensive property in London and its environs; if the object of the exercise were to redeploy jobs where they were most needed, then another part of Wales would have been chosen in preference to the comparatively affluent Newport. Third, the number of posts being relocated has turned out to be substantially fewer than the 1,200 originally claimed, in part because relocations are cancelled out, to some degree, by reductions in existing staffing as part of the Gershon 'efficiency programme', launched at the same time as the Lyons process. According to the Public and Commercial Services union (PCS), Gershon and other central government job cuts have cost Wales a net reduction of some 5,000 civil service jobs in the four years to 2008,[18] with many more scheduled to follow, even before the government announced its £37 billion cuts package for 2011–14. Many of these cuts have been delivered by shutting government offices in already impoverished areas, thus undermining the creditable efforts of the Assembly government itself to redistribute work and opportunities, not least by transferring posts from Cardiff to three new regional offices, in Merthyr Tydfil, Aberystwyth and Llandudno Junction (a process managed far more smoothly and collaboratively than Lyons).

In principle, however, the targeting of public sector jobs (especially when newly-created) away from London and the South East should be regarded as a good thing – and it should include senior policy positions, as well as more junior operational staff. Ash Amin, Doreen Massey and Nigel Thrift argue persuasively that this would be beneficial not just in terms of the immediate redistribution of work and opportunity, but also because it would help to break up the long-standing concentration of economic and political power in London. The latter contributes toward a skewed perspective in economic policy-making, with an assumption that what is best economically for London and the South-East is also best for the country as a whole. Institutions (such as museums) located in and around London often receive a much higher level of public subsidy than their equivalents in 'the provinces', because they are seen as a 'national', not just a 'London-regional' resource. There is, Amin, Massey and Thrift maintain, an undeclared 'London/South East' regional policy. These cogent observations provide a fitting response to the claim – now made increasingly frequently – that the 'efficient, productive' South-East is subsidising Wales, Scotland and the North of England. Even Peter Hain, for example, responded to the Assembly government's decision to review the Barnett Formula – on which its funding is based – by saying: 'I don't see it as an attractive proposition for

English taxpayers to be invited to spend more of their money in Wales than they are already'.[19] Rather than accede to those who apparently regard taxation and public spending as a system of charitable giving, Hain should be reaffirming the case for the distribution of resources based on need. It is in this that the Barnett Formula fails – as Ron Davies and others have pointed out[20] – determining the annual growth in the Assembly's block grant by giving it the same per capita increase as the equivalent English departments, despite the fact that there are greater calls on public spending in Wales, due to its more impoverished state. The Assembly government's review of the formula is, therefore, very much to be welcomed.

The other major aspect of Welsh Labour's economic development policy is, of course, its stewardship of European structural funds. European support for Britain's disadvantaged regions has become much more significant since the 1980s, when the Tories cut back the British government's own regional funding by 75 per cent. Labour can (and does) claim credit for securing 'Objective One' EU structural funds for West Wales and the Valleys and for the beneficial impact of their subsequent deployment. Following decades of economic decline, the Objective One area – covering thirteen of Wales' 22 local authorities and accounting for nearly two-thirds of the Welsh population – qualified for these funds by having a per capita gross domestic product (GDP) of less than 75 per cent of the EU average. This has resulted in more than £1.5 billion being committed by the EU – rising to £3 billion with match-funding – for investment in a range of projects that, it is claimed, have helped to create or safeguard over 70,000 jobs. This funding is very much time-limited, however. Wales' economic performance has gradually improved relative to the EU as a whole and the accession to the Union between 2004 and 2007 of twelve new member-states – mostly poorer countries from eastern and central Europe – has lowered the overall average GDP per head. Wales, along with Cornwall (but unlike two other regions – Merseyside and South Yorkshire) narrowly qualified for a continuation of Objective One (now renamed 'Convergence' funding) from 2007 to 2013, but only because the calculation was based on the years 2000–2002. It will certainly not qualify for a further extension post 2013.

Meanwhile, it has proven difficult to make a definitive assessment of the impact of Objective One funds to date. The author of an independent mid-term evaluation of the programme commissioned by the Welsh Assembly Government comments that 'In many cases, European funding was being used to enhance the quality and intensity of activities, rather than to generate wholly additional outputs', while a more recent commentary notes that the programme has failed to raise the level of gross value added (GVA) per capita in West Wales and the Valleys relative to the UK, only arresting the sharp relative decline that occurred between 1995 and 2000. Moreover, it appears that many of the jobs created by Objective One did no more than replace other jobs being lost elsewhere in the private sector.[21] Thus, the programme could be seen as having added more water to a leaking bucket; the bucket would, of course, have emptied a lot faster without it but in the long-run the hole needs to be plugged. With EU enlargement, there are many more poor countries seeking assistance from a diminishing structural funding pot; rather than fight over the scraps offered up by the wealthy 'core' regions and nations, Wales should be joining together with other impoverished parts of the Union to demand an augmented funding programme with sufficient resources to promote regeneration on a lasting basis.

What kind of jobs?

In addition to considering the true extent to which unemployment has been reduced in Wales, there is also the question of the *type* of jobs that have been created in recent years. In particular, it should be acknowledged that a large part of the attraction for potential investors is that, notwithstanding the minimum wage, Wales remains a low-wage economy, compared to the rest of Western Europe and even much of the UK. The relatively high wages paid to Welsh manual workers in sectors like coal and steel meant that average earnings in Wales compared favourably with most English regions in the early 1980s; the destruction of these industries left Wales at the bottom of the pay league by the end of the decade.[22] The latest statistics demonstrate the limits of the recovery in pay levels that has taken place since the 1990s: in 2008, average male full-time gross earnings in Wales were £28,208, compared to £36,110 in England and £31,454 in Scotland. Although ahead of Northern Ireland (£27,410) and the North-East (£26,610), Wales does not compare well even with some areas with a similar socio-economic profile, such as South Yorkshire (£30,364) and Merseyside (£31,110). A particularly striking, and sobering comparison, because of its proximity, is with the city of Bristol, where the figure is £32,930.[23] Before the election victory of 1997, the CBI lobbied for the valleys to be exempt from the minimum wage. More recently, a report by an academic at Derby university has called for regional variations in the minimum wage, including a cut of almost 10 per cent in the rate in Wales, on the grounds that the south-east is subsidising the poorer regions and people in the latter have insufficient incentive to find work.[24] Disturbingly, it was reported that Gordon Brown had been 'persuaded' of the economic virtues of such a reactionary policy and was actively considering how it might be implemented.[25] In the meantime, the current minimum wage is still well below the original European Decency Threshold of 68 per cent of the average wage within a national economy. Moreover, the government is already moving to introduce regional pay rates within the public sector – beginning with the Ministry of Justice, with the result that courts staff throughout Wales are being paid less than colleagues in Bristol, Birmingham or Liverpool for doing the same job. A report by the Bevan Foundation in 2004 predicted that regional pay would lead to a downward spiral of incomes in areas where lower rates were paid, but the government has so far proven deaf to such concerns.[26]

In addition to wage levels, there is also a question about the quality of the jobs that have been created. During Wales' supposed inward investment boom in the 1980s and 1990s, a large proportion of the manufacturing work located here was of the 'branch plant' variety – routine assembly operations – while firms kept their headquarters and research and development departments elsewhere; Wales had comparatively few managers, engineers, scientists and technicians. Similarly, private services jobs in Wales have tended to be in declining sectors with lower pay rates:

> Typically, Wales gains direct-line insurance brokers and financial product telesales workers but loses regional bank headquarters ... while the higher-paying service sector non-manual jobs are created on the other side of the Severn...[27]

The predominance of low-paid, low-skill assembly line or call-centre work may have lessened somewhat in the last few years: Welsh Labour cites examples like General Dynamics Systems at Oakdale, EADS in Newport, Logica CMG in Bridgend, the Institute of Life Sciences at Swansea University and the forthcoming Defence Training Academy at St Athan (although three of these are engaged in the 'defence' industry, raising serious ethical questions – see Appendix 1). Nevertheless, the current Assembly economic development strategy acknowledges that Wales still has 'an adverse occupational and industry mix, with relatively few high value-added jobs, whether in company head offices and research and development departments or whether in sectors with high rewards, such as financial or professional services [and] a correspondingly unfavourable qualifications profile in the workforce as a whole…'[28] There is little hope of improvement in this regard in the short term: the recession has already claimed good quality jobs at long-established Welsh plants such as Hoover's in Merthyr and Bosch at Miskin, and Corus' several Welsh sites.

The Assembly's strategy does not comment on the proportion of Welsh workers on short-term contracts, working long or unsociable hours, lacking decent employment benefits, or having poor/non-existent career progression prospects. There has been far too little research carried out in this area, although the experience of trade unionists and anti-poverty campaigners would indicate that all is not well. It can certainly be said that workers in Britain (including Wales) are easier to sack and easier to ignore than elsewhere in the EU. Although the Charter of Fundamental Rights, incorporated into the draft EU Constitution (now reborn as simply a Treaty), ostensibly defends the rights of workers within the EU, it is only to be interpreted in accordance with 'national traditions'. By virtue of a last-minute amendment in the EU Constitution negotiations, vigorously lobbied for by the CBI, those 'traditions', as far as Britain is concerned, apparently include the most restrictive anti-union laws of any western democracy.

Tackling the transnationals
But, it might be argued, jobs are jobs, and aren't lower wages and restrictions on the right to strike and organise a price worth paying for the impressive rate of job creation seen until recently? If Wales is attractive to international capital, and has optimum conditions for private enterprise to flourish, surely everyone will benefit? The problem is that such a strategy is based on a wing and a prayer, relying on the goodwill of big business – which, after all, recognises no other obligation than to its shareholders. Any commitment to the workers and their communities will be maintained only to the extent that it is compatible with healthy profit margins. To cite an obvious example: when, in January 2001, Corus decided to reduce costs by cutting 2,500 Welsh jobs, closing the Ebbw Vale and Bryngwyn steelworks and scaling down operations at Llanwern and Shotton, the Assembly government could only plead with the company's bosses to reconsider. There followed a desperate scramble to secure whatever financial inducements might be allowed within the tight constraints of European competition legislation and which

could be offered to Corus. When it dawned that nothing was going to change the minds of Corus management, AMs lined up to condemn the company's chairman, Sir Brian Moffat for his lack of a social conscience, but what exactly did they think capitalist multinationals were *for*? (Moffat's widely reported comment that he was interested in making money, not steel, should have given them a clue.[29])

It is true that there is little preventative action that the Assembly itself, with its limited powers, could have taken. However, the consensus in the Assembly seemed to be that there is nothing that *any* layer of government can do to prevent transnational corporations like Corus from 'downsizing' and devastating communities in the process. Almost all accepted the received economic wisdom that globalisation leaves national governments powerless in the face of corporate tyranny. It is true that capital is more footloose now than it was 30 years ago but, to a large extent, this is the result of decisions by governments and by the international institutions (IMF, EU, WTO, etc.) that governments have created, and which depend on their participation. Measures like the removal of capital controls are *political* decisions that can be reversed: they do not flow automatically from some inexorable economic logic. International economic rules that limit governments' freedom of manoeuvre have been established at the behest, or with the consent, of those governments (or their predecessors). As the satirical website, *WalesWatch*, commented at the time of the Corus decision:

> The Blair administration is not 'powerless in the face of globalisation' as they claim, usually with an embarrassed shrug. They choose to do nothing. If you accept laissez faire economics, embrace the market as the one true God, and earnestly seek the approval of corporate business, then you have no armoury of sanctions to turn to when a company takes advantage of your largesse.[30]

What should have happened? One proposal, which was at least raised by Plaid Cymru and by Ron Davies, was for the UK government to take the threatened plants into public ownership. This was, of course, dismissed out of hand by both the Westminster and Cardiff administrations, yet it is hard to think of a clearer example of the case for nationalisation in the public interest. Corus' actions were supposedly prompted by the loss of £226 million in the first half of the 2000–01 financial year, yet, as Rhodri Morgan pointed out at the time, the company had paid out £700 million to shareholders a year earlier, following its merger with British Steel. The social irresponsibility of business decisions such as this makes a mockery of claims that private enterprise is more efficient and less wasteful than the public sector. For New Labour, nationalisation was – until recently! – a policy supported only by cranks and left-wing extremists, yet in 1971, the *Conservative* Heath government responded to the financial problems of Rolls-Royce by nationalising the company; such a prestigious firm, on which so many jobs depended, could not be abandoned to the vicissitudes of the market. Four years later, the Wilson Government took a similar course of action in regard to British Leyland. Yet, in 2001, to show the same willingness to defend the interests of Welsh communities dependent on steel jobs could not be countenanced if it meant trespassing on the sacrosanct property rights of Corus shareholders. Even in the autumn of 2008, as Britain headed toward recession, it was only the financial institutions that had become so central to the British economy, which could expect to be bailed out – not the likes of Corus', Hoover's and Bosch's Welsh operations – although Lord Mandelson talked in December 2008 about a new policy of 'industrial activism' that might involve government assistance to struggling manufacturers.[31]

The Corus workers were also disadvantaged by lacking the statutory rights to information and consultation from their employer that were enjoyed by workers in almost every other EU state – and the Blair government was in no hurry to remedy this. When an EU Information and Consultation Directive was introduced in 2002, the UK and Ireland secured a delay in its implementation until April 2005 for organisations with 150 or more employees, April 2007 for those with 100 or more members of staff and April 2008 for those with 50 or more.

The Corus situation was, of course, far from unique. There was also the murky affair of LG in Newport, which hoovered up over £200 million in sweeteners before closing, having produced a fraction of the jobs promised. On a smaller scale, in 2002, Dewhirsts' closure of its factories in Swansea, Cardigan and Fishguard, to transfer production to Morocco – where wages were 50p an hour, compared to £4.50 in Wales – provoked a similar admission of impotence from our elected representatives. More recently the proposed closure by Burberry of its Treorchy factory in favour of cheaper pickings in Asia has prompted, at three levels of government, protests and allegations of bad faith on the part of management, letters of protest from Welsh Burberry-wearing celebrities, and, among the public at large, a wave of revulsion against rapacious global capitalism interested only in maximising shareholder value –

without a single job being saved. The Assembly government was quite right to demand the return of over £600,000 in grant aid by Dairygold Food Products, which in 2006 made 115 people redundant when it decamped from Felinfach in Ceredigion. Most AMs would no doubt like to be able to do more to defend Welsh jobs, yet feel they are circumscribed by economic and political constraints that have no power to change. Yet any progress demands a readiness to challenge the current situation, in which capital controls people, and not – as it should be – the other way around.

In the absence of a more robust lead from government, the best defence that might have been available to Welsh steelworkers was indicated by the Dutch union, FNV Bondgenoten, which represents the Corus workforce in the Netherlands. The union offered strong support for ISTC efforts to prevent the closures and job losses – including a pledge to boycott any orders from Britain. The ISTC does, not, however, seem to have responded to this exemplary solidarity with more than polite gratitude, pinning its hopes instead on plans for a workers' buyout that swiftly fell through. Nevertheless, in an age of 'globalised' capital, united trade union action across national boundaries is the best means of defending jobs against the threat of 'downsizing'. Otherwise, the more that Welsh workers' wages increase, the more likely it is that companies like this will up sticks and move to where wages are lower. If Latvia is too expensive, they will move to Turkey, or Morocco, or Cambodia, because they will always be able to find somewhere cheaper: an unsustainable and unedifying race to the bottom.

A pioneering example of international union activity took place in 1997, when Renault workers in Belgium, France and Spain took co-ordinated strike action (albeit only for an hour) and organised joint demonstrations in response to company 'restructuring' plans, involving the closure of its one Belgian plant, at Vilvoorde, and major job cuts elsewhere. More recently, unions have begun to see the need for permanent international links. Britain's largest union, Unite, has signed an agreement with the US-Canadian United Steelworkers Union, as the first step towards merger and eventually a global 'super-union', including developing countries as well as the first world. Although the initiative here usually rests (quite rightly) with the workers' organisations, there is a role for progressive government, whether at national, regional or local level. Welsh Labour could look to the example of the Greater London Council (GLC) in the 1980s, which, when faced with downsizing threats from transnationals like Ford and Unilever, used its limited powers to boost worker and community resistance. Among the measures taken were: support for international union liaison; organisation of seminars for stewards; the establishment of trade union resource centres and a Transnational Information Centre – London (TICL) to undertake research into the challenges posed by international capital; a public inquiry into plans by Ford to close its Dagenham foundry; lobbying through the EEC and the European Parliament; development of a set of demands for action – including legislation – by the national government; and linking-up with another local authority in France, which was facing problems with a common transnational (Kodak).[32]

With economic sectors of strategic importance, like steel, the Assembly government should be working with unions and with administrations in other countries to establish a coordinated, Europe-wide plan for production, counteracting the tendency of global capital to play off regions and countries against each other and to shift resources across borders in the interests of short-term profitability. Companies should be obliged to sign planning agreements, guaranteeing long-term investment and decent pay and conditions, or face nationalisation.

Towards a socialist economic strategy

When all is said and done, the Assembly government should be given credit for trying to increase the living standards of the people of Wales by every means that it considers to be available. In particular, it is absolutely correct that the top priorities of its economic development strategy are to 'increase employment' and to 'raise the quality of jobs, so that annual earnings increase'. However, these goals should be seen very much as necessary but not sufficient. It is notable that, whereas Welsh Labour's education and health policies are very much informed by identifiably socialist (or at least social-democratic) goals – such as equality of outcome – the same cannot be said for its economic policies. That is to say, Welsh Labour's economic policies are not transformative – they do not seek to change society, simply to make the existing economic order as bearable as possible. This is not just a matter of limited powers, since policies can and do incorporate aspirations that go beyond what can be delivered in the here-and-now. Nor would it be entirely fair to blame limited horizons on the part of the Assembly Ministers and policy-makers, whose personal commitment to equality and social justice we do not doubt. The real problem is that in economic policy, above all other fields of governance, the idea that 'There Is No Alternative' to the free market dogma first applied comprehensively under Thatcher, has really taken

120

hold. New Labour's absolute adherence to this mantra seems to have dispelled any lingering hopes within the Welsh Labour leadership that an alternative path – however desirable – might be permissible. As a result of a series of conscious political decisions, and a number of simultaneous and connected conscious processes – the removal of trade barriers and of controls on the movement of capital, the increased power of multinational corporations and the European Union's own competition rules, to which its own leadership has been an active party – New Labour has 'modernised' itself back into the 1850s. It is a large part of our purpose to challenge this thinking and to seek to embolden Welsh Labour to advance that challenge. The comments we have made here do not pretend to constitute an alternative socialist agenda for the Welsh economy; they are simply a series of largely defensive measures that could also contribute to a new perspective on economic development. The worsening economic situation makes such a new perspective increasingly urgent.

Transport: the challenge of geography

New Labour does not seem to have anything as coherent as a transport *policy*. Those with long memories might remember from 1997 an extravagant promise from John Prescott: 'I will have failed in this if in five years there are not many more people using public transport and far fewer journeys by car. It is a tall order but I want you to hold me to it.'[33] This was quickly abandoned, leaving New Labour with little more than the Tories' destructive privatisation and deregulation policies, and a series of pragmatic concessions to suit the interests of the road and aviation lobbies. With frustrated rail users returning to their cars in despair at the overcrowded, unreliable, fragmented and prohibitively expensive train service, New Labour's transport 'policy' is well and truly through the looking glass.

It was not difficult to improve on this. Welsh Labour, without all the money or the power that it really needs, and beset by Wales' geographical and demographical difficulties, has nevertheless taken some modest but worthy steps towards a coherent transport policy. In 2003 it brought economic development and transport into one portfolio – a logical decision, given the obvious relationship between the two. The devolution of further powers to the Assembly gave it a new strategic role in respect of transport services. Welsh Labour has launched a 15-year, £8 billion transport strategy, increasing investment in transport by 150 per cent from 2001, to £500 million a year.

One obvious result has been the expansion of the rail network. The Vale of Glamorgan rail link now connects the capital city to Cardiff-Wales airport. The rail link from Cardiff to Ebbw Vale, the first railway to be opened in Wales since the 1960s, is a welcome replacement, for those without a car, for a two-hour bus journey. The establishment of a single Wales and Border rail franchise means that there is a direct and frequent north-south rail service. Free train travel for the over 60s, currently piloted in some rural areas, promotes rail use and combats the isolation suffered by the elderly in those areas.[34] The policy obviously complements the highly successful introduction in Welsh Labour's first term, of free bus travel for the over-60s and for disabled people and their carers, a policy which has benefited an estimated half a million people. The scheme to extend concessionary travel to 16–18 year olds addresses the mobility needs of the other major group in society without access to a car or the resources to own one. Welsh Labour has also boosted community transport and local bus schemes through the Local Transport Services Grant. All these initiatives are part of an Assembly government plan, which appears to be succeeding, to increase bus travel in Wales.

The problem is that the Assembly government's worthy aims run into the buffers of Tory transport policy, left untouched by New Labour. Bus deregulation, introduced by the Tories' 1985 Transport Act, was a wanton act of political vandalism by the rich against the interests of the poor. It means that local authorities can no longer provide a bus *service*, with all the benefits for mobility and integration that that word implies. Socially necessary but unprofitable routes can only be subsidised under certain circumstances, and with local authorities paying private companies to run them. This policy resulted in a collapse in bus use (except in London, where the rules did not apply) and a huge increase in fares. The implications for Wales are obvious. In urban areas the high fares and the inevitable gaps in the service act as a disincentive for bus use; in rural areas, those without a car face almost complete isolation. Communities dependent on car ownership become unviable as communities. In the absence of affordable social housing they die a slow death by isolation, or become colonies of second home owners from England.

The other giant obstacle is the lack of an integrated, publicly-run railway system: the Tories' scorched earth privatisation and New Labour's refusal (beyond winding up Railtrack) to take the system back into public control and end the racket by which the taxpayer, in the form of subsidies, puts money into the pockets of rail company shareholders. The UK's rail system, previously starved of investment but just about adequate, is now widely regarded by the travelling public as hopelessly dysfunctional. Within Wales, the Assembly government has managed to negotiate an all-Wales franchise, but that still leaves out the service connecting South Wales with England – subject to widespread (and justified) criticism from the public and politicians alike.

For Welsh Labour's transport policies to be realisable – including the laudable aim, set out jointly with Plaid in *One Wales*, of an expanded, integrated transport network, to reduce car dependence – the twin nettles of bus deregulation and rail privatisation must be grasped. These are issues on which Welsh Labour can and should be working with socialists elsewhere in the UK, as well as with the trade unions and passenger groups.

Energy: keeping the lights on – sustainably

It is in energy policy where the weaknesses and ambiguities of the existing devolution settlement become all too clear. The Assembly's devolved responsibility embraces economic development, transport, the environment, planning and the countryside and it has a legal commitment to promote sustainability. It is obviously essential that there be clear consistency in strategy between these areas, not least in relation to energy policy. However, energy is not fully devolved: planning applications for projects producing up to 50MW of electricity are dealt with by the Assembly government, beyond which threshold they remain with Westminster. Control over key energy policy areas, involving major projects, is therefore retained by the UK government. The Assembly government voiced its concern at this anomalous state of affairs back in 2003, but in November 2007, addressing Welsh MPs, the then Welsh Secretary, Peter Hain, dismissed any prospect of extending devolution in this area. In fact, Westminster seems intent on less, rather than more, accountability. The 2008 Planning Act takes decision-making for large-scale planning projects, known in England and Wales as Nationally Significant Infrastructure Projects (NSIPs), away from the UK Department for Business, Enterprise and Regulatory Reform, handing these over to a new quango, the Infrastructure Planning Commission (IPC), which works within policy guidelines, or National Policy Statements, from Westminster. The legislation replaces the numerous different consents previously obtained from different regulators under different statutory regimes with a single consent. The purpose of this 'streamlining' is to make life easier for big business. Thus, in relation to NSIPs which are not in devolved areas, Wales will have less power than

Scotland and Northern Ireland, leaving the people of Wales essentially unrepresented in the face of huge projects such as the LPG pipeline and – crucially – nuclear power stations.[35]

Largely due to the calculated political spite of Thatcher and Major in closing down the UK's coal industry, and the decline in North Sea oil and gas production, Wales, like the rest of the UK, is heavily dependent on imported oil and gas, the rapidly fluctuating cost of which threatens increased fuel poverty and economic crisis. Wales still has many years' reserves of coal, but coal production, in its traditional form, was environmentally disastrous. Therefore, Wales needs a sustainable and coherent energy policy, which balances the needs to reduce CO_2 emissions, reduce dependence on imported fossil fuels, banish fuel poverty and conserve energy supplies.[36]

Energy Route Map Wales, published by the Welsh Assembly government in 2005, advocates a strategy based on these principles, whereby Wales' energy needs are met by a combination of 'clean' fossil fuels, such as gas and clean coal, and renewable energy sources – principally, wind power. Regarding the various 'clean coal' technologies, a rigorous scepticism is necessary in the face of the 'greenwashing' claims of the government and the energy companies. In particular, the much-touted carbon capture and storage (CCS) may not be viable for years, if ever. Provided that 'clean coal', in some form, can be what it says it is, there is little in *Energy Route Map Wales* to quarrel with. Wales, with its hills and long coastline, appears well suited to play a leading role in exploiting sources of renewable energy. Jane Davidson, appointed environment minister after the 2007 election, has argued that a range of 'cutting edge tidal power projects', potentially including tidal lagoons off the coasts of Swansea and Rhyl, could help Wales become a self-sufficient energy producer.[37] *Renewable Energy Route Map for Wales*, sent out for public consultation in February 2008, argues for just such a perspective: renewable energy being derived from wind power, tidal and wave power, and sustainable biomass. Even the often critical Friends of the Earth Cymru described this plan as 'ambitious, but it is the right ambition.'[38] Certainly, the clean energy from the proposed Severn tidal barrage in whatever form could provide 5 per cent of all the electricity needs of the UK. However, the project carries with it the risk of damaging the unique eco-system in the Severn estuary. In October 2007 the Sustainable Development Commission set tough conditions for any support for the project: public ownership to avoid short-termism in decision-making, full compliance with European directives on habitats and long-term commitment towards creating compensatory habitats and further, wider government action on climate change remaining a priority.[39]

A Nuclear-free Wales!

However, *Energy Route Map Wales*, and the thinking behind it, are flawed in two ways. First, as noted above, its context is the incomplete devolution settlement. Wales was therefore included in the recent energy white paper, in which the Westminster government committed itself to a nuclear power programme. This was itself the result of a 'review' widely regarded as being rigged in favour of the nuclear option. While in office, Blair reminded Wales that there was no 'opt-out' in energy policy. Wales therefore faces the imposition of a nuclear power programme, whatever the wishes of its people or their elected representatives. Both Jane Davidson and her predecessor, Andrew Davies, have made clear their opposition to nuclear power on environmental and cost grounds. However, Welsh Labour's November 2006 final policy forum document which dealt with energy policy retreated from this *de facto* anti-nuclear policy by recognising nuclear power as an 'option'. Moreover, *One Wales* – which has good things to say about renewable energy and microgeneration – is silent on the nuclear issue.

To erect a new generation of nuclear power stations across Wales would be a terrible mistake. Even if it is accepted that the new reactors would be better designed, built and maintained than those at Chernobyl, any embrace of nuclear power flies in the face of the obvious dangers of environmental catastrophe as a result of accident or terrorism, the risk of theft of weapons-usable material, the insoluble problem of where to put the waste, and the fact that the nuclear industry has always required a hefty government subsidy to keep it afloat.[40] How can the commitment to sustainability, enshrined in the Government of Wales Act, be reconciled with the existence, for millennia to come, of deposits of radioactive waste? How 'sustainable' is the ever-present threat of a leak like that of 1957 at Windscale, not to mention something far worse? We recognise that nuclear power has its supporters in the labour movement, particularly on Anglesey, where it is important as a source of energy for local industry and as an employer. However, it would be a mistake to allow the nuclear industry and its supporters to dictate the terms of any discussion about how we live our lives. Conversely, the adoption of a nuclear-free policy would have ramifications far beyond Wales, acting as an example to other countries, which in turn would be in Wales' interest. After all, as the Chernobyl catastrophe demonstrated, a nuclear-free Wales would still be vulnerable to fall-out from a disaster anywhere in Europe. Irrespective of any other political differences with them, Welsh Labour must support the SNP government in Edinburgh in its determination to keep Scotland nuclear-free. Socialists, trade unionists and anyone who cares about our environment and the welfare of future generations needs to make sure that Wales becomes and remains nuclear-free.

Energy Route Map Wales's second flaw is that it sees the free market as the mechanism for the delivery of its energy policy objectives. Having proudly boasted that the 'UK has the most competitive energy markets of all EU and G8 countries', the document then claims to able to square the circle of 'securing affordable energy supplies and attaining much greater efficiency' through a 'market-based approach'. The elimination of fuel poverty, energy conservation, the reduction of CO_2 emissions and the development of a coherent, sustainable and, therefore, planned energy policy which benefits the whole of society, are directly at odds with a system based on profit and the interests of shareholders. In any event, the free market in energy so idealised by *Energy Route Map Wales* does not exist, due to the manipulation of prices and gas flows by the big European energy firms, something that has exercised the regulator, Ofgem, and the Business and Enterprise Select Committee and which has led Welsh MEP Eluned Morgan to campaign for an 'unbundling' or separation of the European energy supply and transmission markets, to address an obvious conflict of interest. However, as their solution would be a 'free' – as opposed to a rigged – market, they can offer no fundamental solution to the problems we face. Having connived at corporate greed since 1997, New Labour is unlikely to do anything to bring the energy companies under any kind of real control. Welsh Labour must, therefore, campaign not only for complete control by the Welsh Assembly government of energy policy, but also for a publicly accountable energy industry – which would involve a return to public ownership, combined with active support for community-owned microgeneration schemes, such as wind farms and tidal lagoons. Households which fit low or zero carbon (LZC) technology could be rewarded with a 'feed-in tariff', paying them for electricity fed back into the grid. Generous subsidies and incentives would be required to put LZC technology units, such as solar panels, within the realistic financial range of most of the population (following proposals in *Renewable Energy Route Map for Wales*, the Assembly government intends to relax planning controls to make this easier). Such initiatives must be combined with making Welsh homes more energy-efficient – by insulation, for example – which would reduce fuel poverty and cut carbon emissions.

It might be objected that, even if it were willing to work towards the twin objectives of a nuclear-free Wales and a publicly owned and accountable energy industry, an Assembly government – even *with* devolved control of energy policy – would not have the power to realise them. Yet the obstacles to such ambitions represented by Westminster and by the EU and WTO competition rules are also obstacles placed in the path of socialism and democracy more generally; if Wales is to have a sustainable, environmentally-driven energy policy which meets all its people's needs, the struggle for their removal must start now. We will look at these issues in more detail in chapter ten.

Sustainability: Wales leading the world?

Section 121 of the Government of Wales Act 1998 bestowed on the Welsh Assembly a legally binding duty to promote sustainable development, and Wales thus became one of only three countries in the world to have such a duty enshrined in their constitution. This seemed exciting: Wales was going to break away, consciously, both from the Tory and New Labour position of allowing business to dictate the terms of economic development and from the traditional Labour position, which was that the purpose of economic development was to create jobs, regardless of any environmental considerations (and often any social considerations) that might be involved. The Assembly government would be the first to use the concept of the 'ecological footprint' (the amount of productive land and sea required to produce the resources we consume and to dispose of our waste) as a benchmark of sustainability. That Wales was consciously looking to the future in this way was significant. Wales was, to a large extent, the first industrial country. But it was a country whose considerable wealth had largely been extracted from it for the benefit of people elsewhere. Wales' industrial development, based primarily on extractive and heavy industries, at an appalling cost to its environment and to the health and well-being of its people, was as unsustainable as it is possible to be. The responsibility for this does not just lie with heavy industry. The distinctive landscape of much of rural Wales is artificial – the result of the destruction of most of the native deciduous forest and scrub, its replacement by fast-growing, non-native conifers, and centuries of intensive sheep-grazing.

The greening of the valleys and the numerous blue flag beaches in Wales do not mean that the problems associated with past industrial development have gone away. The supporters of nuclear power are making the claim – which we have already shown to be spurious – that it is 'clean' energy. The economy of West Wales is largely dependent on the oil terminal at Milford Haven, bringing with it the ever-present danger of an ecological catastrophe akin to the *Sea Empress* oil spill, and there is the possibility that oil rigs may soon dot Cardigan Bay. Wales is despoiled by open-cast mining, quarrying, landfill sites and toxic waste dumps. Such 'externalities' of heavy industry, along with poor quality – and therefore energy-inefficient – housing stock, mean that the level of carbon emissions per person in Wales is the highest in the UK. Away from the M4 corridor, many communities are heavily dependent on private car ownership.

Contradictory aims

Meanwhile, it does not seem to occur to New Labour that calling itself 'green' is anything to do with what it actually does. While Tony Blair liked to talk 'green', Gordon Brown's record is, if anything, even less distinguished. As chancellor and as prime minister, Brown has displayed unwavering support for big business, and in particular the roads and aviation lobbies. His changes of tack on the fuel duty escalator are motivated more by the demands of middle England and the motoring lobby, and by the needs of the Treasury, than any environmental considerations. While renewable energy in Germany makes up 9 per cent of the total and in Denmark 15 per cent, the figure for Britain is a pathetic 2 per cent. Much of New Labour's highly publicised reduction in carbon emissions in fact represents the unintended consequence of Tory policies: the destruction of the mining industry and the collapse of manufacturing over the course of two recessions. Indeed, once shipping, aviation and imported goods are accounted for, emissions are 49 per cent higher than reported.[41]

The Westminster government's readiness to spend £3 billion – or £1,000 per inch – on widening the M6 (40 times the cost of its low carbon buildings programme), the growing gap between the cost of a journey by rail and by car, the building, at Kingsnorth in Kent, of the first new coal-fired power station for 30 years[42] and the carelessness of government departments as to where they buy the wood for the costly and unnecessary refits for their offices – all this suggests that, for all its rhetoric, New Labour regards sustainability as a soundbite, or at best a distant aspiration. Its various piecemeal measures, such as the tweaking of car tax and increases in air passenger duty, are completely inadequate and in areas like rural Wales, any increase in the cost of motoring without a corresponding increase in affordable, integrated public transport provision would be understandably unpopular.[43]

In November 2007, Brown appeared to confound many of his critics, restating his commitment to the EU's target, set earlier that year and endorsed by Blair, that 20 per cent of all European energy should come from renewable sources by 2020, committing the UK to an emission cut of 60 per cent by 2050 (a target subsequently increased to 80 per cent), and talking about a future 'low carbon economy'.[44] However, the government has since been caught out attempting to undermine EU legislation giving renewable energy access to the National Grid,[45] and just two days after Brown's announcement, the government appeared to have no qualms about announcing the environmentally disastrous proposals since confirmed for the expansion of Heathrow Airport. Consequently, the Assembly government is faced not just with the legacy of Wales' past, but with some very real contemporary dangers as well. And, as in so many other areas, much of the power to make a real difference resides not in Cardiff, but in Westminster or Brussels or with other international or supra-national bodies.

From the outset, the Assembly set itself the groundbreaking task of integrating the principles of sustainable development into its policies and its day-to-day work, and subjecting itself to an inclusive process of consultation. The initial result, published in 2000, was *A Sustainable Wales – Learning to Live Differently*, described by Friends of the Earth Cymru as 'a commendable, if utopian vision that gives a flavour of the many interrelated issues that come within the remit', but which read, 'like an "all things to all men" [sic] wish list that is not easily grasped as a concept or policy tool'.[46] There followed an independent effectiveness report, a revised scheme and an action plan, which, in a refreshingly honest manner, reflected the effectiveness report's judgement as to the weaknesses in the original scheme. The action plan acknowledged the difficulties in achieving the level of integration required, and the limitations of a Wales-only approach. It recognised the problems posed by the increase in economic activity for the need to reduce CO_2 emissions, the hitherto modest record on renewable energy generation, the implications for sustainability of economic inactivity, deprivation and inequality, and the limited progress, compared to other European regions, in waste management, recycling and public transport provision.

Turning words into action?

The action plan contained a number of specific commitments. By 2010, all Assembly buildings would run on 100 per cent renewable energy; the Assembly and its agencies would encourage 'indigenous microgeneration renewables' in Wales; there would be an investigation into the promotion of the uptake of alternative fuels; and energy efficiency standards would be above those currently required by building regulations for all new homes built by social landlords using the social housing grant. Finally, contract specifications for school meals would have to address 'health, nutrition and seasonality'. All the commitments set out in the action plan would be subject to monitoring and review.

The revised scheme and action plan won praise from the Sustainable Development Commission for Wales for its emphasis on 'leadership and implementation', as well as its participatory approach, while Jonathan Porritt acclaimed the Assembly's 'unique ... clarity of vision and commitment to embed sustainable development at the heart of everything it does'.[47] By the end of the Assembly's second term, however, the Sustainable Development Commissioner, Peter Davies, commented that 'the rhetoric [is] outweighing the tangible progress by some degree', despite 'a myriad of speeches, reports, action plans and strategies'.[48] This note of caution reminds us that, despite the recent reaffirmation of many of the above commitments and the *One Wales* pledge to establish a climate commission for Wales, it would surely be wrong to take the government's pronouncements purely at face value, without subjecting its record to the necessary scrutiny and criticism.

One difficulty is that, while everyone now seems to be in favour of sustainability, there is no clear consensus as to what it is. The most famous definition of sustainability – and the one which was accepted by the Assembly government – comes from the 1987 Brundtland report to the World Commission on Environment and Development (*Our Common Future*): 'development which meets the needs of the present without compromising the ability of future generations to meet their own needs'. The Assembly attempted to clarify the somewhat vague Brundtland definition, declaring that 'we will take social, economic and environmental issues into account in everything we do'. It has since refined its definition thus: 'improving people's quality of life and well-being, while using environmental resources sustainably, so that development does not compromise the quality of life of future generations'.[49] The Assembly – and specifically the Assembly government – needs not only to clarify its conception of sustainability, but to set out clearly what it is trying to achieve, and to fight for it. However worthy or ground-breaking a political initiative may be, it is unlikely to secure popular support for Welsh Labour (or Plaid Cymru) if, as recorded by a 2003 survey, 73 per cent of the people of Wales are 'relatively or completely unfamiliar' with the term sustainable development[50] and, as Peter Davies comments, 'it would be difficult for the vast majority of people in Wales to recognise that this commitment to sustainable development is a distinctive element in their devolved government'.[51]

In 2007, the new coalition government, emphasising its claim to put sustainability at the heart of its energy, transport and food production and procurement policies, created a department for sustainability, the environment and housing, headed by Jane Davidson. At the same time, a cross-cutting scrutiny committee was established to oversee the efforts of all ministers to incorporate sustainability into their portfolios and policies, and to hold the Assembly government to account. There has subsequently been an increasing urgency in the government's pursuit of its agenda. In October 2007, for example, a target for 70 per cent recycling and composting of household waste by 2025 was announced. Already, by 2008, Wales had reduced by 20 per cent over the previous three years the amount of biodegradable waste sent to landfill and Wales was already below its European target allowance for 2009/10, the first year in which local authorities have to report on their performance to the EU (and incur financial penalties if they miss the target).[52] February 2008 saw the launch of the *Renewable Energy Route Map* consultation document, referred to earlier in this chapter (and described by the usually circumspect Peter Davies as a 'commendable vision').[53] In November, the Assembly government announced a green building charter involving a 'coalition of the willing', comprising 43 organisations from the public and private sector, with the aim of achieving a built environment with low or zero net carbon emissions as soon as practicably possible, thus earning Jonathan Porritt's praise for Wales' 'foresight and ambition to accelerate progress towards a sustainable built environment'. The aspiration is for all new buildings built from 2011 to be zero carbon in space heating, lighting, and hot water, and to increase energy efficiency in buildings to bring about a reduction of 3 per cent per year from 2011, in order to achieve a total reduction of 80 per cent by 2050.[54] At the same time, the consultation began on the renewed sustainable development scheme, in which the Assembly government set itself the goal of 'using all its devolved powers to make every part of the public sector sustainable for the benefit of the environment and the people of Wales.'[55] From now on, sustainable development would be the 'single organising principle for all parts of the public sector': the Assembly government would 'use all its devolved powers ... to lessen Wales's environmental impact on the world, and help protect our country for future generations'. Whereas, at present, the people of Wales are using 2.7 planets' worth of resources to sustain our lifestyles – set to rise, if unchecked, to 3.3 planets by 2020 – Wales would be committed to becoming a 'one planet nation'.

The Assembly government has a crucial role to play in educating, informing and co-ordinating the activities of the people of Wales on sustainability issues. Many people want to do the 'right' thing, but, beset by conflicting advice and information – often from those selling 'green' products – or with no information at all, do not know what the 'right' thing is. In the renewed sustainability scheme, the Assembly government identifies one of its 'core principles' as the *involvement* of people and communities. Its three-year media campaign to help people tackle climate change at home – including a guide for householders, launched in July 2008 – has the potential to help to empower people in Wales, so that they are less likely to think that there is nothing they can do to make a difference, or that the problems faced are so huge as to be beyond them. The various proposals, apparently thwarted by Whitehall, to ban or impose a tax on single-use plastic bags would, if implemented, have put Wales in the forefront of efforts to preserve the environment for future generations, while also performing an educational function.

There is an obvious need for the Government to co-ordinate sustainability issues in economic development, transport, local government, health and education, making it clear that sustainable development is not simply a 'green' issue – a widespread misconception highlighted by the 2003 Davidoff Report[56] – but informs all social, economic or environmental activity in Wales. The renewed sustainability scheme attempts to counter this thinking by advancing, as another 'core principle', the *integration* of economic, social and environmental considerations. A concrete example of this in action is the Assembly government's linking of its campaign against fuel poverty to the issue of energy-efficient housing and the adoption of its code of sustainable homes, as part of the green building charter.

The Assembly government's position is therefore, quite rightly, that sustainability is not merely an environmental question, nor a bolt-on extra, a luxury to be discarded in the face of economic considerations. If it were merely to 'take into account' environmental issues – or, like New

Labour in Westminster, to defer to the market and 'choice' – the default position would be for narrowly economic considerations – and inevitably, the interests of big business – to prevail at the expense of all others. In particular, the worsening economic situation might well bring to the fore the familiar argument that environmental considerations are an expendable luxury when times are hard. Sustainability must therefore resemble a three-legged stool, in which environmental, social and economic factors cannot exist without each other. The widely-held misconception that sustainability, including environmental concerns, is somehow in conflict with economic development and job creation must be challenged. Rather than seeing economic growth as a way of producing the wealth to provide the resources to deal with inequality and environmental degradation, it must be recognised that increased equality and better protection of the environment can bring about a direct increase in people's quality of life. There are obvious ways in which this approach can be promoted, such as the development of industries relating to renewable energy, recycling, nature conservation, energy conservation, organic farming and sustainable tourism. This is the intent behind the Assembly government's recently launched 'green jobs strategy', aiming to make existing jobs in Wales more sustainable and carbon-efficient and to help generate a range of new jobs in emerging green technologies and products.

A Welsh Labour Policy Forum document of September 2008 takes a further step in the right direction in this respect, arguing against the 'boxing off' of sustainability into one discrete policy area, and against the false dichotomy of 'jobs versus environment'. In contrast to Westminster's combination of inertia and heavy-handedness, it advocates active government support for greater community engagement in environmental issues, such as the transition towns network. Significantly, it recognises that it is not a lack of individual will that keeps people in their cars, particularly in Wales' dispersed or rural communities, but the lack of integrated and affordable alternatives to car use.[57]

A different idea of 'progress'

It is necessary to challenge the notion that gross domestic product (GDP) is the only way of assessing economic development. GDP focuses on economic growth only – not the social or environmental cost of that growth. (An example is the cost of dealing with the pollution caused by the Sea Empress running aground off Pembrokeshire being regarded as a contribution to GDP rather than the cost that it so obviously was.) A broader measure of progress is possible, such as the Index of Sustainable Economic Welfare (ISEW), which takes into account economic, social and environmental factors such as the depletion of non-renewable resources, the destruction of habitats, pollution and the inequality of income distribution, in order to arrive at an assessment of wealth and progress. The Assembly government already has four 'headline indicators' of sustainability – economic output, social justice, biodiversity conservation and ecological footprint – and, for its renewed sustainability scheme, plans to add a fifth measure of 'wellbeing in Wales'.

In Westminster, the New Labour government is 'streamlining' the planning process. As we have seen, this will involve making the planning process easier for New Labour's friends in big business at the expense of democracy and accountability. Wales has the opportunity to go the other way, at least for those planning matters where power resides with the Assembly. There should be a 'third-party' right of appeal, so that individuals or community groups affected by a planning decision made by a local authority, which fails to comply with the Assembly's sustainability policies, can appeal against that decision. This may make the planning process more complicated, but will also make it fairer, and more democratic.

Unfortunately, there remains a gap between the Assembly government's aspiration or rhetoric on sustainability, and what actually happens 'on the ground'. Three examples should suffice. First, there is the proposal for a new M4 relief road which, if built, would cut through the environmentally important Gwent Levels, much of which is a Site of Special Scientific Interest (SSSI). The Levels are already a refuge for some of the wildlife displaced from Cardiff Bay by the destruction of the SSSI there as a result of the building of the barrage and the construction of an artificial lake – an environmentally disastrous project, to which Labour's initial opposition (albeit in pre-Assembly times) melted away. The relief-road proposal seems to be an example of the disastrous 'predict and provide' approach: increase the provision to meet predicted demand, the demand rises to fill it, so even more provision is needed, and so on. The proposal is in direct contradiction to the aim of increasing public transport provision as a disincentive to car use, and to the necessary aim, set out in the consultation paper referred to above, to not only protect biodiversity, but to use it, in the form of wetlands and peat bogs, as a weapon in limiting the effects of climate change, as part of a 'response to climate change predicated on sustainable development principles, with biodiversity at its centre.'[58]

A second blemish on the Assembly government's sustainability credentials will be apparent to those residents of Merthyr Tydfil who live less than 40 metres from the Ffos y Fran open-cast mine. Ffos y Fran, which supplies Aberthaw power station, outrageously 'greens' itself by claiming to be 'land reclamation by coal extraction'. Open-cast coal mining is, by virtue of CO_2 emissions and other externalities, one of the most unsustainable activities there is. The most recent planning application for this project was granted in 2005 by the Assembly government, which survived a challenge at the Court of Appeal the following year, brought by local residents. The Assembly government is now insisting that that in future, as in Scotland, opencast sites are at least 500 metres from the nearest houses. This will not be retrospective, and therefore, offers little comfort to the people of Merthyr who will suffer from the noise and dust caused by this huge hole in the ground for many years to come. A final example, and a negative development from the point of view of CO_2 emissions, noise, and all the other unwelcome by-products of the seemingly out of control aviation industry, is the introduction of a heavily-subsidised north-south air link. Even Wales' difficult topography merits a better solution than this. Only if progress is judged purely on GDP, and economic factors are, when push comes to shove, allowed to trump all other considerations, do these projects have any real logic, albeit not one that sits easily with the 'sustainability' agenda of the government.

The whole field of policy relating to sustainability is, then, highly dynamic, both in terms of the information available, and of the political priorities adopted by governments and non-governmental organisations alike. The sustainability agenda pursued by the Welsh Assembly government reflects this dynamism, and the progress made since 2000 largely does it credit. While, however, this progress should be recognised by socialists and environmentalists in Wales, they must reserve the right to scrutinise, to be critical, and to ensure that the government's practice matches its aspirations.

Chapter 7

Community and identity

In Welsh Labour's agenda under Rhodri Morgan, and in its current joint programme with Plaid Cymru, there has been a clear break with the New Labour fashion of glossing over social differentiation, in order to avoid giving offence to the 'aspirational' floating voters of 'Middle England', and suggesting that government can simultaneously serve the interests of all sections of society, without prioritising any of them. The political leadership of Wales has consistently acknowledged that Welsh society is stratified by class and has sought to use its powers (limited as they are) to offset the accumulated disparities of power and privilege that shape people's life chances. The concept of 'progressive universalism', which underpins much of the Assembly government's agenda, recognises an overriding duty to the most disadvantaged. Yet our society is not, of course, divided solely along class lines but also by age, gender, ethnicity, culture, language, religion, sexuality, physical and mental capacity – and in countless other ways. Over the last 30–40 years, a major goal of progressive politics has been to ensure that nobody is prevented from attaining their full potential in life because of their individual identity, while also avoiding the imposition of a spurious homogeneity. Since the 1970s, *formal* equality in many spheres has gradually been secured with the passage of legislation outlawing discrimination; underlying structural inequalities have, however, proven more difficult to eradicate. New Labour has an exemplary record in extending more robust legal rights to groups that have previously suffered discrimination or exclusion: the Civil Partnerships Act being one recent example. In many of its other policies, however, it has worsened the position of certain disadvantaged groups. For example: in allowing the gap between rich and poor to widen, it has exacerbated the relative deprivation of ethnic minorities, who remain disproportionately represented among the poorest. In its prosecution of the 'war on terror' it has risked criminalising whole ethnic and religious communities. And in its treatment of asylum-seekers it has put the approval of the right-wing media before the humane treatment of desperate and persecuted people.

As with sustainable development, the National Assembly has a statutory duty, under the Government of Wales Act 1998, to promote equality of opportunity. Its Equality of Opportunity Committee diligently oversees its efforts to discharge this responsibility, while the Assembly government records its own efforts in its Annual Report on Equality and Diversity, the most recent edition of which was published at the end of 2007. This lists a number of worthy schemes and initiatives, ranging from a scheme to encourage disabled people into enterprise to projects that tackle barriers to participation in community activities for people with sight and hearing loss and overcome sensory barriers to using computers.[1] In supporting such a wide variety of disparate interventions to address inequalities, the Assembly recognises the complex pattern of particular needs that exist in Welsh society. Addressing such needs will, however, always be difficult in a society that is driven primarily by profit and by competition for resources – rather than one in which services are planned and resources organised to cater for the needs of all citizens. The situation, at any one time, of particular sections of society is always heavily influenced by narrowly economic factors. For example: many employers avoid hiring people with disabilities, rather than make the workplace alterations that might be required to accommodate them; economic migrants from poorer countries are often employed principally because they will accept lower wages and can therefore be used to undercut an indigenous workforce; women (in particular) with childcare commitments, or who plan to start families, are passed over for promotion in favour of colleagues who are 'unhindered' by such 'baggage'.

The most significant manifestation of this general tendency for the fortunes of particular groups to be determined by economic forces has been the mass entry of women into the workforce in Wales over the last 40 years. During the 1970s, the number of women in paid employment increased by more than 100,000, at a time when the male workforce was in sharp decline, rising to almost 38 per cent of the total by 1979, compared with less than 32 per cent ten years before.[2] Women now make up more than 47 per cent of the Welsh workforce (but around 43 per cent of these work part-time – four times the proportion of male part-timers[3]). In its long-term social consequences, this 'feminisation' of the workforce has been empowering of women and generally beneficial in terms of the greater diversity it has brought to the working population. In its origins, however, it was driven by the need of capital in new manufacturing industries to exploit previously untapped reserves of labour – particularly those whose 'second-earner' status and/or lack of previous employment meant they had lower expectations in terms of pay, hours and conditions and a lesser disposition towards trade union militancy. Consequently, women's employment in Wales was long characterised by significantly lower wages and a lower-skill profile.[4] Even today, while the gender gap has increasingly narrowed in terms of economic activity, women's average earnings are 10.9 per cent lower than men's – although this gap is lower than in England and Scotland (but higher than in Northern Ireland) – and the difference is much greater for managers (20.5 per cent) and in skilled manual work (24.5 per cent).[5] Legal advances and cultural change have certainly improved women's relative position in the workplace but the persistence of patriarchal attitudes and authority-structures, and the continuing convenience for business of a gender-division of labour in at least some areas of the economy, mean that the struggle for substantive equality still has a long way to go.

Women's political representation has also advanced in a slow and uneven fashion. The organised involvement of women in the Labour party goes back almost to the party's beginnings, with the establishment of the Women's Labour League, which had branches in around fifteen South Wales towns by the time it was absorbed into the mainstream party organisation in 1918. From this point onwards, the Welsh party had a full-time women's organiser and this role was discharged energetically by Elizabeth Andrews for three decades. By the 1930s, women represented well over 40 per cent of Welsh party membership and played their full part in activism – yet they generally played a subordinate role in the party, only very rarely running for elected office.[6] This began to change decisively from the late 1960s, with the rise of the women's liberation movement and the entry of women into the workforce in large numbers. By the early 1980s, women were at the forefront of the some of the major political struggles. On 27 August 1981, 40 members of the peace organisation, 'Women for Life on Earth' set off on a 120-mile march from Cardiff to the RAF base at Greenham Common, Berkshire, to oppose the decision to station 96 US Cruise nuclear missiles there. They were to establish the internationally-renowned

Women's Peace Camp which remained in place, outside the perimeter fence, for nineteen years. The women of South Wales' mining communities played a crucial part in the great strike that began in March 1984, establishing support groups in every colliery town and village on the coalfield. In the course of the dispute, their role expanded from important but subordinate functions, like co-ordinating food supplies, to encompass the full range of political leadership activities within the campaign, stiffening the resolve of the strikers and acting as roving ambassadors for the union and their communities.[7] The support groups continued after the end of the strike and some of their leading activists would later achieve prominence in other areas of Welsh public life – such as Siân James, now MP for Swansea East. Women also organised the support group that supported the quarrymen of Blaenau Ffestiniog through the seven-month strike of 1985–86.

These developments fuelled the demand to smash the 'glass ceiling' that prevented women from attaining the highest levels of responsibility in politics – as in other areas of life. Although the first woman MP had been elected in 1918, the level of women's parliamentary representation remained stuck at around 3–5 per cent of House of Commons membership in the 40 years after 1945. In Wales, the position was even worse, with only three women elected between 1929 and 1970 (and one of those, Dorothy Rees, MP for Barry, served only one very short term, in 1950–51). From 1970 until Ann Clwyd's by-election victory in Cynon Valley in May 1984, there were no Welsh women MPs at all and Clwyd was not joined by another woman for a further thirteen years. When significant progress was made, in 1997, it was because Labour had begun to introduce all-women shortlists to select its candidates in certain seats that had fallen vacant.[8] In that year's general election, the number of women MPs doubled from the 60 elected five years earlier to 120 (18.2 per cent of the total); 101 of these were Labour, four of them representing Welsh constituencies.[9]

With the arrival of the Assembly, the opportunity to select a full set of constituency candidates at once enabled Labour to introduce the mechanism of 'twinning', whereby constituencies were paired and asked to conduct a joint selection to choose one woman and one man in each case. This procedure proved highly controversial, with a 'Campaign Against Twinning' ranged against the 'Twin to Win' group, which supported the policy. Its adoption contributed to the election of 24 women at the outset of the first 60-member Assembly, a figure that rose to 30 in 2003, dropping back slightly to 28 four years later. The Assembly now has a higher proportion of women than almost any parliamentary body in the world, including those in Scandinavia; for a while, there was also a slight majority of women in the Welsh cabinet. Twinning, then – like all-women shortlists – may have been something of a blunt instrument, but it was a necessary one, to secure the gender equality absent, until 1999, from Welsh political life. The greater prominence of women in Welsh politics, compared to Westminster, is also reflected in the fact that the Assembly keeps family-friendly hours. Women's position has been bolstered by the highly effective, high-profile work of ministers like Jane Davidson, Edwina Hart, Sue Essex and Jane Hutt and opposition or backbench politicians like Helen Mary Jones, Leanne Wood and Kirsty Williams.

There is far less cause for celebration over the record on black and minority ethnic representation in Welsh politics. There was a complete absence, during the Assembly's first two terms, of any AM from an ethnic minority and there are still no black or brown faces among Wales' 40 Westminster MPs. According to the 2001 census, 2.2 per cent of people in Wales belong to an ethnic minority, and in both Cardiff – which has one of the longest-established black communities in Britain – and Newport, the percentage is substantially higher. Yet, until the election in 2007 of Plaid Cymru's Mohammad Asghar, not a single Assembly member, nor any MP representing a Welsh constituency, belonged to an ethnic minority. This situation undermines the legitimacy of the Assembly as a body claiming to represent the people of Wales. For Labour, in particular, it must be a matter of concern that none of the party's first-past-the-post candidates in the 2003 or the 2007 elections was from a non-white ethnic group. It is true that in 2003, the black Cardiff councillor, Cherry Short, was placed in the only winnable regional list position – number one in Mid and West Wales – and that it was (ironically) only the narrow victory by Labour's Catherine Thomas in Llanelli that prevented the party from qualifying for the extra seat that Short would have occupied. It should not, however, be left to the vagaries of the additional member system to ensure representation that should be forthcoming at constituency level – if no CLP is able to select a black or Asian candidate, then Labour has a problem. In 2007, the party did not allow itself even the slim chance of black representation that had existed four years earlier: the only highly-placed ethnic minority 'top-up' seat candidates were in areas where Labour would almost certainly not qualify for such a seat. Ironically, this was because black candidates were allocated to higher list positions in regions (South Wales Central and South Wales East) with large black communities – yet the party is consistently over-represented at constituency level in these same regions and thus never qualifies for a top-up seat. Apparently, this self-defeating approach was dictated by legal advice: to assign a particular list position to a black candidate purely on the basis of likely success would fall foul of equality legislation. Once again, however, this underlines the inadequacy of relying on the additional member system. There is a strong case for the guaranteed inclusion of at least one minority ethnic candidate on all parliamentary and Assembly selection shortlists and even for all-black shortlists in areas like Cardiff and Newport. It seems likely that such measures will be necessary if Labour's candidates are to be genuinely representative of the areas they seek to represent.

Of course, it is not only in the political arena that Wales' black communities find that they have to battle for equal treatment with the white majority. Only in sport and in certain limited spheres of commerce do people from ethnic minorities in Wales have any real visibility: in the arts, academia, the media, much of the economy and even in trade unions, they have very little public profile. As the Commission for Racial Equality (CRE) pointed out in its final report, published in September 2007, rates of employment for ethnic minorities across Britain have remained stubbornly lower than those for the working-age population overall: 60 per cent, compared to 75 per cent – and the rate is even lower for those of Bangladeshi (44 per cent) or Pakistani origin (45 per cent) or of black African descent (57 per cent).[10] In Wales, the economic inactivity rate (excluding students) for ethnic minorities was 46 per cent higher than for the white population – somewhat lower than the 58 per cent difference for the UK as a whole, but still a huge margin.[11] Only 2.4 per cent of all FTSE 100 company directors belong to ethnic minorities. And while approximately 300,000 businesses in the UK are owned by people from ethnic minorities – contributing some £20 billion to the economy annually – these businesses are likely to be located in the most deprived areas and to find it more difficult to gain opportunities to tender for contracts in both public and private sector supply chains.[12] Ethnic minority Britons are more likely to experience poor health than the overall population, reflecting their greater experience of relative poverty. The CRE cites some startling disparities:

> Mortality at or around birth among babies of Pakistani- and Caribbean-born mothers is almost double the national average; people of Pakistani, Bangladeshi and African-Caribbean origin are between three and six

times more likely to have type two diabetes; and smoking is most prevalent among men of Bangladeshi (44 per cent of whom smoke) and Irish (39 per cent of whom smoke) heritage.[13]

In addition, black people are six times more likely, and Asian people twice as likely, to be stopped and searched by the police; black people are over three times more likely to be arrested than white people; ethnic minority groups make up a quarter of the male prison population; and annual recorded racist incidents have increased dramatically since the mid-1990s.[14]

Most of these figures are for the UK as a whole but there is no reason to suppose that they are unrepresentative of the situation in Wales. The Welsh cherish their reputation as a welcoming and tolerant people but, while there are certainly examples of harmonious and well-integrated multi-ethnic communities, there have also been some ugly episodes of prejudice and hostility. Two recent examples have been the violent clashes between white residents and Iraqi Kurds on Wrexham's run-down Caia Park estate in June 2003 and the racist murder of Kalan Kawa Karim in Swansea the following year. It is, of course, no coincidence that the far-right British National Party (BNP) stood candidates in both Swansea East and Wrexham in the 2005 general election. Fortunately, although a couple of candidates were elected unopposed to community councils in 2008, the BNP has yet to see any of its candidates win an election in Wales, but there are no grounds for complacency: in the 2007 Assembly elections, the party's regional list vote in areas like Wrexham – where it exploited tensions over an influx of Polish migrant workers – was as high as 10 per cent. There has, however, been a robust and determined response to the far right from across the political spectrum in Wales, embracing even the Tories, notwithstanding the readiness of Monmouth MP and former AM, David Davies, to make political capital out of attacking the 'equal opportunities industry'. (There has also been less readiness in Welsh politics than in the UK as a whole to exploit the tensions around the presence of asylum seekers – see Appendix 2). Opposition to racism and fascism, and the pursuit of the interests of minority ethnic communities generally, cannot be left to an almost exclusively white political establishment, however; the representation of black and Asian people must, therefore, be seen as an urgent priority.

To discuss the involvement of black and minority ethnic people in Welsh public life is to prompt questions of identity and belonging – in particular, the dichotomy between multiculturalism and integration. At the level of Westminster politics, the promotion of 'Britishness' has been an increasingly persistent theme, elaborated on by Gordon Brown, Jack Straw and Ruth Kelly, among others. Their insistence on an overriding identification with, and acceptance of, the majority culture and social norms seems worryingly intolerant. In 1990, progressive opinion was united in condemning and ridiculing Norman Tebbit when he put forward his 'cricket test' as a means of gauging acceptable standards of 'loyalty' on the parts of immigrants to the host nation; yet, in the age of the 'war on terror' it seems that it is legitimate to demand that minority communities demonstrate their reliability. Ruth Kelly's insistence that families of foreign descent should speak English even at home is perhaps the most extreme example of the new intolerance – at least, from a mainstream politician.

In the light of this, it is notable that there have no serious attempts to define Welshness in a prescriptive or exclusive way. The availability of Welsh identity to all who live within Wales' borders seems to be the only generally accepted criterion of our national community. In the light of the persistent insinuations that the Welsh nationalism of Plaid Cymru is somehow comparable with the 'British nationalism' of the BNP, it needs to be emphasised that Plaid has been as committed as any other section of political opinion to the idea that Wales and Welshness must be inclusive, above all. The fact that it is a Plaid Assembly Member who is the first from an ethnic minority is surely significant. Of course, there must certainly be racists among Plaid's members, supporters and voters – just as there undoubtedly are for the all other parties – but there is no evidence to suggest any inherent link between Welsh nationalism or patriotism, on one hand, and racism on the other. To say this is not to make an uncritical defence of Welsh nationalism, which – like the nationalisms of other small, stateless nations – is a limited ideology, given unity and cohesion by the overriding demand for the right to establish a self-governing state. As we have argued above, socialists should be sympathetic to such a demand, especially where it commands mass popular support, but it cannot serve as a surrogate for the broader ambitions of the socialist project. Nor, in supporting the legitimate aspirations of the Welsh people for national self-determination, do we subscribe to romantic 'blood and soil' notions of the eternal destiny of the Welsh, or their inherent nobility compared to the English. It hardly needs saying that the Welsh are not, as a people, fundamentally more decent, progressive, altruistic – or whatever – than any other nation. On the other hand, the suggestions – especially from many in the Labour party – that Welsh nationalism is fundamentally parochial and reactionary are unwarranted (and such critics usually end up endorsing *British* nationalism by default). There is no necessary contradiction between having a strong sense of 'local' identity and recognising one's citizenship in a global community; indeed, it has become almost conventional to observe that small-scale community fellowship has become all the more important in an increasingly 'globalised' world.

The area in which Welsh nationalism is most frequently accused of elitism and intolerance of outsiders is its fight to sustain and promote the Welsh language and particularly its efforts to defend the cultural integrity of Welsh-speaking communities in North and West Wales, whose character is threatened by the large-scale in-migration of English incomers. To a large extent, the issue over the Welsh language as such has been resolved – in principle, at least – in favour of its supporters. The idea that Welsh was a dying language, which should not be resuscitated, was falsified by the results of the 1981, 1991 and 2001 censuses, which saw the long-term decline of the language arrested and then begin to be reversed. The gradual reawakening of Welsh cultural pride was assisted by developments like the establishment of S4C, the 1993 Welsh Language Act and the introduction of Welsh as a core curriculum subject in schools up to the age of sixteen. The 2001 census revealed that the proportion of people in Wales able to speak Welsh had risen to 21 per cent, with 20 per cent able to read the language, 18 per cent able to write it, and 24 per cent capable of understanding spoken Welsh. The highest proportion of Welsh speakers was among young people: 39 per cent of children aged 10 to 15 could speak, read and write Welsh, compared with 25 per cent of 16–19 year olds.

However, the percentage of Welsh speakers in areas where Welsh is spoken by the majority is still in decline. Communities in which young people can find neither long-term employment nor affordable housing have increasingly found their homes, and sometimes their businesses, being bought up by affluent incomers who possess no affinity with the culture and traditions of the local area. In some cases, they attempt to learn the language and otherwise 'assimilate' but all too often they exhibit an arrogant disdain for the speaking of Welsh and for their adopted communities generally. In circumstances like these, to attempt to preserve the language is not to hang onto the badge of an exclusive club, but rather to try and sustain one of the principal remaining adhesives holding together an economically declining community. This is as much a socio-economic as a cultural issue; if it were happening in the East End of London (as, indeed, it as been) it would be called simply 'gentrification' or 'yuppification'. The fact that those adversely affected by it are rural Welsh communities, not the urban-industrial working class of English inner cities should not diminish the sympathy and support of would-be progressives. The measures in the *One Wales* agreement that seek to address this issue should therefore be warmly welcomed: in particular, the use of Language Impact Assessments for planning purposes in areas of housing pressure; giving local authorities the ability to secure 100 per cent affordable housing in development sites in such areas; providing grants for first-time house-buyers and extending housing protection for rural workers; researching population shifts to promote balanced populations; and increasing support for Welsh-medium print and electronic media.[15]

'The Welsh language,' says *One Wales*, 'belongs to everyone in Wales as part of our common national heritage, identity and public good.'[16] This is an important declaration, which should be borne in mind whenever 'British unionists' in the Conservative and (sadly) the Labour party use the language as a stick to beat Plaid Cymru, denouncing 'preferential' treatment for the bilingual minority at the expense of the monoglot majority. It is also a reminder that any socialist political project for Wales must respect and embrace the diversity of our national community. The left is primarily concerned – with good reason – about issues of material wellbeing; yet, we cannot simply assign people to amorphous categories such as 'the working class', 'the poor' or 'the socially-excluded', however objectively valid these designations may be. The struggle of women for gender equality, of black people for racial equality and of numerous other social groups, which we have not even considered here – like disabled people and the LGBT community – are no less important than the fight for equality and social justice as such. To its credit, the Assembly has recognised this, as its many equality strategies and initiatives – limited and piecemeal as they are – bear witness. The socialist left has to build on the good work that has been done and forge an alliance for radical and lasting social change that is genuinely inclusive and representative of all sections of the people of Wales.

Chapter 8

Why party democracy matters

We have been discussing the sort of policy agenda that we would wish to see in Wales – and doing so from the perspective of Labour party activists. Yet some readers who may sympathise with our views will see the Labour party as a problem, not as any part of the solution. We have ourselves been very critical of the record of New Labour in the preceding chapters. Our ongoing commitment to working through the Labour party reflects not only the more progressive approach of the Welsh Labour leadership but our conviction that the majority of party members retain a belief in the possibility of a qualitatively fairer and more equal society. The fact that their views are often not reflected by the Westminster leadership is, in large part, a consequence of the undemocratic internal character of the Labour party. Over many years, the party's leaders and top officials have proven adept at circumventing – or, where necessary, amending – the provisions for accountability in the party rules, to ensure that power over decision-making remains firmly at the centre. Some will argue that this demonstrates that Labour is fundamentally dysfunctional. Our view, however, is that, as long as millions of people look to Labour to advance their interests, efforts to democratise the party have a broader relevance.

The rise and fall of Labour party democracy

Contemporary conflict over Labour party democracy goes back as least as far as the Wilson Governments of 1964–70, whose performance in office gradually dispelled the initial enthusiasm with which they had been greeted by socialists. Particularly unpopular was *In Place of Strife*,

Barbara Castle's white paper on industrial relations, which attempted to clamp down on union rights. Although eventually shelved, the damage to the party's standing that these proposals caused among trade union members undoubtedly contributed to Labour's election defeat in 1970. Three years later, the Campaign for Labour Party Democracy (CLPD) was established by activists to secure the adoption of constitutional safeguards that would give ordinary party members some control over policy and the ability to hold their representatives accountable. In the early 1980s, following the downfall of an even more disappointing Labour government, the CLPD and its co-thinkers won some important battles, giving party members the right to reselect their parliamentary candidates, and making the election of the leader the prerogative of the whole party, rather than just the MPs. Already, by the later years of Neil Kinnock's leadership, these achievements were being undermined by simply bypassing the official channels of party decision-making, establishing a shadow power structure whose apex was the leader's office. Subsequently, under Tony Blair and Gordon Brown, a more overt attack has been carried out on party democracy, which has not merely rolled back the gains of the 1980s but has left party members with fewer democratic rights than they have held at any time in Labour's history.

The most significant innovation of the New Labour period has been the change in the character and status of party conference, which has been stripped of any real authority over party policy. To say this is not to hold up the pre-Blair conferences as a paragon of transparency and accountability. They certainly saw more than their fair share of manoeuvring and stitch-ups – not least in the 'compositing' process, where several motions on the same subject would be welded into a fairly banal amalgam that eliminated the more controversial points of its original constituents. In this pre-New Labour period, however, it was at least possible to discuss and vote on a fairly clear proposition, on most of the major policy issues of the day. This all changed with the introduction in 1997 of a new policy-making process called 'Partnership in Power' (PiP).

The avoidance of debate
Under PiP, policy development is primarily the prerogative of the National Policy Forum (NPF), a body elected at conference every two years, on which all sections of the party are represented, but which also includes, as of right, members of the NEC and the Cabinet. The NPF establishes sub-committees (policy commissions) for each of the major

policy areas and these draw up documents that are presented to conference and which are supposed to form the basis of the Labour's programme in government. For the party leadership, anxious to avoid embarrassing public displays of 'off-message' views by activists, the NPF has many advantages over party conference. Its meetings are held behind closed doors, at residential sessions where there are ample opportunities for protracted negotiations over controversial issues with influential participants (usually from the unions). The NPF and its constituent commissions have all-encompassing discussions on particular policy areas, which are then written-up by party officials to reflect the 'general consensus'. Needless to say, the written summaries tend to reflect the leadership's view (or to skate over controversial points altogether) and the onus is then on dissident elements to demand detailed re-drafting.

Every year, party conference spends most of its time discussing, in turn, the documents that have emerged from the NPF process. At the end of each discussion, however, there is usually only one vote: to accept or reject the document in its entirety. Conference cannot amend the documents on its own initiative. It can, *very* occasionally, choose between a majority and a minority position arising from the NPF, on a particular issue within a particular policy document. This happens when the NPF has failed to arrive at a 'consensus' and a proposition, which the leadership has tried to kill off, has nevertheless received more than 25 per cent, but less than 50 per cent, of the vote at a crucial Forum meeting. In 2004, for example, there were minority positions calling for rail renationalisation and for the 'fourth option' in council housing (i.e. giving councils a level playing field to borrow money to renew their housing stock in-house, rather than transfer it to the private or 'third' sector). Conference duly supported both of these minority positions, only to have them rejected out of hand by the relevant ministers.

Conference debates on policy forum documents hardly resemble debates at all, since the subject under discussion (e.g. the entire field of health and social care) is generally so broad that consecutive speakers are likely to address completely unconnected points. There is, therefore, no sense of collectively getting to grips with an important issue. This is exacerbated by the fact that many speakers – often aspiring MPs – will use their three minutes in the spotlight not to raise a matter of real concern to them, but simply to present the 'party line' on an issue, sometimes with 'drafting support' from party officials. These people can often guarantee that they will be called to the rostrum, because the list of speakers is largely determined beforehand, with aspirants approaching officials, having their seating position and distinguishing features noted and passed to the chair. The latter then goes through a pantomime of peering at the sea of upheld hands – seemingly trying to select a representative selection of speakers – and then simply identifies those on the pre-arranged list (sometimes displaying a remarkable ability to see through barriers and around corners). At the end of the 'debate', the policy document is always approved – usually virtually unanimously – because to take the other alternative and reject it would leave the party without a policy at all.

From bad (under Blair) to worse (under Brown)

After 1997, the only resolutions allowed at conference were on emergencies and 'contemporary' issues – that is, issues too recent to be covered by the NPF documents. Every year, the resolutions submitted – if considered sufficiently 'contemporary' by the Conference Arrangements Committee – would be categorised according to the issues they covered and a ballot of delegates would choose four issues for debate (a rule change in 2003 allowed the top four selected by the unions and the top four chosen by the CLPs, to allow someone other than the general secretaries of the 'big four' unions to get a look-in). All resolutions submitted under the chosen headings – or composites of two or more of them – would then be discussed and voted on by conference. At the September 2007 conference, however – Brown's first as leader – all this has changed again, after conference passed a set of rule changes proposed by the leadership under the Orwellian rubric, *Renewing and Extending Party Democracy*. Now, even contemporary resolutions have been abolished. Conference may decide only which issues to refer to the NPF, from those submitted by party units and affiliates and then whittled down by conference. The NPF will then consider these issues and report back to the following year's conference. For anything other than a very long-running issue, the process is pointless. It will, however, achieve the aim of eliminating any controversy from conference and allowing the party to appear united in the eyes of the media and the general public. The vote in favour of the rule change was carried – after a typically stage-managed debate – by over 80 per cent in both the CLPs' and the affiliates' section, the 'big four' union leaders having struck a deal with Brown at the previous week's NEC meeting, in the interests of party unity in the pre-election period. They may already regret having been so accommodating.

Post-democracy, Welsh style

Much of the above also applies to the Welsh Labour policy process, since 'Partnership in Power' was introduced in Wales too, after a brief hiatus. Unfortunately, this transplantation of the English model has not been treated by the Welsh party collectively as an alien imposition that offends against the democratic and transparent culture of the Welsh labour movement, since the latter was never much in evidence at Welsh party conferences anyway. In Wales, the trade union bureaucracy has acted as a consistently conservative force and 'regional' secretaries have relished their role as 'fixers', becalming rank-and-file rebellion, delivering conference majorities for leadership-approved policies and generally keeping everything running smoothly. Under 'Partnership in Power', then, the already rigid, top-down structures of Welsh Labour decision-making have been overlaid with an additional set of New Labour mechanisms that likewise function to impose a false 'unity', to marginalise dissent and to limit the opportunities for activists to exercise real influence (for the more complex case of Blaenau Gwent, see Appendix 3). This is not to say that there is no *discussion*: the Welsh Policy Forum process provides ample opportunities, over the four-year cycle between Assembly elections, for party units and affiliates to discuss draft documents and for Forum delegates to suggest modifications. In recent years, there have even been signs of a greater openness to such changes on the part of Welsh party officials compiling the final-stage documents. The fundamental problem, however – as at the British level – is that when those final documents are presented to conference, there is no opportunity to amend them. Until this changes, there will be no real accountability.[1]

An additional problem within Welsh Labour decision-making is that devolution itself has been used as an excuse to limit discussion and block rank-and-file initiatives. Welsh Labour conference had always been reserved, quite reasonably, for the discussion of Welsh issues but this was usually interpreted to include anything that had a significant bearing on Wales. The 1998 Welsh Labour conference decided, however, that the advent of the Assembly meant that only subjects that fell within the devolved policy areas should be deemed a proper subject for discussion in future. The difficulty with this is that a large number of areas of public policy in Wales – including some of those that impinge most sharply on popular concerns – are beyond the Assembly's competence.

A very clear example of this came with the March 2003 Welsh Labour conference, held a matter of weeks before the start of the war in Iraq. No fewer than five contemporary resolutions were submitted by constituency parties opposed to the war, all of which emphasised the real impact that the conflict would have on Wales: by diverting much-needed funding from Welsh public services to military uses; by inflaming ethnic and religious tensions in Welsh communities; and by putting Welsh people at risk from retributive terrorist attack. Despite the enormity of the subject and the reasonable character of the arguments, the conference standing orders committee stood firm: rules were rules. Thus, Welsh Labour was perhaps the only political organisation of any size *not* to be discussing the most pressing issue in world affairs at that moment. Anxious to avoid any repetition of this fiasco, Welsh Labour Grassroots supporters – with backing from Unison and a few other party units and affiliates – have made repeated but unsuccessful attempts at subsequent conferences to force a change in the party's standing orders, to allow non-devolved matters to be discussed. This must be addressed: at stake is not just the right to discuss the Iraq war – or, indeed, *any* specific subject – but the right of the party in Wales, like any other political party worthy of the name, to have the discussions that its members consider important.

Political radicalism, organisational conservatism

The 'clear red water' agenda, which has given substance to devolution, has also exposed the tension between the radicalism of Welsh Labour's substantive policies and the bureaucratic immobility of the party apparatus. In government, Welsh Labour is able to implement policies that constitute a clear alternative to those of New Labour in Westminster. However, the Welsh party is no more democratic than that in England. Its structures and processes were, of course, designed in London and there would probably be resistance from the leadership if Wales attempted to amend these structures unilaterally. It might even be said that Welsh Labour's ability to plough its own furrow in policy terms is conditional on there being no relaxation of the rigid, top-down internal regime which characterises today's Labour party. It is clear, also, that the 'Welsh way' has not yet been able to arrest the decline in party membership in Wales, or to reduce the number of moribund, or permanently inquorate, branches.

In June 2008, in the wake of a disastrous set of local election results, Labour's Welsh Executive Committee (WEC) circulated a set of proposals for reorganising party structures in Wales, which seemed at first like a very New Labour attempt to clamp down on the residual influence of rank-and-file members over policy and decision-making. This included the abolition of county parties, the virtual elimination of ward branches in their existing form and an end to the delegate-based structure of constituency general management committees. The WEC's near-complete climbdown in response to a furious reaction from activists suggests that the intent had quite likely been to streamline structures in recognition of a rapidly-declining membership-base, rather than to use the latter as a pretext to stifle dissent. Suspicions to the contrary were understandable, however, in the light of recent experience and the evident distaste of the UK leadership for anything resembling participatory democracy.

New Labour's internal regime is part of a project by the Blair-Brown leadership to replace parties based on mass mobilisation and participation with those based around well-funded elites, developing policies by way of manipulated, undemocratic focus groups and media grandstanding. 'Partnership in Power', for its part, is little more than a manoeuvre designed to shunt into a siding any demands from the membership on the leadership. But in Wales, the policies pursued accord far more with the beliefs of party members, so what does the leadership have to fear? In fact, it is almost certainly not the elected *political* leadership of Welsh Labour that is primarily responsible for restricting democracy and silencing dissent. There is a division of labour (no pun intended!) between, on one hand, Welsh Labour politicians and, on the other, party officials based in Cardiff but answerable to London. When attempts to open up the party are frustrated, it is not, therefore, on the orders of Rhodri Morgan – but as long as he and his ministerial colleagues tolerate the current state of affairs, they risk undermining the commitment of their natural constituency: the activists who share their enthusiasm for radical reform but expect to have a real say – expressed in the form of a free vote – in policy development.

New Labour or Welsh Labour?

The contradiction between progressive policies on the one hand, and top-down bureaucracy on the other is unsustainable, in the long run, in any political party claiming to be socialist or social-democratic. If we have learned anything from the twentieth century it is that you cannot have socialism without democracy. Without a healthy, lively, internal life, involving the right to discuss, deliberate, and disagree and to call the leadership to account, progressive policies cannot be developed and fought for. The Policy Forum process was created, it would seem, to foster the illusion of such participation. Within Wales, the illusion is sustained by the matey informality that is ingrained in the Welsh party culture and what is probably a genuine willingness, on the part of most ministers, to listen to members' views. The party machine still refuses, however, to risk a genuinely free vote on anything that might make a difference when it comes to the all-important conference. In the glare of the TV cameras, the façade of unity must be maintained and, if a potentially divisive motion should actually make it onto the order paper, the block votes of Unite and the GMB will ensure that there are no upsets. The Welsh party leadership should not allow activists to become resigned or cynical about their ultimate capacity to control their own party. Without an informed and animated rank and file, who will defend the apostles of the Welsh Way if they come under attack from Westminster? Who will give comradely criticism when they are mistaken, and support them when they are right? Eventually, something will have to give. For the sake of its own its own vitality, and the future of a distinct, progressive, Welsh agenda, the party's radical impulses must prevail over the conservatism of the apparatus.

Chapter 9

Allies and adversaries

No lasting progressive change can be brought about solely by the actions of a handful of politicians and their advisors – however well-intentioned – or even by the membership of a political party. When power in society is concentrated in the hands of a few, who have the means to sustain and enforce their authority, it will take major political upheaval to wrest control and resources from their grip. The governments that have achieved the most – particularly, in Britain, the post-war Attlee governments – were responding to a demand for change for which many thousands of people had organised themselves to fight. Progress towards socialism will come when masses of ordinary people recognise that they have a collective interest in bringing it about and that presupposes that they are organised so as to give force to their demands. The greatest reserves of potential 'people power' are concentrated in the trade unions; despite decades of decline and defeat, they remain the backbone of the labour movement and of any progressive social project. In Wales today, they represent nearly 36 per cent of employees – a higher proportion than in England or Scotland (but lower than in Northern Ireland) and higher than in any English region except the North-East.[1] The Wales TUC claims an affiliated membership of 465,000.[2] While those members are far more heavily concentrated in sectors like public services and manufacturing than in, say, financial services, that is still a substantial reserve of strength.

The prospects for socialism in the 21st century are, then, greatly dependent on the resolve and vigour of the labour movement – yet it is within that movement that one encounters some of the most immediate obstacles in day-to-day efforts to advance a socialist agenda. New Labour in Westminster, notwithstanding recent changes within and outside the party, remains intent on driving through a quasi-Thatcherite programme and uses its control of the party apparatus to block resistance. Moreover, while the affiliated trade unions have often opposed particular government policies, especially in areas like privatisation and employment rights, it must be acknowledged that the Blair-Brown leadership could never have sustained its project without trade union support. While most union leaders are keen to distance themselves from identifiably New Labour policies, they have been far from consistent in their support for an alternative and have often sided with the party leadership against attempts to democratise the party and to win it to socialist policies.

New Labour and the trade unions

Following the election of Margaret Thatcher in 1979, the irresolution and disunity of the union leadership, exacerbated by the ineffectuality of its parliamentary allies, allowed the Tories to defeat the labour movement, industry by industry and union by union. The defeat of the steel strike in 1980 cleared the way for the devastation of that industry. Next, car workers, at Longbridge and Cowley in particular, were defeated and prominent shop stewards sacked. When the 1980–81 recession, combined with the savagely deflationary economic policies pursued by Margaret Thatcher and her Chancellor, Geoffrey Howe, wiped out great swathes of engineering industry across Britain, the TUC and its leading affiliates failed to provide the decisive leadership that was needed to save jobs. Nor did they offer much resistance to the legislative attack on union rights: the Employment Acts of 1980 and 1982 restricted the closed shop, picketing, and secondary action and the Trade Union Act of 1984 made it compulsory to hold secret ballots for elections, and before strike action. Significantly, the TUC had, in 1983, failed to give the necessary support to striking print workers who were up against the anti-union laws.

By the time of the last great defeat, that of the miners, the trade union leadership could offer the strikers and their communities enough food and money to prevent them from starving, but not the support and solidarity that could have helped them win. It was on the back of the miners' defeat that Neil Kinnock, together with like-minded union leaders, was able to promote 'new realism' – in other words, acceptance of the outlawing of solidarity action, or any other effective union activity. The new laws provided the union leadership with an excuse not to lead any action in defence of jobs and services. They could use the threat of sequestration of union funds to refuse to support any solidarity action, while the elaborate procedure necessary for strikes to escape illegality served to defuse any rank and file spontaneity. The leadership could then focus its attention on less risky activities, like selling car insurance and credit cards to the membership. While millions of workers were angered by the rollback of their wage rates and conditions, and by attacks on the public services on which they relied, the actions of the Tories and the inaction of their own leaders increasingly left them with no realistic means of doing anything about it. By the 1990s, the level of strike action had sunk to its lowest ebb since the 1890s, and a whole generation of younger workers appeared to accept as normal the outlawing of effective trade unionism. Onto this blighted landscape emerged Tony Blair, climbing onto the summit of the Labour party from the shoulders of Margaret Thatcher and intent on transforming the party into a version of the US Democrats and its membership into a supporters' club.

The last ten years have seen the welcome emergence in a number of unions – Aslef, the CWU, the FBU, Natfhe (now part of UCU), the NUJ, PCS and the RMT – of a leadership prepared to take on the New Labour leadership in defence of its members' interests. Not all of these, of course, are Labour affiliates and two that had been affiliated at the start of the New Labour period – the FBU and RMT – have now left the fold (in one case voluntarily, in the other by expulsion). There was also considerable initial optimism on the left about the current leadership of the 'big four' unions – the TGWU and Amicus (now merged to form Unite) plus the GMB and Unison; the election of Derek Simpson as general secretary of Amicus, over the Blairite, Sir Ken Jackson, occasioned particular jubilation. While these leaders have used a more assertive language than their respective predecessors, however, they have shown little consistent readiness to use their collective weight in the party to push for pro-union policies (notwithstanding the much-hyped 'Warwick accord'). In fact, they used their power to help Blair avoid embarrassing conference votes on more than one occasion and they have now assisted Gordon Brown in abolishing conference resolutions altogether.

The shift to the left, such as it is, has not noticeably been replicated at a Welsh level – perhaps unsurprisingly, given that most 'regional' secretaries are appointed by their London leaderships, rather than elected by their members, having already worked their way up the full-time apparatus. In general, the Welsh union leadership combines old fashioned machine-politics with strategic conservatism. Its role in the recent history of the Welsh Labour party is clear enough. The TGWU, GMB and AEEU, none of which had balloted their members, all delivered their block votes for Alun Michael.[3] The unions played a crucial role in the shameful avoidance of a conference debate on Iraq in 2003 and in defeating attempts by activists at every Welsh conference since 2004 to increase party democracy (the principal exceptions being Unison and the CWU – largely, it would seem, on account of their more democratic structures).[4] Clearly, the struggle within the Labour Party for democracy and socialist policies is intimately connected to the struggle within the workplace for an effective trade unionism that is able to defend jobs and services. Bridging the two is the effort to democratise the unions, strengthening the accountability of full-time officials to rank-and-file members.

The obstacles within the Welsh labour movement to the success of a socialist agenda are not solely related to the control of the bureaucracy; there are also clear ideological differences, with a section of the Welsh Labour party (almost certainly a small minority, but with a degree of influence at parliamentary and Assembly level) identifying more closely with the Blair-Brown agenda than with Rhodri Morgan's distinct 'Welsh Way'. From time to time, critics like Chris Bryant MP have publicly urged the Welsh Labour leadership to embrace New Labour policies;[5] in 2007, Eluned Morgan MEP (not previously regarded as being on the right) ignited a fresh round of intra-party debate with the comment that Welsh Labour might need to ditch its 'clear red water' policy stance in order to appeal to more 'aspirational' voters and win back constituencies like Cardiff North. Our own view hardly needs repeating at this point but it is worth adding that the left needs to be prepared to fight for the defence and extension of the 'clear red water' agenda, as the right will certainly display its customary ruthlessness if it gets anywhere near control of the Welsh party and its policy programme.

'Devo-scepticism' and 'party patriotism'

The nine weeks of negotiations that followed the 2007 Assembly election exposed a further fault-line within Welsh Labour: between those who wanted to take Welsh devolution forward and those (the 'unionists') who did not. The latter comprise, first, those who had always opposed the devolution project in any form; and second, those who had been persuaded to support it on the basis that it would be a one-off

157

event, not a developing process (once an Assembly had been set up – with limited powers and under perpetual Labour control – that, they hoped, would be that). The immediate practical question which brought this division to the fore was whether Labour should enter a coalition with Plaid Cymru or attempt to continue as a minority government. The coalition agreement was conditional on a referendum by 2011 on whether Wales should have a Scottish-style parliament with primary legislative powers, a prospect that was anathema to the Labour 'unionists'.

Four Labour AMs publicly opposed the coalition, manifesting the visceral hostility towards Plaid that is felt among a significant section of party members in Wales' eastern belt and in parts of the valleys. A majority of Welsh Labour MPs were also opposed – reflecting their concern about the impact of further devolution on their own status and numbers – and used their influence to the full in an attempt to dissuade the party from endorsing the agreement. While the MPs' self-interest warrants little consideration, the attitude of the 'refusenik' AMs – who had a more direct interest in the complexion of the Assembly government – raises more serious questions as to what they believe they are in politics *for*. Electing Labour governments is surely not an end in itself, but a means to help to improve people's lives and the *One Wales* agreement preserved every commitment from Welsh Labour's 2007 manifesto, along with some elements of Plaid's. Yet the almost pathological hatred of 'the nationalists' shown by these AMs and their supporters was such that they would have been prepared to jeopardise the implementation of Labour's manifesto: within weeks, if not days, Rhodri Morgan's minority administration would have been ousted by a three-party 'rainbow coalition', raising the prospect of Tory ministers running Welsh public services once again.

Among ordinary Labour party members and trade unionists in Wales, the divisions between unionists and devolutionists are not necessarily set in stone. There are many who, in 1997, voted against the Assembly, or voted 'yes' with little enthusiasm, but who now accept that that devolution is here to stay and appreciate its benefits. Similarly, there will no doubt be some who opposed the red-green alliance but may be prepared to change their minds as they see the coalition government delivering Labour policies. But, while there are exceptions, the devolutionist-unionist division increasingly mirrors the left-right division in the party. Those on the devolutionist left and centre-left appreciate not only the process – the greater democracy resulting from devolution – but also the results: the 'made in Wales' policies, which are closer to their own ideals than New Labour's neo-liberalism. Some on the unionist right proclaim their own 'socialism' and 'internationalism' in opposition to Plaid's 'narrow nationalism' – but, at Assembly level they tend to be those least enamoured with the 'clear red water' agenda, and most sympathetic to New Labour. Nor are they arguing in favour of some sort of world government: their opposition to greater Welsh autonomy means – if only by default – endorsement of the reactionary and over-centralised 'United Kingdom', with all its medieval trappings, such as the monarchy and the House of Lords.

Just as there are adversaries within the Labour party, there are, in our view, also allies, or potential allies, outside it – including in other parties. In order to take advantage of the opportunities to build a bloc for socialism in Wales, it is necessary for members to abandon the 'my party right or wrong' mentality which sees, in an undifferentiated way, all other parties as equally dangerous, and conversely, any Labour party member as somehow 'better' – no matter what their position might be on the Iraq war, or privatisation.

Plaid: allies or enemies?

Plaid Cymru has been attacked – rightly, in our view – for its readiness to countenance a 'rainbow coalition'. There had already been ongoing co-ordination between the three opposition parties after Labour's loss of Blaenau Gwent had reduced it to minority status, and this ended only in December 2006, when Plaid agreed to support Labour's budget, to the consternation of its erstwhile allies. In the post-election period, the Plaid leadership clearly saw the 'rainbow' project as a short-cut into government. The willingness of a significant section of the party – including, at one point, a clear majority of its Assembly group – to consider a coalition with the Tories cannot be excused. For a party pledged to uphold the interests of Wales to do business with the party that had visited such destruction on the country in the 1980s and 1990s would have been a huge betrayal. Nevertheless, a share of the responsibility for the rainbow coalition's resurrection must lie with those in the Labour party whose anti-Plaid tribalism led them to declare any deal with Plaid impossible. Chief among the culprits here was Peter Hain, who, despite being a Westminster MP, seemed to imagine that he had a veto over any governmental arrangements made by the Assembly Labour leadership and publicly ruled out any coalition with Plaid even before the election. Throughout the difficult post-election period, several other MPs and AMs continued to do their best to scupper any arrangement, be it a coalition or a stability pact, with Plaid.

Four Plaid AMs,[6] supported by Jill Evans MEP, publicly opposed, as a matter of principle, any deal between their party and the Tories and ultimately succeeded in winning a majority for a coalition with Labour. Yet they gained little credit for this among Labour's tribalists. Indeed, the venomous abuse directed indiscriminately by the latter against all 'nationalists' aided those within Plaid seeking to secure the 'rainbow' deal, as long as this remained an option.

The very idea of a coalition with Plaid has always been anathema among many Labour party members, but it has logic on its side. Two of the four parties represented in the Assembly – Welsh Labour and Plaid Cymru – have a formal commitment to socialism, while the other two do not. In these terms, the red-green alliance certainly has more coherence than the 'partnership' between Labour and the Liberal Democrats in the Assembly's first term. A common response to this is the allegation that Plaid's supposed commitment to socialism is merely an opportunistic tactic to secure electoral support in South Wales, with its more conservative stance in the north and west being held up in support of this claim. Yet, while no major party is above electoral opportunism, the reality is that Plaid is itself a coalition of left and right tendencies – united by their commitment to Welsh self-government, but divided on their social programme – and that its history has been marked by the tension between the two. Plaid started life in 1925 as a right-wing nationalist sect whose leaders, Saunders Lewis and Ambrose Bebb, admirers of Mussolini and Franco, advocated de-industrialisation and the construction of a neo-medieval society of small property-holders as the cure for Wales' ills. So central was the Welsh language to Plaid's nationalism that Lewis actually opposed carrying out propaganda in English-speaking parts of Wales. Plaid's politics, in that form, were clearly utterly irrelevant to the vast majority of the people of Wales, whichever language they spoke. Plaid's politics subsequently moved on, especially after Saunders Lewis' replacement as party leader, in 1945, by the more progressive – and ultimately more influential – figure of Gwynfor Evans. Nevertheless, many Labour party members, still use Lewis' idiosyncratic brand of right-wing obscurantism as a stick to beat Plaid.

Under Gwynfor Evans, Plaid began to look more like a modern political party, campaigning on a range of issues of general relevance to the people of Wales and duly reaping the electoral benefits, beginning with Evans' 1966 victory in the Carmarthen by-election. There had been attempts to commit the party to some form of socialism as early as

160

the 1930s and these finally bore fruit when Plaid's 1981 conference voted to amend the party constitution to incorporate such a commitment.[7] This remained controversial, however, and throughout the 1980s there were fractious internal debates between left and right, which mirrored, to some extent, those taking place at the same time within the Labour party. The 'National Left', which was led by Dafydd Elis Thomas and welcomed non-Plaid members, aimed to maintain and develop Plaid's socialist commitment, while the more conservative 'Hydro' group sought the renunciation of any ideological affiliation beyond nationalism itself. Neither group survived into the 1990s but it was the left that proved more successful in influencing the party's agenda. Its conception of socialism was never elaborated very coherently, beyond stressing that it was a decentralist 'community socialism' – in contrast to the perceived state-centralist socialism of the Labour party. In practical terms, however, Plaid increasingly associated itself with progressive causes beyond its traditional concerns, such as the anti-nuclear movement, support for the striking miners and opposition to the poll tax.[8] In the late 1990s, renewed debate over policy gave rise to the emergence of a new Plaid left, the leading figures of which were predominantly working class and from the south, including the MEP, Jill Evans (who had also been part of the National Left); Adam Price, who was to become an MP in 2001; and Leanne Wood, then a Rhondda-Cynon-Taff councillor and now an AM. At the same time, Plaid consciously oriented itself to the labour movement, and made energetic attempts to attract trade union activists disenchanted with New Labour.

The continued success of the Plaid left was reflected in the party's 1999 Assembly election manifesto, which called for the restoration of the student grant and the link between pensions and earnings and exerted a stronger appeal to many working-class voters than Labour's insipid quasi-Blairite programme, contributing to an 80 per cent increase in Plaid's vote, in absolute terms. Later, when Welsh Labour was still building up the confidence to declare its divergence from New Labour, Plaid was calling for re-nationalisation of the railways and the steel industry and took a principled stand against military action in Afghanistan and Iraq. It is true to say, however, that the left in Plaid has not had things all its own way in recent years: the most right-wing candidate, Ieuan Wyn Jones, easily won leadership elections in 2000 and 2003 (latterly in a collective leadership with Dafydd Iwan). Moreover, as we have seen, Plaid was happy to work fairly opportunistically as part of a combined opposition in 2005–07 to inflict a series of defeats on Welsh Labour in the

Assembly chamber and was subsequently poised to enter into a coalition with the Tories after the Assembly elections. And in the local authorities that it has controlled, Plaid has often been as conservative and self-serving as the worst of its opponents. Overall, however, Plaid is clearly a progressive party, with a strong socialist wing, and shares much common-ground on policy with Welsh Labour, as the *One Wales* agreement demonstrates.

Labour party members should therefore put aside crude 'Nat-bashing' and attempt to engage with Plaid politically. This would, in turn, strengthen the position of the socialists within Plaid in their efforts to turn the party leftwards and undermine the 'cultural nationalists' who seek to reduce Welsh politics to questions of language and independence. It would also put pressure on Plaid to recognise Welsh Labour's progressive agenda, undermining the efforts by some Plaid members to blur the distinctions between Welsh Labour and New Labour. It would never have been easy to overcome the hostility that has characterised relations between the two parties but the present coalition in Cardiff Bay has created the most favourable possible conditions for a rapprochement between the two major currents in left politics in Wales.

A red-green alliance

A 'red-green' alliance need not be a solution only to electoral stalemate. The issues that the *One Wales* agreement seeks to address will not have been resolved by the conclusion of the present Assembly term and Welsh Labour should therefore consider the possibilities of a longer-term political relationship with Plaid Cymru. This need not – and *should not* – mean ignoring real differences or forswearing electoral competition but it ought to involve, at a minimum, identifying Plaid as Labour's preferred coalition partner in advance of further Assembly elections, on the basis of the two parties' political common-ground. It could also, we would suggest, extend to the establishment of bi-partisan policy commissions to develop a longer-term governmental programme for Wales and to encouraging rank-and-file members of both parties to work together on issues where they can reach agreement. This sort of arrangement could begin to lift Welsh politics above the usual trivial point-scoring, driven by the pursuit of electoral advantage, and pool the intellectual and political resources of the two parties of any size in Wales that claim to stand for socialism and equality. It could yoke together the two principal challenges facing the Welsh left: the need to bring about a more equal, democratic and sustainable society than this and the need to end Wales' status as a poor and peripheral part of the United Kingdom. It could reconcile the supposedly irreconcilable interests of urban and rural Wales, north and south Wales and English-speaking and Welsh-speaking Wales. It could isolate the Tories for the foreseeable future. In so doing it could set a progressive, left-of-centre agenda in Welsh politics for years to come.

An ongoing Labour-Plaid alliance *could* do all of these things – and more – but this would not necessarily be the result of a friendlier relationship between the two parties. A less desirable outcome would be the kind of political culture that often results in situations of long-term coalition-politics: cooperation between the most complacent and self-serving elements of both parties in their mutual interests, to the detriment of the people, and the concentration of power in the hands of the party apparatchiks. To avoid this would require socialist activists in Labour and Plaid taking responsibility to ensure the accountability of their respective leaderships and a consistent focus on implementing progressive policies. They could also discuss a longer-term socialist agenda and work together around particular campaigns. To a limited extent, this has happened before. There was joint work between socialists in both parties during the 1997 referendum campaign, under the banner, 'Socialists Say Yes', including a well-attended conference in Cardiff Bay, which attracted probably the broadest range of left activists that Wales had seen at a meeting (as opposed to a demonstration) since the miners' strike; the following year, the same alliance was involved in building a major demonstration at the Cardiff EU heads of government summit.

A progressive alliance need not be reducible to Labour and Plaid. Who else might be involved? The 'partnership' with the Liberal Democrats in 2000–03 gave Welsh Labour a breathing-space to proceed with its 'clear red water' policies. Moreover, it is true that the Liberal Democrats are more consistently devolutionist than Labour, and they were largely responsible for the setting up of the Richard Commission. Their preference for proportional representation over first past the post has the advantage of being consistently democratic. On many social issues, they are no worse than Labour and their record on civil liberties is better than Labour's. However, Adam Price was right to describe the Lib Dems as 'political weather vanes'. At local level, their slippery opportunism, which can manifest itself in right-wing policies, is well-known and they have earned the enmity of many socialists in Wales by going into coalition with the Tories on several councils. Their recent policy-change on tax cuts indicates a turn to the right from the election campaign of 2005. This does not mean that their support should not be sought for progressive policies, on an issue-by-issue basis; their record at Assembly level suggests that such support would probably be forthcoming more often than not. Moreover, individual Lib Dem politicians have behaved in a principled way – such as Peter Black and the new leader, Kirsty Williams, who both opposed a rainbow alliance with the Tories. Nevertheless, as a party they are too unreliable to be part of any ongoing progressive alliance worthy of the name.

The Greens are a different proposition altogether. Of all the parties, they have, of course, the most sophisticated and coherent positions on environmental issues but they have also developed a range of policies which would not disgrace any democratic socialist party – although the party as a whole does not claim to be such. Coexisting with the socialists among the Greens are those who advocate only individual, as opposed to collective, solutions to the problems we face, and who do not see socialist democracy as the way to prevent environmental catastrophe and build a sustainable society. The Green party's contribution to questions such as climate change and sustainable development, and the way in which that contribution informs its position on transport, agriculture, energy and other questions, suggests that it would be a natural partner in any broad, progressive alliance with Welsh Labour and Plaid Cymru (indeed, it had a close ongoing relationship with the latter during the 1990s, when Cynog Dafis sat in Parliament as a joint Plaid Cymru and Green MP).

Other parties further to the left generally lack significant support in Wales, with the partial exception of the Communist party, which, despite its small and ageing membership, still exerts a degree of influence in the trade unions, in particular – not least through the pages of the *Morning Star* – and has consistently played a constructive role in progressive campaigns and initiatives. The newer left groupings like Arthur Scargill's Socialist Labour Party and the ill-fated Respect, have fallen far short of their objective of displacing a rightward-moving Labour party, consistently attracting only a derisory vote, although their members have played a positive role in a range of campaigns, not least the anti-war movement. As for Forward Wales, it proved to be no more than a vehicle for John Marek and Ron Davies following their break from Labour – a vehicle that was soon abandoned on the hard shoulder. The members of all these groups should be encouraged to become part of a red-green alliance based on a renewed Welsh socialist project. They need not leave

164

their existing organisations – so long as those organisations abandon any pretence of being themselves the 'vanguard' of the Welsh working class and agree to play a constructive role in a broad alliance headed by the socialists who command real mass support: those within Welsh Labour and Plaid Cymru. The trade unions also have a central role to play, along with the cooperative movement and organisations representing women, minority ethnic and faith communities, lesbian and gay communities, pensioners, disabled people and a whole range of progressive campaigns on the environment, international solidarity, animal welfare and innumerable other issues. The politicians of the centre-left can provide a lead, some focus and co-ordination – but socialism can only ultimately be won by the conscious, determined action of the huge majority who have a stake in a fairer, more equal society.

Chapter 10

21st century socialism: Welsh recipe or international cookbook?

A sharp-eyed observer would have noticed that '21st century socialism – a Welsh recipe', the November 2006 speech in which Rhodri Morgan once again distanced Welsh Labour from Westminster, was delivered at almost exactly the same point in the electoral cycle as his 'clear red water' declaration: six months before an Assembly general election.[1] As we observed in chapter four, it is at least arguable that the 2002 speech yielded a political dividend in assisting the recapture of Rhondda, Islwyn, Llanelli and Conwy the following year, allowing Labour to form a majority government; four years later, the first minister had a tougher job on his hands. Although many voters experienced, on a day-to-day basis, the benefits of a specifically Welsh agenda, the 2007 election showed that to a large extent, they still considered politics in all-British terms. We would not suggest that the Assembly's own policies were universally popular – particularly in areas like health service reconfiguration – but evidence from the doorstep strongly suggests that Labour's Senedd majority was not lost, primarily, in Clwyd West or Cardiff North, but in Iraq, Lebanon, Westminster, and on the Downing Street sofa. A non-Blairite administration was punished electorally in an anti-Blair backlash. Some voters may have been hazy about the division between the different levels of government when they voted against Labour. Others no doubt understood the distinction well enough: they may have been happy with the free bus travel and free prescriptions; they may have thought Rhodri Morgan nevertheless a decent and honest politician, but they made a priority of punishing Labour over Iraq.

Even if it did not sufficiently differentiate Welsh Labour from New Labour to secure an Assembly majority, that need not, of course, invalidate the political principles set out in the '21st century socialism' speech. The political clarity with which those principles were expounded makes the speech a convenient starting-point for an analysis of Welsh Labour's overall project. The first minister's distancing of his own programme from that of New Labour was judiciously worded, but unmistakable: the latter had been 'the most successful electoral project in the history of the party ... but like any project it is the product of its own time, 1994–2007, and its own circumstances'. He then proceeded to set out the ingredients, as he saw it, of his 'Welsh recipe'. What an unappetising dish it must have seemed to the Blairites and their few Welsh outriders! One by one, the nostrums of New Labour and its Thatcherite predecessor were emphatically rejected, as Morgan reasserted the role of the state as a force for good in politics, emphasising the importance of universality and the solidarity of interest that is reinforced by universal provision. The Welsh socialism of the 21st century would be 'more participative than passive', with the structures in health and education revised so that 'users are at the heart of decision making' and so that the door of the welfare state is no longer shut in a retreat 'to the city centre, or the call centre'. In emphasising the importance of combating inequality, Morgan did not merely register a philosophical difference with New Labour; he exposed the greatest failure of its record in office: the increase in inequality since 1997, about which both Blair and Mandelson had publicly expressed their blithe unconcern. In reaffirming his government's commitment to equality of outcome, he openly acknowledged the influence of the Nordic countries, thus implicitly rejecting the Atlanticism of Blair, Mandelson and Brown.

What sort of 'socialism'?
But did the first minister's speech set out a coherent strategy for the realisation of its stated aim, a Welsh socialism for the 21st century? How we answer this question depends on which end of the telescope we look through. We have argued throughout this book that Welsh Labour has demonstrated – not just in its leader's speeches, but through its everyday policy delivery – that a practical alternative exists to the policies pursued by New Labour in England, directly contradicting the claims of Blair

and Brown that theirs is the only feasible programme for the centre-left. That the New Labour leadership so often gets away with saying this (and there are, of course, many people in the Labour party in England who know full well that there is an alternative) relies, in part, on the indifference of the English media towards Wales and on Welsh Labour's reluctance, for comprehensible reasons, to shout its differences from the rooftops. However, it also depends, more fundamentally, on the low level of fighting spirit and political consciousness among working people. Many people passionately desire a qualitatively fairer and more equal society than the one we have, but see no practical way of achieving it. The very fact that the Welsh first minister could make a speech like '21st century socialism – a Welsh recipe' is a welcome indication that Blair has failed in his apparent ambition to exclude the very mention of socialism from the discourse of practical politics.

But what, on the other hand, about all the things that Rhodri Morgan did not say? He did not, for example, comment on the transfer of council housing stock. As we pointed out in chapter five, the Assembly government appears to have quietly acquiesced to Westminster on this issue, despite the successive votes in Labour conference. Yet the right to affordable, secure housing, with an accountable social landlord should be at the heart of any recipe for 21st century socialism. While Morgan is limited in this area, among others, by the devolution settlement, that need not preclude some indication of what would be desirable if the means were available. There was no mention of the Iraq war, nor indeed, more generally, of New Labour's catastrophic foreign policy – yet this continues to cast a shadow over every Labour election campaign. The failure publicly to condemn the war, when most Labour AMs disagreed with it in private, cannot be justified by the evasive and pedantic argument that it is not a devolved matter. Not only was there a moral imperative to denounce such savage injustice, but this would surely have won back many disillusioned former Labour supporters. In contrast to the party's general timidity on such issues, the strong public statement against Trident replacement in March 2007 by the then education minister, Jane Davidson, supported by the outgoing finance minister, Sue Essex, was both principled and courageous. Davidson quite correctly took the view that taking a stand on a matter of such significance was more important than protocol about devolved and reserved matters.

Ultimately, the fine detail of what was or was not in the first minister's speech is less important than whether Welsh Labour's current programme and its leader's declaration of intent, taken together, live up to the rubric, '21st century socialism – a Welsh recipe'. Most significantly, we should acknowledge that Morgan assumes (in common with the whole Welsh Labour leadership and the vast majority of Labour MPs) that the means of production are to remain, fundamentally, in private hands. This is a significant limitation, because the exercise of the Assembly's powers on the basis of a commitment to equality and social justice – while entirely laudable – falls a long way short of the introduction of socialism. Socialism involves nothing less than placing the means of production, distribution and exchange of goods and services under the democratic control of working people – the majority of the world's population. Such control has to go beyond the formal, unaccountable model provided by 'Old Labour' nationalisation, on the basis that you do not really own what you cannot control, any more than you can control what you do not own. Only with such democratic control can production and distribution be carried out according to need and not private profit, so that there can be an end to the present obscenity of hardship and deprivation in the midst of plenty. Only with production planned and organised for need, rather than in the interests of shareholders, can the resources of our planet be used responsibly, so that they can be handed on to future generations.

What about the second part of the title: 'a Welsh recipe'? The supposed distinctiveness of Welsh circumstances is the usual public explanation given by Welsh Labour for its divergence from New Labour orthodoxy: Wales is different; we have our own way of doing things. Much is made of Wales' radical traditions of solidarity and egalitarianism – and there is something in this, as we have ourselves argued in chapter three – but then every country has its own traditions of struggle and solidarity. Moreover, the specific form of Wales' economic and social problems may be unique but the fundamental character of those problems, and the kind of solutions to which they might be susceptible, are more general. Thus, the corollary of the 'Welsh way' is that in England, New Labour can get on with a neo-liberal agenda, provided that it leaves Wales alone. However, if, as Rhodri Morgan once declared, the policies of the 'choice' agenda are amoral, then they are as amoral in England – or anywhere else – as they are in Wales. The struggle for socialism is not the exclusive prerogative of working people in Wales, or any other country. It is an international struggle, fought simultaneously on many fronts, but it is a struggle in which Wales can – and, hopefully, *will* – play its part.

In saying what we believe full-blown socialism would necessary involve, we do not dismiss those policies which, in themselves, fall short of that vision. A national health service, free at the point of delivery and untainted by the mechanism of the market, is an important part of what a socialist society would look like, as is a comprehensive, affordable and sustainable public transport system and an education system based on equality of outcome, aimed at unlocking the potential of every human being. Insofar as the Welsh Labour leadership's policies are based on these principles, they must be supported. First of all, they must be supported because they can improve the quality of life of the majority of people in Wales, including many communities which have known only poverty. Second, they demonstrate – as the deregulated free market becomes ever more discredited – that there is a practicable alternative. Third, the experience of fighting for, winning and defending such progressive policies will raise the consciousness and increase the morale of working people so that they can go on to make further conquests.

A change of direction

However, the realisation, at a British or international level, even of policies equivalent to those already pursued by Welsh Labour, would require what would be, by today's standards, a political earthquake: a fundamental change in direction not only by the leadership of the Labour party and the trade union movement in Britain, but also the labour movement leadership elsewhere. We therefore have to proceed from an examination of those policies which are beyond the ambition of a Welsh Labour administration to those which, under present conditions, are beyond its capacity.

One of the main obstacles in this regard – as we have acknowledged elsewhere in this book – is a shortage of public finance. The widely-acknowledged inadequacy of the Barnett formula highlights the wider problem that the Assembly is in competition with numerous other branches of government, many responsible for providing vital public services to needy people, for a limited share of a restricted funding pot. One of the principal characteristics of the neo-liberal era has been a government commitment to permanent austerity (or 'the end of the old tax-and-spend policies', as they prefer to call it). Of course, that austerity affects some sections of society far more profoundly than others: after well over a decade of New Labour government, the poorest 20 per cent of people in Britain pay a higher proportion of their income in tax than the richest 20 per cent and people on comparatively modest incomes find themselves in the same tax bracket as billionaires. The poor pay a huge amount of tax, relative to their income, in indirect taxes such as

VAT, on which governments increasingly rely because of the reduced tax-take from the very rich. Corporation tax, levied on company profits, was reduced in the 2007 budget from an already generous 30 per cent to 28 per cent. The British tax system is therefore profoundly regressive. Worse still, governments (not just this present one) turn a blind eye to tax avoidance by the very wealthy and by large corporations, resulting in an estimated £97 billion to £150 billion going uncollected every year.[2]

There is also, of course, the murky world of the offshore economy and tax havens. By virtue of its various territories and crown dependencies, such as Jersey and the Cayman Islands – ostensibly independent jurisdictions, but closely tied in with the City of London – Britain is a tax haven state. One third of the assets of the global rich are estimated to be tied up in the offshore sector which, due to its secrecy, provides what the Tax Justice Network calls an 'interface' between the legal economy and such sectors as drugs, arms and money laundering. It is estimated that the stock of undeclared private wealth held offshore by rich individuals is worth about $11.5 trillion, yielding an annual income of $860 billion and lost annual tax revenue of $255 billion.[3] How much could be achieved if a Labour government were simply to deal with the offshore racket, close the tax avoidance loopholes, such as the claim of 'non-domiciled' status, and pursue tax evaders as energetically as it presently pursues the nearly-always-poor 'benefit cheats'? How much more would be achieved if a Labour government were to make changes to the existing tax structure so that the rich paid more in relation to their income? To address this problem, the Labour Representation Committee called in 2005 for two new rates of income tax, of 50 per cent at £60,000 and 60 per cent at £100,000, which would raise £14 billion annually.[4] This is what a Labour government should be doing.

Tackling inequality

A Labour government could also levy a so-called Tobin tax on stock market activity. It could impose a windfall tax on the obscene bonuses paid in the City of London, a tax on the golden handshakes and share options paid to retiring directors of large companies. Recent levels of executive pay represent little more than a glorying in rampant inequality for its own sake: it has no possible purpose other than to demonstrate how much richer are the rich than the rest of us. It is this culture of greed and reckless risk-taking, facilitated by the 'light-touch' regulation favoured by the Tories and New Labour, which, in 2008, brought the global financial system to its knees.

An equitable, progressive taxation system, and the imposition on the financial sector of, at the very least, a far tougher regulatory regime, if not outright public ownership, would not amount to socialism but at least the rich would no longer be allowed to continue simply accumulating wealth at the expense of any obligation towards the rest of society. It could ameliorate the appalling and destructive inequality which, for almost three decades, has virtually been government policy, but which has helped to make the UK a profoundly unhappy, dysfunctional society. Set against the institution of a socialist society, a fairer and more redistributive tax system and a degree of financial regulation common until the Thatcher era seems a modest ambition. However, New Labour shows little inclination to introduce either. One should not be deceived into thinking that October 2008's £50 billion recapitalisation – effectively a partial nationalisation of Britain's banks – and the total nationalisations of Northern Rock and the Bradford & Bingley[5] represent any fundamental change in economic strategy on the part of New Labour or any sign of the necessary democracy and accountability in financial decision-making; the return of Peter Mandelson to the cabinet in the reshuffle of October 2008 only underlines this. The recapitalisation is an emergency response to the sheer enormity of the crisis of confidence in the banking system. The banks are being bailed out – effectively saved from the consequences of their own actions – with taxpayers' money, which could have been used for health, education, transport or social housing. The individual nationalisations were an ad hoc response to the crisis resulting from those banks' own irresponsibility and greed – in turn, a consequence of New Labour's refusal to regulate. Given the position of the financial sector in the economy, it was simply not an option to let these banks go under; had these lame ducks been in the manufacturing sector, the government would have displayed considerably less understanding. Tellingly, the backlash against the City's greed culture is more evident in the right-wing media than in Gordon Brown's cabinet. While Brown has started to rail against the immorality of this culture, the government's recapitalisation does not give it the power to oversee executive pay. The government's measures therefore fall far short of what is really necessary: the nationalisation of these banks, the establishment of democratic control over banking decisions and democratic representation on boards.

Informing New Labour's approach is not just an awe of wealth and the wealthy, although that undoubtedly exists. There is the ever-present threat of capital flight: corporations taking their investment, and the jobs that go with it, elsewhere, where taxes are lower, where there is less regulation and where they can get a better return. This is the theme of the CBI's incessant agitation for lower taxes and a reduced 'burden' of regulation. Yet, as we argued in chapter six, there is always somewhere in the world that is cheaper, and so the reality is that national governments end up in a race for the bottom while corporations try to contribute as little as possible to the local infrastructure, from which they benefit, and to the well-being of the workers who make their profits for them. But, while the arguments justifying it are fallacious, tax competition is a reality for open economies; it cannot be dealt with in purely national terms. The answer is not tax competition between countries, but tax solidarity, something which we will deal with below.

Getting where we need to be

We have said what we think is wrong with the present economic system. We have set out what we believe socialism is. We have stated our support for policies which, while not in themselves amounting to socialism, can improve in all sorts of ways the lives of working people. We have looked at some of the forces which can participate in the struggle for a better future, and some of those standing in the way of that struggle. The crucial question, however, is how do we get from where we are now to where we would like to be? How do we build a 'bridge' between mobilising working people to vote for a progressive Labour administration in Cardiff Bay and taking power into their own hands? How can we, in Wales – one small country buffeted by the cold winds of globalisation – enact policies which can help us to transform socialism from an ideal into a realistic possibility?

We could start by trying to change the way politicians relate to people, and the way people relate to the political process. There is a widespread disengagement with political parties, not just in Wales, nor in Britain, but throughout the western world. This is reflected in the declining membership of political parties and decreasing turnouts in elections. The general perception is 'they're all in it for themselves', 'they never listen', or 'they make promises and then do the opposite', 'they're all the same', or even 'why should I be in a particular party? There are things that all the different parties do or say that I agree with'. This is not the same, however, as disengagement with politics *as such*. Millions of people marched against the Iraq war. Millions care desperately about the threat to their environment, either from global warming or from road or air pollution. They want a decent, affordable, integrated public transport system, good schools they can walk to, and a National Health Service which concentrates on getting them better (or, better still, prevents them getting ill in the first place) in clean hospitals which are not over-staffed with target-obsessed managers.

There are signs that the established political parties are aware of this. New Labour is forever talking about talking to people, but stunts like the 'big conversation' demonstrate that it will only talk about what it wants to hear. On the typically New Labour assumption that people can only be motivated by greed, Hazel Blears has recently suggested 'incentives' to get young people to vote, such as the chance to win an ipod, but if people vote because they actually want things to change, they will be disappointed. Privatisation, 'best value' and the steady centralisation of power have left local councils almost irrelevant, huge sectors of the economy are in private hands and the three main political parties at Westminster all agree on the primacy of the free market. Idealism, the desire to make the world a different and better place, has been replaced by technocratic managerialism.

So, how do we make state institutions and public services more accountable? Back in the 1980s, the Tories' answer to this question was the supposed responsiveness and dynamism of the market. The Tories, New Labour loyalists and the former public sector managers who have enriched themselves through privatisation may still believe this; almost no one who uses or works in public services would agree with them. So, how do we ensure, in Rhodri Morgan's words, that the Welsh socialism of the 21st century will be 'more participative than passive', that 'users are at the heart of decision making' and that the door of the welfare state is no longer shut in a retreat 'to the city centre, or the call centre'?

'Participative democracy'

2007 saw the introduction of the Assembly's petitions committee, which allows people to ask the Assembly government to address issues that they consider pressing. This is a good idea as far as it goes, but if Welsh Labour really wants a socialism that is 'more participative than passive' then it should rely far more on the practical knowledge and enlightened self-interest of Welsh communities. The Senedd, and all the other sites for governmental decision-making throughout Wales, should open their doors to ordinary people, facilitating genuine popular partic-ipation in political decision-making. In the running of health, education and transport services, users, patients or students' bodies could work with those who provide the services so that they are truly accountable and responsive to the needs of those who depend on them. The managers and technicians whose expertise is necessary to run those services should have to engage with the views of the community in making their decisions. Under the rubric of 'co-production', this model is increasingly recognised – although not by government – as an effective and socially desirable way to deliver and improve services.[6] In our view, it needs to be applied consistently all major areas of public policy. Decisions on environmental and planning issues, such as the location of a factory, an office block, a new road or a recycling plant, could also be opened up to trade unions and to community and environmental organisations. There could be popular participation in the setting of budgets and the determining of economic priorities.

This is not pie-in-the-sky; there are precedents. The Greater London Council (GLC) experimented with popular participation in the 1980s, involving communities in planning decisions. More recently there has been a more profound and durable experiment in participative democracy in the Brazilian city of Porto Alegre. When, in 1989 the Workers Party (PT) took control of the municipality, it asked community organisations for their suggestions and proposals for improving the city. The resulting 'participative budgets' – now an established fact of life in the city – have brought about in improvements to the city's housing, infrastructure and public services and environment and considerable redistribution of public investment towards where it is most needed. Brazil is a notoriously unequal society, yet many of the middle-classes of Porto Alegre have come to accept that the participative budget is here to stay. The series of meetings involved in the budget process attract tens of thousands of people. Significantly, for Brazil, municipal corruption is down. The experiment has been taken up in other cities in Brazil, Argentina and Uruguay.[7]

There is no reason why this could not be adopted in Wales. While the respective situations of a South American city and a country such as Wales are obviously different (although, in population terms, they are of similar size) each would recognise in the other the problems of neglect and inequality, and the need to redirect investment and assistance to those who need it most. Invariably such an experiment, if applied in Wales, would not always work perfectly. There would be disagreements; differing needs and priorities would have to be reconciled. Not everyone or every community would get what they wanted, when it wanted it. Like much else that has been proposed here, it would kick incessantly against the confines of the present devolution settlement. Such participative democracy would have to be combined with representative democracy, if only to ensure that the loudest voices did not get listened to at the expense of all others. But these problems would be the price well worth paying for the people of Wales to be able to decide how to govern themselves rather than ask someone to do it for them.

The longer-term agenda for the left must also embrace the expansion of the public sector beyond the residual services that have survived 30 years of privatisation. Making real progress towards a socialist society would involve increasingly superseding the organisation of economic activity on the basis of commodity production and exchange. We will ultimately transcend the dysfunctionality of capitalism only by freeing our working lives and inter-personal relations from the dictates of the market. Thus, the creation of new forms of productive activity on a publicly or cooperatively run basis would help to establish stronger foundations for the kind of society that we would like to see. The Assembly government's (re-)creation of free public goods in areas like NHS prescriptions, school breakfasts and museum access has also contributed to this process, as well as being beneficial in its own right. Yet, as long as such gains are seen as 'handed down from above' by the state, there is a danger that they will be perceived as a form of charity, providing no more than a safety net for those too impoverished to procure what they need through the market. Popular involvement in the control and distribution of these resources – as described above – would help to reinforce their true status as commonly-owned goods, to which all citizens have an inalienable right, simply by virtue of their humanity. Such processes of de-commodification must be consciously presented as the seeds of a new society, not as the defensive preservation of rights won in better times. The expansion of the area of material activity that lies beyond the reach of the market and is subject to conscious human control – whether through the direct intervention of the state or the promotion of grassroots cooperative initiatives – would constitute a truly radical direction in which the Assembly government might take Wales.

Raising our sights

It will be objected that much of which is advocated here, while desirable in itself, is simply not practicable. Even a Welsh Assembly with primary law-making powers, our critics may argue, is several years away, and even when that goal is realised, Wales will still be a part of the UK and therefore subject not only to its laws, but also to its membership of the EU and the WTO. It could further be argued that, even without these treaties and obligations, Wales' power to enact its own laws to the benefit of its people, or to protect its own economy from the depredations of global capital, would be purely academic, given the liberalisation of currency markets and the dangers of capital flight and tax avoidance. We can do everything to make Wales an attractive place for industries to locate, but – as we have seen in chapter six – we cannot keep jobs in Wales if a particular firm wants to move somewhere else. Wales is a small nation with an open economy, bound by a complex latticework of international treaties and obligations as well as the economic facts of life.

The economic order referred to as 'globalisation' is not a force of nature, but the interplay of a number of connected economic processes, which are, in turn, the product of conscious human design: the removal of controls on the movement of capital and of trade barriers, and the increased power of transnational corporations. In other words, it is the internationalisation of the policies of deregulation and privatisation pursued domestically by Thatcher and Reagan, during the 1980s. Moreover, we should not forget that in many parts of the world – beginning in Chile in 1973 – these policies have been imposed through the barrel of a gun on a cowed and terrorised population. The world economy has been restructured around three poles: the USA, the EU and Japan, the rest of the world – with increasingly important exceptions, notably the loosely-allied 'BRIC' countries (Brazil, Russia, India and China) – remaining marginalised. Bodies such as the WTO have acquired sweeping powers in recent years, but they are made up of representatives of individual countries, dominated by the most powerful – above all, the USA. The latter, in particular, represents its own agenda – the agenda of its leading corporations – as the agenda of the 'international community'. Although it is often said that nation-states no longer matter, they have not lost control; there is simply a different kind of control. Therefore, as ever, powerful states get their own way, and less powerful ones do not. Wales straddles this divide, forming part of a powerful state within one of the three great blocs but, on its own, small, weak, and – by West European standards – relatively poor. Even insofar as the treaties referred to above have been entered into by democratically elected governments, this has been without the consent of their people – including the people of Wales. No one has asked us whether we want to be subject to the rules of the unaccountable WTO or International Monetary Fund (IMF), or the competition rules of the EU.

We need, therefore, to strip away globalisation's mystique, recognising that it is not beyond comprehension or challenge but that the processes to which it refers confer even greater power on the world's dominant states and classes: the power to destroy even the relatively large economies of Latin America and South-East Asia. Clearly, a small country like Wales cannot go it alone. To become a Celtic version of North Korea would not be possible, even if it were desirable. Complete independence for Wales is not on the agenda but, even if it were, it would no more solve Wales' problems than the achievement of national sovereignty has proved a panacea for any other small country in Europe. In developing the devolution process and a progressive 'Welsh agenda' we should not be turning our backs on the rest of Europe but strengthening the ties of solidarity with working people throughout the continent, as the only realistic way to combat the neo-liberal globalisers. In the fight to defend jobs and public services, the bonds of solidarity must extend not just over Offa's Dyke and Hadrian's Wall, but over the Channel and the Atlantic as well.

The European Union: problem or solution?

The European Union has long been a vexed question for the British labour movement. For many years, the idea that the EU, or its predecessor, the European Economic Community, was a 'bosses' club' was sufficient justification for many trade unionists to line up with some of the most reactionary sections of British society in opposition to it. But Britain is just about the only country in the EU (with the possible exceptions of Poland and Austria) where the opposition to European integration comes predominantly from the right – and such a standpoint is in direct opposition to the cross border solidarity we need. In any case, that Euro-sceptic opposition is weaker in Wales than in England, largely because during the Tory years, Brussels provided the money for regeneration and development that was not forthcoming from London and has continued to provide support in the form of Objective One funding. Many in the labour movement have, in recent years, erred in the other direction, seeing the European Union as a place of safety from the deregulatory agenda pursued in the USA and Britain. The general popularity of the EU, in almost all member-states, is based less on what it actually does than on what it seems to represent: international cooperation, free movement of goods and travel, and an alternative to war. After the ravages of two world wars in 30 years, European unity – in any form – had enormous reserves of goodwill on which to draw.

If, then, we are to develop effective solidarity throughout the European Union, it is necessary to acknowledge the complexity of the

EU project and to be clear as to what we support and what we oppose in that project. The British Euro-sceptic right, as well as its free-market fundamentalist co-thinkers in the USA, sees the social chapter as proof that the EU is, at least, semi-socialist. This view is given plausibility by the fact that the EU has offered some defence of social and employment rights against rabid neo-liberals like Blair and Berlusconi who have campaigned hard for greater 'flexibility' (i.e. reduced labour costs and social provision) in an effort to make the EU more like the 'Anglo-Saxon' economies of Britain and the USA.

After the Second World War, with the West European states in ruins, almost bankrupt, struggling to hold onto their colonial empires, and faced with the overwhelming economic might of the USA, economic restructuring could only take place on a continental scale. European integration was based on the need to internationalise West European capital in the face of US dominance. Private property could not be adequately defended within the framework of a French or Italian – still less a Dutch or Belgian – state. The various laws and regulations operating in the EU do not contradict the free market: they give it a legal and institutional basis. EU institutions reflect the influence of social-democratic and Christian-democratic parties in the foundation of the original EEC. In the context of the Cold War, they wanted to defend the market economy (and, in the case of the social democrats, their own position in the labour movement) against the perceived threat of communism, hence the emphasis on welfarism and full employment. This, in turn, was made possible by the pump-priming policies of reconstruction following the Second World War, aided by the US dollar, in the form of Marshall Aid, in the context of the long, post-war, economic boom. This boom disguised to some extent the fundamentally free market nature of the EEC, which was laid bare by the end of first the post-war boom and then the cold war, which pushed to the fore the deflationary and deregulatory nature of the project.[8]

The Stability and Growth Pact (SGP) is at the heart of what socialists should oppose about the EU. The SGP enforces the 1992 Maastricht Treaty's convergence criteria for monetary union. Governments are prohibited from running an annual budget deficit of more than three per cent of gross domestic product; the penalties for non-compliance are huge fines. Thus, even if they might want to, governments are prevented from borrowing money, above a certain level, to spend on public services, welfare and job creation. The SGP makes fiscal austerity and deflation a corollary and a precondition for monetary union, setting in stone the Thatcherite creed that governments should not spend themselves out of a recession. The pact is therefore no mere detail, which could be amended out of existence (although maybe some European politicians, beginning to realise what they have signed up to, wish that it could be); it is at the heart of the monetary union project. Why? Because the euro, to serve its purpose as a competitor to the currencies of the other two economic blocs, the dollar and the yen, needs to be a 'hard' currency. For it to be viable in these terms, currency union requires attacks on public services, welfare, social security, and the right to organise. It involves privatisation, the liberalisation of markets, casualisation, and 'flexibility'. In short, it requires the dismantling of a whole swathe of valuable gains made by the working class across Western Europe since the Second World War (a process that has, in any case, already proceeded further in Britain than in most other EU countries).

The existence of a single currency over most of the pre-enlargement EU has aggravated already existing uneven economic development. It has enabled advanced production to be concentrated more and more in certain areas. The consequence is the relative – and, in some cases, absolute – decline in other areas, resulting in their deepening poverty there and increasing inequality throughout the EU, with the poorer regions ending up as exporters of migrant labour. These problems, serious enough already for the EU's existing weaker economies such as Portugal, Greece, and parts of Britain, have only worsened with the accession of twelve new states in 2004–07, the supposed unification of the continent actually deepening existing divisions. Enlargement has enabled employers to move capital where labour costs are lower, an example being the 2006 transfer by Peugeot from Coventry to Slovakia. Workers can therefore be browbeaten: accept attacks on wages and conditions or we will move the factory somewhere else. Peugeot will now be able to make the same ultimatum to Slovakian workers, this time threatening to relocate to Bulgaria or Romania.

The EU reform treaty, agreed in June 2007, has replaced the constitution signed in 2004, but abandoned following its rejection in referenda in France and the Netherlands. It has to be ratified by all member-states by mid-2009.[9] It retains many of the institutional innovations of the constitution, while, as a sop to its opponents, eliminates 'state-like' symbols and terminology. It proposes to give the EU full legal personality, allowing it to sign international agreements. The European Commission will therefore have the sole right to enter into negotiations at the WTO through the General Agreement on Trade in Services

(GATS) process, which aims to open up public services all over the world to privatisation. The treaty yokes together the dominant features of the European integration process: neo-liberal economics (notwithstanding Nicholas Sarkozy's success in eliminating 'free and undistorted competition' from the list of treaty objectives) and, in the reduction of areas of national veto, a profound democratic deficit. The extension of qualified majority voting (QMV), to be phased in between 2014 and 2017[10] (with Blair having secured an exemption for Britain in respect of Home Office powers) is justified by the expansion of the EU to 25 and then to 27 states, but the conflict between expansion and the existence of a national veto could have been dealt with by an increase in the powers of the only directly-elected body in the EU: the European parliament.

The appointment of Peter Mandelson as EU trade commissioner was entirely in keeping with the direction taken by the EU. As his predecessor, Pascal Lamy (himself no friend of the poor) suggested at the time, Mandelson's role was to act as a trojan horse to promote Anglo-US neo-liberal policies. This is exactly why Mandelson got the job; he is an enthusiast of the 'Lisbon process' which emerged from the summit held under the Portuguese presidency of 2000, described in approving terms by Blair as a move away from the 'social regulation agenda of the 1980s and instead [in] a direction of enterprise, innovation, competition and employment'.[11] Lest any Europhiles wish to clutch at the straw of the charter of fundamental rights, this is not incorporated into the Treaty, but merely an annexe to it. Moreover, as a leaving present to the people of Britain, Blair obtained an opt-out, so that it will not encroach upon or create new rights in UK law, presumably to preserve Thatcher's punitive anti-union laws and Britain's grim long-hours culture.

The establishment of a European central bank to take the management of the euro away from elected politicians is no mere blip, or administrative accident. Over the past 50 years, the process of European integration has involved the establishment of non-accountable supranational institutions, in recognition of the difficulty in running a market economy purely within the framework of a French, German or Italian state. European integration has, from the outset, tried to reconcile formal democracy with technocratic government, by which real decision-making is effectively insulated from the democratic process – hence, the limited powers of the European parliament. The independence (i.e. unaccountability) of the central bank proceeds from the conviction that the way to avoid rampant inflation is to keep financial policy away from politicians. A sign of the Blair government's commitment to the euro project – despite not having joined in the first wave – was Brown's handing over the control of interest rates to the Bank of England, in line with the requirements of the convergence criteria. Even New Labour's enemies on the right hailed this as a 'masterstroke'; suddenly, 'unelected bureaucrats' did not seem so threatening! Thus, European technocratic government converged with New Labour's managerialism: what is important is not ideology, but 'what works'. While no state is too keen on allowing much democratic control over its financial policy, there was previously, at least, a measure of formal accountability: even Tory chancellors were, after all, elected politicians. Now, formal accountability is replaced by formalised unaccountability. Whether in the eurozone or not, the sacred business of finance has been elevated above mere politics.

Cross-border solidarity

We in Wales should not, therefore, see the EU, or the seductive notion of a 'Europe of the regions', as a panacea for all our economic problems, or as a refuge from the ravages of globalisation. But neither should we go back down the blind alley of withdrawal from the EU. Instead, we should aim to transform the economic and political space of the EU, created for the convenience of the capitalist class, into an arena for the pursuit of working-class and popular interests.

Welsh Labour should use its position in the Assembly and the European parliament to campaign for a united front against austerity and privatisation throughout the EU, and against the 'beggar my neighbour' attitude towards employment and economic development. Employers are able to use divide-and-rule tactics in moving jobs from one part of the EU to another because workers in Wales and, for example, Slovakia, are not talking to each other, let alone working together. Workers in the richer countries are desperate to hold on to the jobs they have, while those in the poorer countries are equally desperate to secure such jobs. The low level of self-organisation and self-confidence among workers and the knowledge that their jobs can be exported perpetuates a feeling of insecurity, which is readily exploited by governments and rarely challenged by trade union leaders, who find it easier to adopt a nationalistic posture than to attack the system that plays groups of workers off against each other.[12] Lacking the will to lead an international fight for workers' interests, the Labour and trade union leadership will rail against the export of jobs elsewhere but claim it as a victory when we in Wales are able to undercut workers elsewhere. This race to the bottom can only be stopped by the internationalisation of the old trade union principle that 'an injury to one is an injury to all'.

A recent step forward has been the announcement of a pact between Amicus (now part of Unite), the German union IG Metall and two US unions, precisely to present a united front against attempts to play workers in different countries off against each other. Their capacity to play that role would be greatly enhanced, however, by the introduction of more democratic structures within the unions themselves, so that the leadership is accountable to the rank and file, not free to make deals over the heads of the members. Trade union action also needs to be reinforced by the political support of the left parties and Welsh Labour should link up with socialist and progressive parliamentarians throughout Britain and other EU member-states, to build and support action in defence of jobs. For such action to be realistic, there needs to be the broadest possible campaign for an end to Britain's repressive trade union laws, under which unions taking part in solidarity action risk the sequestration of their funds.

Defending public services

People throughout the EU also need to link up to defend public services from privatisation and from the cuts forced by the Stability and Growth Pact. We should demand that governments ignore the convergence criteria when setting budgets, and when threatened with fines, refuse to pay them. When the French economy was last threatened with recession, in 2003, the then prime minister, Raffarin, defending a projected 3.7 per cent deficit budget, stated that his main priority was the French economy, and that the eurozone budgetary rules should be applied more flexibly. Raffarin is no socialist, but his readiness to defend 'national interests' shows the potential for opposition to the SGP. In practice, the pact has proven effectively unenforceable against the bigger countries, which were, ironically, its original advocates. The 'no' vote in the Swedish euro referendum in 2003 was also highly significant. In favour of the euro were the 'big beasts' of Swedish politics and big business. The left, including about half the Social-Democratic Party's voters, and the Greens, set the tone for the campaign, showing that it is possible to campaign against the politics and economics of the EU from a progressive standpoint, and without being drawn into the right-wing nationalist culture of opposition exemplified by UKIP.

It is not enough simply to defend those public services threatened with privatisation. Privatisation of services and utilities has already meant a bonanza for directors and shareholders, and increased costs for the users, or 'customers'. Welsh Labour should also be campaigning jointly with socialists and environmentalists across the EU for publicly-owned utilities – transport, postage, telecommunications, energy and water – accountable to the millions of people throughout Europe whose wellbeing depends on them. This is directly contrary to the aim of the EU as it presently exists, but it exemplifies perfectly the need to transform the EU into something that works in the interests of its people. Therefore, Welsh Labour, in common with socialists throughout the EU, should be pushing for the transfer of power from the unelected Commission and the Council of Ministers to the elected European Parliament, to address the democratic deficit in the EU – the basis of much of the opposition to the constitution treaty. In the meantime, socialists in Wales should also be seeking a mechanism whereby Welsh interests might be guaranteed specific representation within the EU Commission and the Council of Ministers, defending Wales' publicly owned and accountable services against any move by Westminster to sign them away as part of the GATS negotiations.

Socialists throughout the EU should be joining together to demand that instead of the cut-throat race for the bottom of tax competition, governments strive for tax solidarity, cooperating with each other concerning the levels of taxation, to prevent capital from playing one off against the other. At the same time, socialists should be demanding that the benefits of development be shared with less wealthy countries, so that they also enjoy a living wage, decent working conditions and good public services. We should also be linking up with workers in those parts of Eastern Europe that are currently outside the EU, as well as further afield, against the reactionary 'Fortress Europe' of the Schengen agreement, in defence of asylum seekers, and those driven by poverty to seek work in the EU, and standing firm against the discrimination and violence shown towards migrants in the EU.

This sounds ambitious, given where we are at the moment, but just as none of the rights enjoyed in the member states – such as the right to vote, to form trade unions, to go on strike, or for decent health and education – were achieved without working people mobilising and fighting for them, so no rights will be won within the political entity of the EU without them being fought for in the same way. There is no guarantee that jobs cannot be 'exported' outside the EU, to the Far East, North Africa or Latin America. However, if working people in the EU can achieve half of what is advocated here, fighting for a peoples' Europe rather than a bosses' Europe, there is no way that it can be 'business as usual' in the other unaccountable and undemocratic institutions which currently rule our lives.

Towards a just world order

Socialism and internationalism are not, of course, reducible to the European Union and Wales' role within it. Welsh Labour has a part to play in building an alliance of socialist and green parties, trade unions and community organisations against the unjust international trade system and the privatising dogma of the 'Washington Consensus', which condemn millions to poverty and starvation.

The Welsh labour movement has a long and proud record in the struggle for peace and disarmament. It was, after all, from South Wales that the marchers who set up the Greenham Common peace camp originally set out. Welsh Labour should be working with CND, Plaid Cymru and the Greens in opposing the dangerous and foolish waste of money which is the replacement of the Trident missile system. Welsh Labour could show its support and solidarity with the governments of Cuba, Venezuela and Bolivia, which are leading the resistance to neoliberalism. It could be working with workers' and farmers' organisations, and non-governmental organisations in Africa, Asia, and Latin America to build practical solidarity and assistance, such as through the provision of health care and education, and helping in the fight against the consequences of debt repayment. Most importantly, it could be campaigning for a new order in the Middle East, attempting to undo the catastrophic damage done by Blair's unhinged foreign policy, calling for the withdrawal of troops from Iraq and Afghanistan, and for justice for the Palestinians. It can reach out to the Muslims, both in Wales and beyond, who, as result of Blair's wars are beleaguered and victimised.

The 'ethical foreign policy' announced by New Labour in 1997 did not last long. But Welsh Labour could have a genuinely ethical foreign policy. To those who object that a country which is not itself independent cannot have a foreign policy at all, we would argue that foreign policy amounts to more than the wars, and the (very bad) diplomacy of Blair, Bush and their like. No constraints of protocol should be allowed to impede the pursuit of socialism, solidarity and internationalism. It might seem that such a small country can make little impact in the wider world but this is not a question of Wales trying to do everything on its own, but rather of becoming 'the threat of a good example', and of working to build global alliances for real change. Wales sent, for its pop-

185

ulation, a famously large contingent to fight fascism in the Spanish Civil War. They did not stop to consider whether, being from a small stateless nation, there was any point. Welsh socialists, as much as Welsh writers, musicians, and sports people, can make sure that our country punches above its weight in Europe, and in the world.

What does this perspective mean for Labour in Wales, as the current, and hopefully future, party of government? Tony Benn has often stated that the Labour Party is the 'buckle' which connects parliament and the streets – in other words, it connects popular protest and a desire for change with means of using political power to bring about that change. Welsh Labour has to aim to act as such a 'buckle'. But to do so would mean breaking openly and decisively from the neo-liberal agenda followed so slavishly by New Labour in Westminster. It would involve abandoning any residual timidity in the face of Westminster, and outgrowing the existing devolution settlement. Never again must Welsh Labour fail to discuss at its conference something as momentous as the Iraq war because it is not 'devolved'. It will have to put aside 'party patriotism' and build alliances with other socialists and other progressive forces. It will have to take some political risks, but they will be risks worth taking.

Chapter 11

Conclusion:
Welsh Labour after New Labour

In this book, we have presented an analysis of the Welsh devolution
process and the progressive governmental agenda to which it has given
rise. We have portrayed these developments as, in the first instance, a
national response to the events of the 1980s and 1990s, during which the
people of Wales were the unwilling participants in a political project over
which they had no control and from which they did not benefit. The
attempt to repair the damage inflicted on Wales during the Thatcher-
Major era and the decades of industrial decline that preceded it has
involved the partial reunification of two political traditions: the movement for Welsh self-government (which is broader than the specifically
nationalist movement) and the socialist movement, which has arisen out
of the organised working class. The political project that has developed
under the auspices of the National Assembly – driven mainly, but not
exclusively, by Rhodri Morgan's Welsh Labour party – has embodied, in
a limited and imperfect way, these national and social aspirations. Thus,
we have been presented with a set of policies whose distinctive character
is explained by reference to their Welsh *context*, but which also differ
from the agenda of Westminster in their egalitarian and collectivist social
content.

We have argued that, in order to understand the character, the ambitions and the limitations of this political project – the 'clear red water'
agenda – it is necessary to consider its historical inheritance. Wales' rapid
and often brutal conversion into one of the first industrial societies saw

workers respond fiercely to the many injustices heaped upon them – initially in sporadic outbursts of militancy but later as a cohesive movement, in the form, especially, of Chartism. The early workers' movement was distinctly Welsh in the folk traditions and notions of social justice on which it drew, as well as in the language through which its activities were conducted. The response from the state was harshly repressive, however, and the revived movement that had grown up by the end of the nineteenth century was generally more cautious and modest in its goals. It was also an all-British movement, which increasingly accepted the leadership of the Labour party and the TUC. As the government and employers offered significant concessions, while sections of the working class benefited materially from imperial expansion, Welsh workers – like their counterparts in England and Scotland – invested their hopes in parliamentary action to secure prosperity and social justice: with a government pledged to represent working people at Westminster, the British state could, it seemed, provide an inclusive and supportive social structure, capable of accommodating the interests of communities in Merthyr or Wrexham.

The basis for this optimism was undermined in the 1970s, however, by the end of the long boom that had followed the Second World War. Whereas continuous economic growth had provided the tax revenues that facilitated the establishment and consolidation of the modern welfare state, the arrival of 'stagflation' promoted a new austerity that saw social gains under attack once again. This took a particularly vicious form after 1979, as the Tories set out to 'modernise' the British economy by shutting down 'uncompetitive' industries, crushing trade union resistance and creating mass unemployment. The exposure of Welsh communities to these attacks on their livelihood and security, with the labour movement leadership entreating them simply to wait for the next general election for deliverance, revived popular support for some measure of Welsh self-government, if only as a defensive bulwark.

As the dire consequences of four consecutive Tory election victories solidified this support, democratic devolution became a core feature of the labour and progressive project in Wales, signifying a profound shift in the relationship between socialism and Welsh national consciousness. The period spanning the unsuccessful referendum in 1979 and the 'yes' vote eighteen years later witnessed a partial erosion of the mutual incomprehension and hostility between, on one hand, those nationalists and devolutionists who lacked a class-political perspective and, on the other hand, those on the left who had viewed the campaign for self-government as a distraction, or even as inimical to the struggle for socialism. While a strengthened left-devolutionist current emerged from the victorious 'yes' campaign in 1997 to occupy centre-stage in Welsh politics, however, new tensions soon developed between the dynamic of democratic devolution and the needs of the New Labour project – between those who regarded the victory of 1999 as the start of a process, and those 'Labour-unionists' who saw it as a one-off concession. The devolutionists won the upper hand with the replacement of Alun Michael by Rhodri Morgan in February 2000 and a distinctive 'made in Wales' political agenda began – slowly and falteringly – to take shape.

Over the subsequent period, this has resulted in a public services regime based on collaboration rather than competition, on the displacement from the public sphere of consumerism by citizenship, and on the reinstatement of equality of outcome – rather than just equality of opportunity – as a central policy goal. The recourse to cheap gimmicks and easy targets, so often characteristic of Westminster politics, has been eschewed in favour of a serious attempt to tackle Wales' complex social problems. Major challenges have been undertaken and ambitious commitments made, in areas ranging from sustainable development to child poverty. Like Ken Livingstone's GLC in the 1980s, Welsh Labour has boldly applied its limited powers in a sustained attempt to offset the cumulative inequality, insecurity and alienation generated by a capitalist market economy. Unlike the GLC, however, the Assembly government has too often failed to convey to its public the radical import of its ambitions and to excite the imagination of those who should be its most passionate supporters. In part, this reflects the political sensitivity of undertaking a programme that diverges so clearly from that of the Westminster leadership, on whose patronage the Welsh party still depends. It also, however, reflects the conservatism and routinism of the Welsh labour movement, within which the radical flame that burned so brightly for a more than a century was all but extinguished as the 'people's party' became the new establishment in post-war Wales. The smouldering embers have flared with a new radiance in recent years but they are, as yet, insufficient to spark a new conflagration. Moreover, Welsh Labour's ambition for social change has been less evident in areas like economic development, where the Assembly's powers are weakest and neo-liberal hegemony strongest; too often, it has seemed merely to embrace anything 'modern' – a faint echo of Harold Wilson's exultation in the 'white heat of the technological revolution'.

If the emancipatory potential of the 'clear red water' is to be realised, then Welsh Labour's regime must be more than an enlightened technocracy. Progressive Assembly ministers must put themselves at the heart of a broad alliance for radical social change, involving unions, cooperatives, community groups, campaigning organisations and activists from all those parties claiming to be part of the left. The *One Wales* coalition has created a tremendous opportunity in this regard, giving rise to a progressive agenda that is not the property of one party alone. Socialists within Welsh Labour and Plaid Cymru should exploit this opportunity to the full, reaching out to the grassroots to cultivate a real popular debate about building a more equal, democratic and sustainable Wales. In the process, they could counteract the influence of the conservative forces within their own respective parties, and within Welsh society in general, and capture the imagination of those people – especially amongst the young – who desperately desire social transformation but have little faith in conventional party politics.

Already, despite all the difficulties it faces, Welsh Labour has demonstrated that there is a practical alternative to the policies pursued by New Labour in England, thus contradicting the claims of Blair and Brown that theirs has been the only feasible Labour programme. When we commenced work on this book, New Labour and the Tories were still loudly proclaiming the triumph of free market capitalism. Those who argued for another way to organise society were dismissed as 'dinosaurs': at best, quaintly utopian, at worst, totalitarian. Yet, the very fact that the Welsh first minister and his cabinet colleagues could routinely make speeches referring to socialism – even in purely aspirational terms – suggested that New Labour had failed in its task of expunging the 's' word from the vocabulary of modern politics. Since then, the global financial system has been brought to the point of collapse by the reckless and irresponsible greed of the rich, indulged for so many years by US and British governments. The inability to afford food, fuel and medicines condemns millions around the world to disease and starvation. In the recession now hitting the British economy, many Welsh people – having barely emerged from the poverty of the Tory years, and already heavily in debt – will lose their homes and their jobs. Such a situation is as clear as possible a demonstration of the failure of the free market.

While the paeans to its majesty have become more muted since the beginning of the present downturn, the free market's enthusiasts nevertheless insist that it is the only 'modern' way to run an economy – and who could possibly be against anything modern? How else, other than by global capitalism, do we come by such essential accoutrements of the new millennium as mini-laptops, ipods and European weekend breaks? But free market capitalism is not a force of nature; it is a social construct, a result of the conscious decisions of those who rule our lives. It is not the best way to organise human affairs, let alone the only way. Its effects in Africa, Asia and Latin America, where it has frequently been imposed on the population through the barrel of a gun, are almost unimaginable poverty and rampant, destabilising inequality. Closer to home, its imposition started with the election of Margaret Thatcher, and continued with the defeat of the trade union movement, and in particular, the miners, with the aid of a battery of anti-union laws and attacks on civil liberties. The short journey from Cardiff Bay to Merthyr Tydfil illustrates better than any book or speech the inequality and insecurity which disfigures the fifth largest economy on the globe. Nor is free market capitalism truly 'modern'. In having millionaire 'philanthropists' run the schools, outlawing solidarity action by trade unionists and plundering the resources of the rest of the planet, New Labour has 'modernised' itself back the Victorian age.

As we have argued, New Labour's quasi-nationalisation measures, in response to the meltdown of the financial sector, are far more a panic-stricken attempt to prop up the existing economic order, than the construction of a real alternative. However, the collapse of the complacent assumptions underpinning the neo-liberal consensus makes the need for that new order increasingly urgent. It is in Latin America, where the neo-liberal experiment was first tried out, that the fightback at government level has started. However, exercising that choice is not easy, as can be seen from the difficulties faced by Venezuela, a large country given some freedom of manoeuvre by its vast oil reserves. Wales' break from neo-liberal orthodoxy is far more modest, but it is nevertheless a reality.

Wales is a small country and, by West European standards, a poor one, with very limited control over its own affairs. Even if and when primary lawmaking powers become a reality, Wales will still be a part of the UK and therefore subject not only to its laws, but also to its membership of the EU and the WTO. Even without these treaties and obligations, Wales' power to enact its own laws to the benefit of its people, or to protect its own economy from the depredations of global capital, would be largely academic, given the liberalisation of currency markets and the dangers of capital flight and tax avoidance. We have recognised that reality, situating the politics of 'clear red water' within the broader global context. The working people of Wales, we have argued, need to join the struggle being waged by socialists and environmentalists from Ireland to the Balkans, to transform the political space of the EU from a free-market, privatised Europe to a people's Europe, based on equality and social justice.

Welsh Labour's detractors think the 'clear red water' agenda is old-fashioned. But while it has its origins in Wales' radical traditions, the refusal to regard the users of services as 'serial shoppers', the emphasis on equality of outcome and the commitment to sustainability are a glimpse into a democratic socialist future, beyond the dysfunctional, unequal and frequently violent neo-liberal present. Welsh Labour, then, has one foot in the future, and the other in the past. It can fall back in line with the increasingly discredited New Labour project, or keep moving forward towards a real socialist alternative. When the history of 21st century Wales comes to be written, 'clear red water' could merit a mere footnote, or a volume all to itself.

Appendix 1

St Athan and the defence industry

One policy over which there is little disagreement in mainstream Welsh politics is the Defence Training Academy planned for St Athan in the Vale of Glamorgan, which is intended to provide non-military training to the three armed services on a single site, currently scheduled to open in 2013. Although it is a UK Ministry of Defence project, it has been strongly supported by the Welsh Assembly Government (both the current coalition and its Labour predecessor) and by the Tories and Lib Dems. When, in January 2007, the MoD selected the Metrix consortium – which had nominated the St Athan site – as the preferred bidder to provide outsourced tri-service training, Rhodri Morgan said that it was a 'red letter day' for Wales, involving the creation of a modern purpose-built training campus of just over 10,000 people, creating 1,500 jobs during the construction phase and employing approximately 5,500 people thereafter, generating over £58 million a year of additional spending power in the regional economy.

There are a number of problems with the Academy, however, which have been raised by peace campaigners and by the PCS trade union:[1]

1. Ethical issues, to do with the military character of the project and some of the companies involved in the Metrix consortium. Most people, aside from complete pacifists, would regard the armed forces as having some legitimate defensive role and would want British troops to have the best training and resources, regardless of the conflict in

which they are engaged, not least to prevent unnecessary casualties. However, we should never lose sight of the daily horror being inflicted on the people of Iraq and Afghanistan, in which Britain is playing a part, and it seems reasonable to demand a moratorium on further expansion of military facilities until our troops are withdrawn from those countries. We should also be concerned, at a time like the present, about the use of 'state-of-the-art training opportunities' as a lure to encourage young people with few other prospects to seek a 'career' in the armed forces. There are also specific concerns about the partners in the Metrix consortium, one of which is Raytheon, one of the world's leading arms manufacturers, whose products have contributed to the carnage in Iraq and Palestine, and which, in the past, has manufactured the delivery systems for cluster bombs – the production of which is now banned under a convention signed by more than 100 countries, including the UK, on 3 December 2008.

2. Political objections to the privatisation aspect of the project and, linked to this, trade union objections to the privatisation and relocation of jobs. The St Athan project would further the privatisation of the 'defence industry', representing one of the most lucrative public-private partnerships yet undertaken. Already, the MoD has seen more than 90 separate privatisation projects in recent years, affecting some 20,000 staff. The US occupation of Iraq makes more use of mercenaries, employed by firms like Blackwater, than regular soldiers. Metrix (which includes Qinetiq, itself the result of a highly dubious privatisation) plans to boost its profits at St Athan by maximising the amount of training it provides, offering its services not just to the British armed forces but to military personnel from other countries – many, no doubt, with dubious human rights records – and to mercenaries. Privatisation also means that the MoD civilian instructors currently providing courses to military trainees at a number of different military bases around the UK (including over 100 already based at St Athan) would be transferred to the private sector, which raises the usual concerns about an employer concerned mainly with profit cutting jobs, pay and conditions. Those existing staff not already based at St Athan would be expected to relocate there and those unable or unwilling to transfer would lose their jobs. For these reasons, PCS – which represents most of the civilian staff involved – is strongly opposed to the plans. Thus, the project does not offer 'new jobs' to the Welsh economy, but existing jobs relocated from elsewhere. In addition, many of

the 'knock-on' jobs in the local economy are likely to be in low-waged, lowskilled occupations like catering and cleaning – not the 'hi-tech' sector.

3. Doubts about the capacity of the project to deliver the jobs and other benefits that have been promised. PFI and PPP schemes, in particular, have a long history of cost and time overruns, with the taxpayer footing the bill and, the St Athan project has already experienced a number of setbacks. The original timetable anticipated contracts being signed in October 2007, with construction commencing on site the following month and the Academy opening in January 2011. In October 2007, however, a revised timetable was announced, which saw construction beginning in 2009 and the Academy opening in 2013. Even this was for Package 1 only – it had been decided that that Package 2 represented 'insufficient inefficiencies' for it to be safe to proceed without further work. In January of this year, it was confirmed that Package 2 had been dropped from the project.

Leaked minutes of a high-level MoD meeting in June 2008 reveal concerns about major risks to the project, including a potential affordability gap as a result of changes in accounting rules that might result in the investment no longer being 'off balance sheet' and also because of a risk that the sale of MoD land, on which the deal depended, might not go ahead at the original price due to delays in planning permission. In addition, 72 per cent of the existing MoD trainers had said that they did not want to move to south Wales and there were concerns that Metrix might not be able to recruit suitable replacements. Subsequently, the economic downturn has exacerbated many of these problems, particularly the risks associated with the PPP aspects of the project. The cost has now increased from £11bn to £12bn, due to the increased cost of borrowing and Metrix's ability to offset rising costs with land sales having diminished – thus wiping out any expected financial savings. And while Metrix submitted a revised proposal in September, which was less dependent on raising revenue through the sales of MoD land, an investment decision will not take place before spring 2009, with the contract signature to come approximately 15 months later – a delay of a year since the contract was awarded to Metrix and by six months from the previous target date. The future of the project looks increasingly uncertain, despite official protestations to the contrary.

Against the evident problems, we have the prospect of 'more jobs for Wales' and 'state of the art training facilities' – although the jobs seem fewer, and in many cases poorer quality, than first suggested. No doubt the cry that we need jobs – any jobs – will be all the louder now that we are in recession and losing jobs at major employers like Hoover, Corus and Bosch – but this hardly seems the most cost-effective way to deliver them. In the 1970s and 80s, unions and peace campaigners argued for the right to *useful* work and shop stewards at Lucas and Vickers, among others, drew up plans to convert military production to peaceful purposes.[2] Surely socialists should be committed to a transformation in the nature and purpose of work? Yet the debate about the character of work has become impoverished, as the experience of neoliberalism (including the destruction of Welsh heavy industry under the Tories) has lowered ambitions. Notwithstanding a greater awareness of environmental externalities, the UK and Assembly governments seem interested only in ensuring that jobs are high-skilled, so that we can compete with India and China. But, even taking this into account, it is difficult to imagine that such an expensive and risky project as the St Athan Academy would have been pursued so remorselessly if it were not connected to the defence industry. President Eisenhower – a Republican and a five-star general – warned the US people, in his final presidential address, about the pernicious influence of the 'military-industrial complex'. The same concerns apply to the UK today. The journalist and environmental campaigner, George Monbiot, has forcefully questioned why Britain needs the second-biggest military budget (in cash terms) in the world. '[T]he bigger the budget,' he writes, 'the more powerful the lobby becomes which can fight for its own survival … [T]he civil servants in the MoD … seem to be defending not the realm but the arms companies.'[3] There must surely be better ways to spend the £12 billion of public money now earmarked for the St Athan Defence Academy, most likely producing more and better jobs in the process.

Appendix 2

Asylum and immigration

Wales has long enjoyed a reputation as a country ready to offer solidarity and hospitality to those fleeing persecution. In the 1930s Wales accepted Republican refugees from the civil war in Spain. Paul Robeson, a victim of political and racial persecution in the United States, forged ties with the Rhondda miners. But at the start of the 21st century, racist killings in Newport and Swansea, violence in Wrexham directed at Iraqi Kurds and findings by the charity, Save the Children, that one third of child asylum seekers in Wales experienced racist abuse have left that image somewhat tarnished. In Swansea and Wrexham, the British National Party has been attempting to exploit tension created by the local media that Wales is being 'overrun' by asylum seekers or by migrant workers from eastern Europe which it cannot cope with. In fact, in 2005, according to the Welsh Refugee Council, Wales had 2500 asylum seekers – less than 0.1 per cent of the population. Many did not choose to come to Wales. It is the policy of the Home Office to 'disperse' asylum seekers, preventing them from gravitating quite naturally to those places, mainly London, where they could take advantage of family and community support. Many have been welcomed here because, of course, people in Wales are no more racist than anywhere else. They have, however, been subject to a constant diet of lies and misinformation from the media and Labour politicians such as David Blunkett and John Reid about the immigration 'problem'.

Immigration and asylum are not devolved, of course; they are the responsibility of the Home Office in London. While it is probably not realistic, at this stage, to call for Wales to have complete control over its own asylum and immigration arrangements, the Assembly government could be (and to some extent already is) making the most of what power and influence it has to give asylum seekers and refugees active support and assistance, and to press the Westminster government to change its hard line.

An example of what can be achieved is with children seeking asylum, or who are refugees. In Wales, collaboration between the Minister for Children and the Minister for Social Justice and Regeneration and a series of meetings between the Assembly government and professionals in the field resulted in provision being made for children and young people being under the Assembly government's 2006 Refugees Inclusion Policy. Refugee inclusion has been promoted through targeted funding for local education authorities and through an Ethnic Minority Achievement Strategy which provides guidance to LEAs and schools on how best to ensure that young asylum seekers are able to reach their full potential. Guidance for teachers has also been developed, including on the issue of how to tackle bullying.

In May 2008, Assembly Health Minister Edwina Hart, struck a blow for decency and humanity when she announced that failed asylum seekers in Wales would henceforth be eligible to free NHS treatment, unlike their counterparts in England, where the Department for Heath was seeking to maintain its policy of charging in such cases, in the face of a court judgement that had challenged the legality of this approach.

Appendix 3

Blaenau Gwent:
How Labour lost its safest seat

One of biggest upsets of the 2005 general election was the defeat of
Labour's Maggie Jones in the supposedly ultra-safe seat of Blaenau
Gwent by Peter Law, the Labour AM-turned independent. Jones, a
Unison official and Labour NEC member, had been selected two years
before from an all-women shortlist. As a means of countering the
under-representation of women in Parliament, the latter is something of
a blunt instrument – but a necessary one, particularly in Wales, which
had only ever had four women MPs prior to 1997. Such considerations
did not, however, cut much ice with party members in Blaenau Gwent,
many of whom boycotted the selection process, rejecting any restriction
on their freedom of choice as a Blairite plot to impose a New Labour
candidate rather than a more independent local person. There can be little doubt that their suspicions about the party machine's motives were
well-founded – after all, an all-women shortlist was not imposed in
other constituencies with a retiring incumbent. It does not follow, however, that they had no other option but to abstain from the selection
process, insisting that Peter Law was the only legitimate Labour candidate, and then backing Law as an independent against Jones; they could
and should have supported a local, socialist, woman candidate. Amidst
an anti-Blair backlash, and against a popular local politician, who had
been in the local papers more or less constantly in his 35 years as a coun-

cillor and more recently as AM, Maggie Jones never had a hope. Supported by numerous Labour activists, Law won the seat with a majority of 9,000. Law presented his campaign as a victorious grassroots campaign against Blairites and the metropolitan elite. Socialists should have been wary of accepting Law's 'working class hero' spin at face value, however. Many of his complaints against the leadership were, of course, justified, but his campaign was focused on opposition to a measure aimed at eliminating inequality in Labour politics (motivated in large part by his own desire to become an MP). Originally, a supporter of Alun Michael and not known as a left-winger, his opposition to the leadership began to develop only when Rhodri dropped him from his cabinet to make way for a Liberal Democrat following the 2000 coalition agreement.

When, less than a year after being elected, Law succumbed to a brain tumour, Labour faced a double by-election in Blaenau Gwent, for the Westminster and the Assembly seats. Having initially responded to the Law campaign by summarily expelling 20 (actual or suspected) Law supporters, Labour performed a volte-face, with Peter Hain 'apologising' for imposing an all-woman shortlist – demonstrating that, for all its rhetoric about equality, the Labour leadership is ready to ditch it as soon as it becomes politically inconvenient. Blaenau Gwent Peoples' Voice, as Law's supporters styled themselves, once again defeated the official Labour candidates in both by-elections. Trish Law, who took up her late husband's Assembly seat and retained it in the 2007 Assembly election, has shown little sign of having a coherent alternative agenda, voting with the combined opposition on virtually every issue prior to the Assembly elections but adopting a less hostile attitude to Labour subsequently. The rebellion against the 'political establishment' embodied by Peter and Trish Law is, however, an increasingly common phenomenon – not least in Wales, where John Marek retained his Wrexham seat as an independent in 2003; non-party candidates performed impressively in Caerphilly, Islwyn and Ynys Môn in 2007; and Labour was displaced from several local government strongholds in 2008 by 'localist' opponents. Explanations for this development can be found in the political confluence of the main parties and the high-handed attitude of Labour's leadership and officialdom for the views of ordinary members and supporters (as well as specific issues like the abolition of the 10 per cent tax rate in 2008). The challenge for Welsh Labour is to demonstrate that it is genuinely responsive to the people who put it in office.

Notes

Preface

1. For more information about WLG, see our website: www.welshlabour grassroots.org.

Chapter 1

1. Even the one-off endowment paid by Scottish students on graduation has now been abolished by the SNP government.
2. Ironically, while the phrase appeared in the printed version of the speech distributed to journalists, it was apparently never actually uttered by the First Minister on this occasion, as he was forced to truncate his remarks after the previous speaker – one Neil Kinnock – overran. The term was first applied to Welsh Labour's policies by the *Guardian*, as the speech acknowledges; the paper had earlier used the phrase in an editorial about Gordon Brown's 2002 budget. The speech can be read online at www.sochealth.co.uk/Regions/Wales/red water.htm.
3. Rhodri Morgan's own riposte to the advocates of a more 'aspirational' appeal is succinct: 'For those who believe that the problem of the Labour movement in Wales is that we are too much like a Labour movement, I have to say that this was not the complaint that was made to me on the doorstep.' (R. Morgan, 'Welsh Labour's Future', in Institute of Welsh Affairs, *Politics in 21st Century Wales* (Cardiff: IWA, 2008), p.14.

Chapter 2

1. R. Fevre, 'The Welsh Economy', in D. Dunkerley & A. Thompson (eds), *Wales Today* (Cardiff: Wales University Press, 1999), pp. 64–65.
2. D.L. Adamson, *Living on the Edge: Poverty and Deprivation in Wales* (Llandysul: Gomer, 1996), p.7.
3. Ibid., pp. 15–16.
4. None of the four MPs who served as Secretary of State for Wales during the ten years after 1987 even represented a Welsh constituency.
5. Quangos are quasi-autonomous non-governmental organisations, officially known as NDPBs (non-departmental public bodies) – or, in Wales, after 1999, as ASPBs (Assembly-sponsored public bodies) – now renamed once more as AGSBs (Assembly Government-sponsored bodies).
6. K. Morgan & G. Mungham, *Redesigning Democracy: the Making of the Welsh Assembly* (Bridgend: Seren, 2000), chapter 2.
7. Ibid., p. 81.
8. See Gwyn A. Williams, *When Was Wales? A History of the Welsh* (Harmondsworth: Pelican, 1985), chapter 7.
9. Ibid., p. 305.
10. J. Aitchison & H. Carter, 'The Welsh Language Today', in D. Dunkerley & A. Thompson (eds), op. cit., chapter 6.

Chapter 3

1. Gwyn A. Williams, *When Was Wales? A*

History of the Welsh (Harmondsworth: Pelican, 1985), p. 300.

2. Figures from Ivor Wilks, *South Wales and the Rising of 1839* (2nd edition, Llandysul: Gomer, 1989), pp. 11–12.

3. See David J.V. Jones, *Before Rebecca: Popular Protests in Wales, 1793–1835* (London: Allen Lane, 1973), chapter 1 & appendix 1.

4. Gwyn A. Williams, *The Merthyr Rising* (Cardiff: University of Wales Press, 1988), p.230.

5. There were also links – especially via the radical Carmarthen solicitor, Hugh Williams – between Chartism and the Rebecca Riots, which set the West Wales countryside alight between 1839 and 1844. Rebecca was a movement of small tenant farmers, rather than of the working class, and a response to the numerous discontents of an established agrarian society exposed to rapid upheaval and economic distress – of which the toll-gates destroyed by the rioters were only the outward symbol. In its final phase, largely under Williams' influence, its increasingly haphazard attacks were partly displaced by mass meetings intended to develop clear political demands. See David Williams' classic study, *The Rebecca Riots* (Cardiff: University of Wales Press, 1986 [orig. 1955]).

6. Eddie May, 'The Mosaic of Labour Politics, 1900–1918', in D. Tanner *et al* (eds), *The Labour Party in Wales, 1900–2000* (Cardiff: University of Wales Press, 2000), p. 66 – citing research by Deian Hopkin. Before the introduction of individual membership in 1918, it was possible to join the Labour party only through an affiliated union or a socialist society like the ILP or the Fabians.

7. See W. David, *Remaining True: A Biography of Ness Edwards* (Caerphilly Local History Society, 2006), p.36.

8. I. McAllister, 'The Labour Party in Wales: The Dynamics of One-Partyism', *Llafur* 3, 2 (spring 1981), pp. 79–89.

9. G.A. Williams, *When Was Wales?* p.288.

10. There were no women MPs in Wales between the elevation to the House of Lords of the East Flint MP, Eirene White, in 1970 and the election of Ann Clwyd in Cynon Valley in 1984.

11. See G. Rees & T.L. Rees (eds), *Poverty and Social Inequality in Wales* (London: Croom Helm, 1980), chapters 2–5.

12. See B. Curtis, 'The Wilson Government and Pit Closures in South Wales, 1964–1970', *Llafur* 9, 1 (2004), pp. 59–70; K. Gildart, *North Wales Miners: A Fragile Unity, 1945–1996* (Cardiff: University of Wales Press, 2001).

13. See Rees & Rees, op. cit., especially chapters 7–10.

Chapter 4

1. Cited by R.M. Jones & I.R. Jones, 'Labour and the Nation', in D. Tanner *et al* (eds), op. cit., p. 257.

2. See R. Griffiths, *S.O. Davies: A Socialist Faith* (Llandysul: Gomer, 1983).

3. In 1947, Morgan Phillips, the Welsh-speaking, Aberdare-born general secretary of the British Labour party, even vetoed the name 'Welsh Council for Labour' as the title of the party's first all-Wales organisation, on the grounds that it was too nationalistic; he insisted on the insertion of the word 'Regional' – which was eventually dropped in 1960. The name was changed again in 1976, to 'Labour Party Wales', to emphasise 'the party's primary commitment to the British Labour Party and secondary commitment to Wales'. (K.O. Morgan, 'Power and Glory: War and Reconstruction 1939–1951', in D. Tanner *et al* (eds), op. cit, pp. 169, 178; I. McAllister, op. cit, p.83.)

4. I. McAllister, op. cit., p. 83.

5. For the steel industry, see Joe England, *The Wales TUC 1974–2004: Devolution and Industrial Politics* (Cardiff University of Wales Press, 2004), pp. 46–57. Other details from Gwyn A. Williams, *When Was Wales?* pp. 297–98.

6. See Morgan & Mungham, op. cit., ch. 2.

7. For details, see Paul Flynn, *Dragons Led by Poodles: the Inside Story of a New Labour Stitch-up* (London: Politico's, 1999) and K. Morgan & G. Mungham, op. cit, ch. 5.

8. Anonymous Wales Labour 'insider', quoted by Morgan and Mungham, op. cit., p.129.

9. Rhodri had spoken more tentatively of a 'Welsh Way' of approaching public services in an earlier address to the Wales TUC. An extract from the 'clear red water' speech appeared as an article in *Agenda* (spring 2003) pp.13–14. In the

following months, the most thorough and perceptive analysis of Welsh Labour's divergence from New Labour orthodoxy was given by the Cardiff University academic, Steve Davies, in a paper for the Catalyst think-tank, *Inside the laboratory: the new politics of public services in Wales* (London: Catalyst, 2003), available online at: www.editiondesign. com/catalyst/pubs/paper17a.html. See also: idem, 'Across the clear red water', *Public Finance* (23–29 May 2003); idem, 'Devolution stirs policy evolution', *Health Matters* 54 (Winter 2003/04); idem, 'The great divide', *Public Finance* (12 November 2004); idem, 'Lost in Translation: Speaking a Different Language', *Public Finance* (November 2005) pp.11–17.

10. Ed George, 'Muddy Brown Water', *Workers Action* 22 (Summer 2003) pp.14–17, available online here: www.geocities.com/edgeorge2001es/my writings/Water.html

11. Quoted on the BBC News website, 31 March 2004: news.bbc.co.uk/1/hi/wales/3586389.stm

12. It should also not be forgotten that, prior to 1996, it had been widely assumed that an incoming Labour government would simply legislate for Scottish and Welsh devolution, without recourse to referenda, taking its general election victory as its mandate; the announcement that referenda would be held was regarded by devolutionists as a significant climbdown by the Blair leadership and led to the resignation of the left-wing Scottish MP, John McAllion, from Labour's shadow ministerial team. In retrospect, the referenda were probably necessary to confirm the constitutional and political legitimacy of the Parliament and Assembly but the need to repeat the exercise now seems much less clear.

13. A. Browne, 'Wales 'is split on extra powers', BBC website, 22 September 2008, news.bbc.co.uk:80/1/hi/wales/wales_politics/7625621.stm

14. Welsh Labour, *Better Governance for Wales* (July 2004), p.4

15. For a useful discussion of the powers created by the 2006 Act and their utilisation, see D. Hill, H. Edwards & L. Jeffes, *The Evolution of Devolution:*

reflections on the operation of our legislative system (Tredegar: Bevan Foundation, 2008).

16. The Act also makes specific provision for a referendum on primary powers, subject to a two-thirds majority vote in the Assembly and a simple majority in both Houses of Parliament.

17. M. Shipton, 'Climate change law row', *Western Mail*, 24 September 2007.

18. L. Wood, 'Independence for Wales back on the agenda', *Western Mail*, 16 August 2007; T. Livingstone, 'Plaid starts to utter dreaded "I" word', *Western Mail*, 24 August 2007; H.M. Jones, 'Independent Wales is our goal for a thriving future', *Western Mail*, 5 August 2008.

Chapter 5

1. *The Labour Party manifesto 2005*, p. 18. Available on the party's website at: www.labour.org.uk/fileadmin/manifesto_13042005_a3/flash/manifesto_2005.swf

2. P. Wintour, 'Real cost of Treasury gamble – a £37bn cut in services from 2011', *Guardian*, 26 November 2008.

3. On this, see D. Harvey, *A Brief History of Neoliberalism* (Oxford: OUP, 2005) and N. Klein, *The Shock Doctrine: the rise of disaster capitalism* (London: Allen Lane, 2007).

4. P. Wintour, 'Mandelson: New Labour still alive', *Guardian*, 27 November 2008.

5. M. Drakeford, 'Progressive Universalism', *Agenda* (winter 2007), pp. 4–7, available online at www.iwa.org.uk/debate/ prog_univers.htm

6. The WDA, the Wales Tourist Board and ELWa. These would later be followed by the examinations and curriculum body, ACCAC, and part of the Countryside Council for Wales. Merger of the Welsh Language Board into the WAG was delayed indefinitely by the three then-opposition parties outvoting Welsh Labour in 2006.

7. Welsh Assembly Government, *Making the Connections – Delivering Beyond Boundaries* (November 2006), p.20.

8. D. Williamson, 'Top civil servants earn more than First Minister', *Western Mail*, 20 August 2008.

9. www.assemblywales.org:80/bus-home/bus-committees/bus-committees-third1/bus-committees-third-fin-home/

bus-committees-third-fin-agendas.htm?
act=dis&id=103910&ds=11/2008

10. *Making the Connections* does, in fact, contain one reference (on p.28) to the possible benefits of public-private partnerships but the tone is fairly noncommittal and it is overshadowed by the oft-repeated preference for collaboration over competition.

11. Julian Tudor Hart recounts that when Sir Keith Joseph proposed marketisation of the service in the 1970s, his own party leader, Edward Heath described him as 'completely mad'. See J.T. Hart, *The Political Economy of Health Care: A Clinical Perspective* (Bristol: Policy Press 2006), pp. 251, 263.

12. C. Webster, *The National Health Service: a Political History* (2nd edition, Oxford: O.U.P, 2002), p. 203.

13. A. Pollock, *NHS plc: the privatisation of our health care* (London: Verso, 2004), pp. 36–40.

14. See news.bbc.co.uk/1/hi/health/6552249.stm.

15. Cited by A. Pollock, op. cit., p. 66.

16. Written evidence by UNISON (dated 13 February 2006) to the House of Commons Health Select Committee inquiry into ISTCs, www.publications.parliament.uk/pa/cm200506/cmselect/cmhealth/934/934we45.htm

17. 'MPs call for more scrutiny of DoH contracts', *Public Finance Magazine* 28 April 2006, cited by A. Nunns, *The Patchwork Privatisation of Our Health Service: A Users' Guide* (London: Keep Our NHS Public, 2006), p. 14.

18. S. Player & C. Leys, *Confuse and Conceal: the NHS and Independent Sector Treatment Centres* (Monmouth: Merlin, 2008).

19. A. Pollock, op. cit., pp. 53–60.

20. C. Webster, op. cit, pp. 210–11.

21. See A. Pollock, 'A Gauntlet for Brown', *Guardian*, 11 April 2007; A. Pollock, D. Price & S. Player, 'An Examination of the UK Treasury's Evidence Base for Cost and Time Overrun Data in Value-for-Money Policy & Appraisal, *Public Money & Management*, vol. 27, April 2007, pp. 127–33.

22. See A. Pollock, *NHS plc*, pp. 209–13.

23. 'NHS "now four different systems"', BBC News (2 January 2008), news.bbc.co.uk/1/hi/health/7149423.stm.

24. The broader definition of the 'clinical team' did not, however, apply retrospectively to the three PFI hospitals (Neath Port Talbot Hospital, Chepstow Community Hospital and St David's Community Hospital in Cardiff) built or commissioned before this policy was introduced – a fact that was brought up by Plaid Cymru in 2007 when Labour announced its plans to bring hospital cleaning in-house, pointing out that the existing cleaning contracts at the three hospitals could not be changed for at least 20 years).

25. *Building a Better Wales*, p. 9.

26. *One Wales*, p. 9.

27. Welsh Assembly Government press release, 'Minister outlines simplified NHS structure in Wales' (16 July 2008), new.wales.gov.uk/news/presreleasearchive/2397782/?lang=en.

28. Welsh Assembly Government, *Delivering the new NHS for Wales – consultation paper II* (December 2008), accessible online at wales.gov.uk/consultations/healthsocialcare/nhswales/?lang=en. The reduction from eight LHBs to seven is due to the proposal to create a single North Wales body, in place of the two originally envisaged.

29. See R.G. Wilkinson, *The Impact of Inequality* (London: Routledge, 2005) and M. Marmot, *Status Syndrome: how your social standing directly affects your health* (London: Bloomsbury, 2005).

30. M. Drakeford, 'To those that have', *Agenda* (spring 2006), pp. 50–51.

31. Welsh Assembly Government, *Designed for Life: creating world class health and social care for Wales in the 21st century* (May 2005), p. 26.

32. Ibid, p.14.

33. The consultation paper and related documents can be found online at new.wales.gov.uk/consultations/closed/healandsoccarecloscons/nhswales/?lang=en.

34. Welsh Assembly Government, *Delivering the new NHS for Wales – consultation paper II*, p.12.

35. For a comprehensive briefing on the proposals, see: www.scottishhealthcouncil.org/shcp/CCC_FirstPage.jsp.

36. C. Bryant, *Transforming Britain: the Politics of Modern Progressive Reform* (London: The Smith Institute, 2005), p.48. The pamphlet is available online here: www.smith-institute.org.uk/pdfs/Transform_Britain.pdf.

37. Welsh Assembly Government press

release, Waiting times at an all-time low (30 April 2008), new.wales.gov.uk/news/ThirdAssembly/Health/2008/2372039/?lang=en.

38. S. Gainsbury, 'England's waiting times no better than Wales,' and P. Robinson, 'Intelligence Report', *Health Service Journal*, 6 March 2008.

39. *One Wales*, p. 8.

40. J.T. Hart, op. cit.

41. The near-adulatory tone of some of this coverage is clear from the articles' titles: 'Great Wales' (*Guardian*, 2 October 2001); 'Another country: how Wales is roaring ahead (*Independent*, 2 October 2003); and 'Welcome to Wales: where one size fits all' (*Guardian*, 1 November 2005).

42. D. Blunkett, 'Diversity and specialism will boost standards', speech to the Technology Colleges Trust, 5 November 1997; cited by M. Drakeford, *Privatisation and Social Policy* (Harlow: Longman, 2000), pp. 160, 205.

43. The 1980 Education Act had already given parents the right to express a preference, and to lodge an appeal if dissatisfied, but the 1988 Act gave this teeth, by obliging schools to increase their pupil intake up to a prescribed level.

44. A 1996 DfEE circular increased this figure to 15 per cent but it was restored to 10 per cent by Labour's 1998 School Standards and Framework Act.

45. See M. Tulloch, 'Grammar schools – can parents decide? How the government is protecting selective education', in M. Hewlett, R. Pring & M. Tulloch (Eds) *Comprehensive Education: evolution, achievement and new directions* (Northampton: University of Northampton Press, 2006), pp. 145–54.

46. In at least one case, in the Doncaster area, a campaign by local parents forced the abandonment of a proposed city academy. See F. Beckett, *The Great City Academy Fraud* (London: Continuum, 2007), pp. 81–82.

47. Ibid, p.138.

48. P. Curtis, 'As 51 academy schools prepare for first day, GCSEs show work still to be done,' *Guardian*, 30 August 2008.

49. L. Ward, 'Taskforce steps in to help privatised education firm', *Guardian*, 20 October 2003.

50. N. Mathiason, 'Can schools survive commercial drive?' *Observer*, 11 February 2001.

51. A. Smithers, 'Labour creating secondary maze,' *Guardian*, 24 May 2001.

52. P. Curtis, 'Academies criticised for expelling 10,000', *Guardian*, 25 June 2008. One Sunderland academy suspended 40 pupils in its initial fortnight alone (P. Curtis, 'Academy criticised for excluding 40 pupils in first two weeks', *Guardian*, 19 September 2008).

53. T. Edwards & S. Tomlinson, 'Selection, diversity and inequality in secondary education', in M. Hewlett, R. Pring & M. Tulloch (Eds), op. cit, p. 132.

54. A. West, A. Hind & H. Pennell, 'School admissions and "selection" in comprehensive schools: policy and practice', in M. Hewlett, R. Pring & M. Tulloch (Eds), op. cit, pp. 71–92. While the government's strengthening of the admissions code in 2006 prohibited some of the worst practices – such as interviews of parents or prospective pupils – the competitive ethos of today's English school system suggests that discriminatory practices are likely to continue.

55. S. Gorard, 'The impact of school diversity', in ibid. pp. 63–70.

56. F. Beckett, op. cit., p. 132; M. Taylor, 'Are city academies really helping the poorest children?' *Guardian*, 31 October 2005.

57. See www.pisa.oecd.org

58. Welsh Assembly Government press release, 5 September 2001 (emphasis added).

59. W. Woodward, 'Great Wales', *Guardian*, 2 October 2001.

60. D. Adamson, 'Still living on the edge?' *Contemporary Wales* vol. 21 (2008), p.54.

61. www.poverty.org.uk/W15/index.sthml. Writing in the IWA magazine, *Agenda*, Jane Davidson acknowledged that the GCSE pass figure had become 'stuck' at around 85 per cent ('Pathway out of Poverty', *Agenda*, summer 2006, pp. 47–49.)

62. Joseph Rowntree Foundation, *Monitoring Poverty and Social Exclusion in Wales* (York: JRF/NPI, 2005), pp. 40–41.

63. www.poverty.org.uk/W17/index.sthml

64. Statistics for Wales First Release SDR 108/2008, 'Participation of young people in education and the labour market (Year end 2006)', 29 July 2008.

65. www.poverty.org.uk/W15/index.sthml

66. For example, David Egan argues convincingly for efforts to smooth the transition between primary and secondary

education and for greater emphasis on developing skills and promoting literacy, rather than inculcating subject knowledge, between the ages of 7 and 14. He also calls for a constructive approach to school rationalisation – as falling school rolls reflect a declining birth rate – to ensure that finite resources are put to the best use, and for far more collaboration and networking between institutions serving 14–19 year olds. D. Egan, 'Education in the third Assembly', a two-part article in the *Bevan Foundation Review*, nos. 9 (spring/summer 2007, pp.32–33) and 10 (spring 2008, pp.34–35).

67. www.sheltercymru.org.uk/shelter/policy/policy.asp

68. Statistics Wales first release SDR 94/2008: 'Homelessness (January to March 2008)', 25 June 2008.

69. Shelter Cymru *Autumn/Winter 2008 Update*

70. Joseph Rowntree Foundation, 'Treasury's housing windfalls "should be used to tackle growing homes crisis"' (press release), 1 December 2005.

71. During the five years, 2002–07, house prices in Wales increased by 92 per cent, while wages increased by a mere 15 per cent (*Wales on Sunday*, 16 September 2007).

72. *One Wales*, pp.17–19.

73. J. Pritchard, 'Towards social justice: ending homelessness in Wales', *Bevan Foundation Review* 9 (Spring/Summer 2007), pp. 30–31.

74. The text of Blair's speech (the Beveridge memorial lecture) is accessible online at www.bris.ac.uk/poverty/Publication_files/Tony%20Blair%20Child%20Poverty%20Speech.doc

75. Members' Research Service, *In Figures: Child Poverty* (National Assembly for Wales, July 2008), p.2. www.assemblywales.org/08-045.pdf The improvement within Wales has been proportionately greater than in the UK as a whole: prior to 2005, Wales had a higher rate of child poverty (after housing costs) than the UK; subsequently, the position has been reversed.

76. L. Elias, 'Valley poverty figure shock', *Cynon Valley Leader*, 9 October 2008.

77. Welsh Labour, *Social Justice & Regeneration*, Final Stage Policy Forum Document (November 2006).

78. Sure Start in Wales amalgamated in 2003 with the Children and Youth Support Fund, Children and Youth Partnership Fund and the Childcare Strategy to become Cymorth – which, in any case, shares Sure Start's holistic premise.

79. Child Poverty Action Group, 'Child poverty: the stats – analysis of the latest poverty statistics' (October 2008).

80. 'Ministers' benefit reform worries', BBC website, 10 December 2008, news.bbc.co.uk/1/hi/wales/7773960.stm

81. Welsh Assembly Government, *A Fair Future for Our Children*, p. 13.

82. At least one pair of indicators is virtually meaningless: 95 per cent of young people by 2015, and 97 per cent by 2020, are 'to be ready for high skilled employment and/or further or higher education' (*Measuring Success*, p.13); as the AMs' own research service points out, progress against these objectives cannot be measured, in the absence of any baseline data or some definition of what 'readiness' means in this context (*In Figures: Child Poverty*, p. 11).

83. A. Crowley & V. Winckler, *Children in severe poverty in Wales: an agenda for action* (Save the Children/Bevan Foundation, February 2008), pp. 40–41.

84. This would be facilitated by the LCO on 'Social Welfare and Other Fields' recently approved by Parliament.

85. The closest thing to a definition is given in the 'Measuring Success' document (p.4): 'A child in poverty lives in a family with resources that are so significantly below the average, that they cannot be seen by others and by themselves to be participating fully in society.'

86. D. Adamson, 'Still living on the edge?', p. 50.

87. It was, perhaps, partly to distance itself from such conclusions about inequality that the government in December 2003 modified its measure of child poverty, adopting a three-tier approach that supplemented relative low income with 'absolute' low income (compared to a 1998/99 benchmark, up-rated only in line with inflation) and 'material deprivation' (lack of certain household necessities). Relative low income continues to be generally regarded as the key measure, however.

88. In a Newsnight interview with Jeremy Paxman on 4 June 2001; transcript here: news.bbc.co.uk/1/hi/events/newsnight/1372220.stm

89. P. Wintour, 'Celebrate huge salaries, minister tells Labour', *Guardian*, 10 March 2008.

90. P. Toynbee, 'We will never abolish child poverty in a society shaped like this one', *Guardian*, 7 July 2006.

91. In 1998 Finland spent 6.2 per cent of its GDP on education as against an OECD average of 5.3 per cent. According to the Gini coefficient, a statistical method of measuring inequality on a scale of 1–100 in which 1 represents perfect equality, Finland's coefficient is 26.9, Denmark's is 24.7 and Sweden's 25.8. By comparison, Great Britain scores 36, the USA 40.8 and Brazil 58. (Source: United Nations Human Development Report 2006). An illustration of Finland's culture of equality, so alien to Britain's culture of greed, is the fact that in 2001 the then-chief executive of Nokia, Jorma Ollila, was paid $1.25 million before stock options. This may seem a lot but it is chickenfeed compared to the obscene bonuses in Britain and the USA: His counterparts at Ford and General Motors were paid $32 million and $22 million respectively (W. Hutton, *The World We're In*, London: Abacus, 2002, p. 301).

92. Crowley & Winckler, op. cit. pp. 33–38; D. Adamson, 'Still Living on the Edge', pp. 54–55; 60–61; 64.

93. See Crowley & Winckler, pp. 42–43.

Chapter 6

1. *Building a Better Wales*, pp. 14–17.

2. Ceri Evans, 'For Welsh Self-Government', South Wales *Socialist Outlook* discussion document, 1996 www.angelfire.com/alt/ceri_evans/writings/self_government.htm.

3. G. Day, *Making Sense of Wales* (Cardiff: University of Wales Press, 2002), pp. 52–53.

4. R.M. Jones, 'Social Change in Wales Since 1945', in D. Dunkerley & A. Thompson (eds), *Wales Today* (Cardiff: University of Wales Press, 1999), p.14.

5. J. England, op. cit., pp. 65–73.

6. A full list of some 350 Acts of Parliament under which powers were transferred to the Assembly at its inception is given in the National Assembly for Wales (Transfer of Functions) Order 1999 (www.opsi.gov.uk/si/si1999/99067202.htm *et seq*). Around a dozen of these relate to economic development and the Assembly government was actually making use of nine in November 2002, when Andrew Davies gave evidence to the Richard Commission (see www.richardcommission.gov.uk/content/evidence/written/adavies/annex1-e.htm).

7. His written evidence is here: www.richardcommission.gov.uk/content/evidence/written/adavies/main-e.htm and his oral evidence here: www.richardcommission.gov.uk/content/evidence/oral/adavies/index.htm.

8. As if to demonstrate the point, the Department of Economic Development and Transport in 2006 changed its name to something resembling a New Labour slogan, the Department of Enterprise, Innovation and Networks, a title typically suggesting progress and modernity but whose meaning is opaque. Fortunately, the new name did not survive the 2007 election. The 2006 name-change exemplifies a tendency to imitate New Labour's attachment to the clunky, indigestible jargon of the management consultant or self-help guru, betraying a difficulty or reluctance to speak clearly to voters.

9. *Building a Better Wales*, p. 15.

10. A. Amin, D. Massey & N. Thrift, *Decentering the Nation: a radical approach to regional inequality* (London: Catalyst, 2003), p. 22.

11. Ibid., p. 23.

12. J. Lovering, 'New Myths of the Welsh Economy', *Planet* 116 (1996), pp. 6–16; idem, 'Constructing the Welsh Economy: Changing Perspectives on Economic Development', The O'Donnell Lecture, 1998; idem, 'Theory Led by Policy? The Inadequacies of "The New Regionalism" in Economic Geography Illustrated from the Case of Wales', paper presented at Economy Geography Research Group Seminar, UCL, 3 July 1998, available online at www.econgeog.org.uk/pdfs/lovering.pdf

13. Statistics for Wales/National Statistics bulletin SB 79/2008: 'Economic Statistics Monthly – December 2008' (19 December 2008).

14. S. Fothergill & J. Grieve Smith, *Mobilising Britain's Missing Workforce: Unemployment, Incapacity Benefit and the Regions* (London: Catalyst, 2005).

15. See C. Beatty & S. Fothergill, 'The

diversion from unemployment to sickness across British regions and districts', *Regional Studies*, 39, 7 (2004), pp. 837–854; C. Beatty, S. Fothergill, T. Gore & R. Powell, *The Real Level of Unemployment 2007* (Sheffield: CRESR, 2007); C. Beatty, S. Fothergill & R. Powell, 'Twenty years on: has the economy of the coalfield recovered?', *Environment and Planning A* (forthcoming, 2007) – all available at www.shu.ac.uk/cresr/publication_downloads.html – plus S. Fothergill & J. Grieve Smith, op cit.; C. Beatty & S. Fothergill, 'The Diversion from Unemployment to Sickness: the Remarkable Case of Wales', *Bevan Foundation Review* 5 (Autumn/Winter 2004), pp. 7–9.

16. C. Beatty, S. Fothergill, T. Gore & R. Powell, op. cit., p.13, citing figures from the DWP and ONS. The Welsh authorities in the list were: Merthyr Tydfil (18.9 per cent); Blaenau Gwent (17.9 per cent); Neath Port Talbot (16.3 per cent); Rhondda Cynon Taff (15.8 per cent); Caerphilly (15.5 per cent); Bridgend (13.4 per cent); and Carmarthenshire (13.0 per cent).

17. Ibid., p.23. The claimant count percentages for the four were 4.6, 3.8, 2.9 and 3.1, respectively (ibid, p. 59).

18. M. Shipton, '5,000 jobs lost in Wales', *Western Mail*, 25 October 2006.

19. Quoted in T. Livingstone, 'Assembly set to review Barnett formula', *Western Mail*, 26 July 2007.

20. R. Davies, 'Where Needs Must', *Agenda* (winter 2002/03), pp. 11–13; Barnett gives his own view in 'Formula for Change', *Agenda* (summer 2007), pp. 26–27.

21. See G.S. Williams, 'Evaluating Objective 1 in Wales: the Experience of the Mid-Term Evaluation', *Welsh Economic Review*, vol. 16, no. 4 (summer 2004), pp. 21–24; E. ap Gwilym, 'Growing Pains', *Agenda* (summer 2007), pp. 23–25.

22. R. Fevre, 'The Welsh Economy', in Dunkerley & Thompson, op. cit., pp. 67–68.

23. ONS, *Annual Survey of Hours & Earnings 2008*, www.statistics.gov.uk/downloads/theme_labour/ASHE_2008/tab7_7a.xls

24. D. Devine, 'Row over call to cut minimum Welsh wage', *Western Mail*, 18 June 2007.

25. P. Hennessy, 'Gordon Brown to vary minimum wage over UK', *Sunday Telegraph*, 23 July 2007, www.telegraph.co.uk/news/main.jhtml?xml=/news/2007/07/22/nwage122.xml

26. *Regional pay, regional poverty? The implications of public sector pay flexibility for Wales* (Bevan Foundation Policy Paper 3, Tredegar, 2004).

27. R. Fevre, op. cit., p. 64.

28. Welsh Assembly Government, *Wales: a Vibrant Economy* (Cardiff 2005), pp. 39–40.

29. As originally cited by O. Morgan, 'Hard man who seeks to bang Corus into shape', *Observer*, 12 January 2001.

30. 'Clueless on Corus closures' (12 February 2001); sadly, the WalesWatch website (not to be confused with the more recent IWA blog of the same name) is no longer online.

31. P. Mandelson, 'The future active state', *Guardian*, 4 December 2008.

32. See M. Mackintosh & H. Wainwright (eds), *A Taste of Power: the Politics of Local Economics* (London: Verso, 1987), ch. 7, for further details.

33. *Guardian*, 6 June 1997.

34. Wales has a particular problem with small unstaffed stations, an obvious disincentive for some people to travel by train. Presumably, adequate waiting areas, security, real-time travel information and a permanent staff presence would cut against the drive to maximise profits and increase shareholder value. However, the Assembly Government should be insisting that they are provided.

35. The best that could be done to address this democratic deficit was an amendment to the legislation, obtained by the Assembly government, that for planning applications in Wales, at least one member of the commission be nominated by Welsh ministers.

36. Fuel poverty, a term applying to anyone who needs to spend more than 10 per cent of their income keeping themselves warm and providing for their other energy needs, is a particular problem in Wales. Poor quality, and therefore energy inefficient housing stock, combined with low wages, dependence on benefits, and soaring fuel prices means that 270,000 Welsh households live in fuel poverty, up from 134,000 in 2004.

37. *Western Mail*, November 29 2007

38. news.bbc.co.uk/1/hi/wales/7251549.stm

39. *Severn Barrage Must Pass Tough Sustainability Tests* Report: Sustainable Development

Commission October 1 2007

40. New Labour's nuclear programme, is at the time of writing, subject to the proposed sale of British Energy to the French energy company EDF.

41. bbc.news.co.uk/hi/sci/tech/7536124.stm

42. Regardless of the 'clean coal' spin emanating from government and the company concerned, E.ON, the planning conditions for Kingsnorth are silent on any carbon capture and storage requirement (*Guardian*, August 6 2008).

43. Whatever its merits, the alternative approach of reducing vehicle or fuel tax in such areas is not, at present, open to the Assembly government.

44. The Climate Change Bill received royal assent in November 2008.

45. *Guardian*, July 24 2008.

46. G. James, *Sustaining Spin: an assessment of the mainstreaming of sustainable development by the Welsh Assembly Government and local authorities in Wales* (Friends of the Earth Cymru, January 2004), available online at www.foe.co.uk/resource/reports/sustaining_spin.pdf, p.10.

47. Press release: 'Sustainable Development Commission Welcomes Welsh Assembly Government's Sustainable Development Action Plan' (20 December 2004), www.sd-commission.org.uk/presslist. php/10/welsh-assembly-governments-sustainable-development-action-plan-2004-2007. The Commission has given a full assessment of the Assembly's policies in *Sustainable Development in Wales: from Pioneer to Delivery* (June 2006), www.sd-commission.org.uk/publications/downloads/Pioneer-to-Delivery_Eng3.pdf

48. P. Davies, 'The Rocky Road to Sustainable Development', *Bevan Foundation Review* 9 (Spring/Summer 2007), p.22.

49. Welsh Assembly Government press release, 19 November 2008.

50. J. Bibbings, *Consumption in Wales: Encouraging the Sustainable Lifestyle* (Cardiff: Welsh Consumer Council, 2003), www.wales-consumer.org.uk/research_policy/pdf/WCC13_Consumption_in_Wales.pdf, cited by G. James, op. cit., p.7.

51. P. Davies, op. cit.

52. 'Councils meet landfill targets', BBC news website. 1 September 2008 www.news.bbc.co.uk/1/hi/wales/7591519.stm

53. Quoted in 'Communiries are urged to contribute to the discussion on making Wales a low carbon economy', Cefn Gwalad website: www.cefngwlad.org/index.php?p+bd5d49c5.13.2

54. 'Wales launches green building charter', Green Building website, 13 November 2008.www.newbuilder.co.uk/news/newsfullstory.asp?ID=2731

55. 'New vision for sustainable Wales revealed', Welsh Assembly Government website: wales.gov.uk/news/latest/081119newvision/?version=1&lang=en

56. E. Davidoff, *Report on the External Perceptions of the First Sustainable Development Scheme of the National Assembly for Wales* (Cardiff: Welsh Assembly Government, 2003).

57. *Building Vibrant and Sustainable Communities* (Welsh Labour first stage consultation document, September 2008).

58. Ibid, p.5.

Chapter 7

1. Welsh Assembly Government, *Eighth Annual Report on work to promote Equality and Diversity for 2006–07* (WAG, 2007). Available online at: new.wales.gov.uk/topics/equality/publications/equalityannualrpt8/?lang=en.

2. R. McNabb & J. Shorey, 'The Labour Market', in K.D. George & L. Mainwaring (eds), *The Welsh Economy* (Cardiff: University of Wales Press, 1988), pp. 111–31.

3. ONS, *Regional Trends* 39 (2006), pp. 126, 130.

4. See R. McNabb, 'Segmented Labour Markers, Female Employment and Poverty in Wales' in G. Rees & T.L. Rees (eds) op. cit., pp. 156–67.

5. Welsh Assembly Government Statistical Directorate, *A Statistical Focus on Men and Women in Wales* (2007 edition).

6. N. Evans & D. Jones, ' "To Help Forward the Great Work of Humanity": Women in the Labour Party in Wales' in D. Tanner et al (eds), op. cit., pp. 215–40.

7. See H. Francis & G. Rees, ' "No Surrender in the Valleys": the 1984–85 Miners' Strike in South Wales', *Llafur* 5, 2 (1989), pp. 41–71.

8. This procedure had to be abandoned following a court judgement prompted by disappointed male candidates but was subsequently reinstated when the incoming Labour government amended the law.

9. House of Commons Information Office Factsheet M4, 'Women in the House of Commons' Members Series (revised October 2006), available online at: www.parliament.uk/documents/upload/M04.pdf.

10. Commission for Racial Equality, *A Lot Done, A Lot to Do* (London: CRE, 2007), p. 18.

11. National Assembly for Wales Statistical Directorate, *Economic Inactivity in Wales 2005* (WAG, 2006) p. 28, cited in WAG, *Eighth Annual Report*, p. 25.

12. CRE, op. cit., p. 19.

13. Ibid., pp. 26–27.

14. Ibid., pp. 31–32.

15. *One Wales*, pp. 16–17; 35.

16. Ibid, p.34.

Chapter 8

1. In time, we may yet even see a Welsh version of *Renewing and Extending Party Democracy*. A package of rule changes was indeed carried at the 2008 conference, which included the introduction of 'contemporary issues', but it was explicitly stated that the right to submit contemporary resolutions 'would not be affected'; this may, however, prove a temporary reprieve.

Chapter 9

1. DTI, *Trade Union Membership 2006* (London: DTI, 2006), p.16.

2. *The Voice of Wales at Work: Wales TUC Annual Report 2007–2008* (Cardiff, 2008), pp. 12–13.

3. The TGWU claimed that an OMOV ballot would be prohibitively expensive but then mailed Alun Michael's campaign literature to all its members in Wales. See K. Morgan & G. Mungham, op. cit, pp. 131–39.

4. More positively, from our perspective, the unions also threw their weight behind the *One Wales* coalition.

5. See the discussion of Bryant's critique in chapter 5 above.

6. The four were Nerys Evans, Bethan Jenkins, Helen Mary Jones and Leanne Wood. Jocelyn Davies also voted to reject the 'rainbow' deal, although her own position was reportedly more equivocal and she did not make her views public.

7. The constitution states that it is for 'a democratic Welsh state based on socialist principles'.

8. See L. McAllister, *Plaid Cymru: The Emergence of a Political Party* (Bridgend: Seren, 2001).

Chapter 10

1. The speech was delivered in Swansea on 30 November 2006, at a meeting organised by Compass, and the text can still be accessed on the Compass website: www.compassonline.org.uk/article.asp?n=338

2. P. Sikka, 'Good pensions', in Left Economics Advisory Panel, 'The Red Papers – 10 years on: whatever happened to equality? (March 2007, accessible at www.l-r-c.org.uk/policy/leap/LEAPMar07.pdf), pp.15–16.

3. J. Christiansen, 'Tackling UK Tax Corruption,' in Left Economics Advisory Panel, op. cit., pp.9–11.

4. Labour Representation Committee, *Programme for a Real Labour Government* (2005).

5. Albeit that Bradford & Bingley's profitable savings business was immediately sold on to the Spanish Grupo Santander.

6. See Z. Gannon & N. Lawson, *Co-production: the modernisation of public services by staff and users* (London: Compass, 2008).

7. For a first-hand account of Porto Alegre's participatory budgeting and a discussion of its wider applicability, see H. Wainwright, *Reclaim the State: experiments in popular democracy* (London: Verso, 2003).

8. See Werner Bonefeld 'European Integration: the market, the politics and class. *Capital and Class* 77 summer 2002.

9. Although now ratified in Westminster, it has been rejected, by referendum, in Ireland.

10. A proposal will have to be backed by 55 per cent of member states and 62 per cent of the population of the EU. A 'blocking minority' must consist of at least 4 member states.

11. I. Black, 'Blair sees 20m net jobs', *Guardian*, 25 March 2000.

12. In the wave of wildcat strikes in the power industry in February 2009, while some workers took at face value Gordon Brown's reactionary and undeliverable promise of 'British jobs for British workers', many strikers refused to blame foreign workers, demanding that they be allowed to organise and receive the same rates of pay.

Appendix 1

1. For a succinct presentation of the main concerns about the academy, see S.

Tannock, & J. Maiden, *St Athan Defence
Training Academy and the Future of Wales*
(Cardiff: Stop the St Athan Academy
Campaign, 2007), online at
www.cynefinywerin.org.uk/fileserve.php?
mediaid=149
2. See, for example, K. Coates (ed) *The Right
to Useful Work* (Nottingham: Spokesman,
2007 [1978]); H. Wainwright & D. Elliott,
*The Lucas Plan: a new trade unionism in the
making?* (London: Allison & Busby 1982)
3. G. Monbiot, 'Only paranoia can justify the
world's second biggest military budget',
Guardian, 28 November 2006.

Select Bibliography

Adamson, David, *Living on the Edge: Poverty and Deprivation in Wales*, Llandysul: Gomer, 1996.

Adamson, David, 'Still Living on the Edge?' *Contemporary Wales* 21, 2008, pp. 47–66.

Amin, Ash, Massey, Doreen & Thrift, Nigel, *Decentering the Nation: a radical approach to regional inequality*, London: Catalyst, 2003.

Beatty, Christina, Fothergill, Steve, Gore, Tony & Powell, Ryan, *The Real Level of Unemployment 2007*, Sheffield: CRESR, 2007.

Beckett, Francis, *The Great City Academy Fraud*, London: Continuum, 2007.

Bonefeld, Werner, 'European Integration: the market, the political and class', *Capital and Class* 77, summer 2002, pp. 117–42.

Bryant, Chris, *Transforming Britain: the Politics of Modern Progressive Reform*, London: The Smith Institute, 2005, available online at www.smith-institute.org.uk/ pdfs/Transform_Britain.pdf

Crowley, Anne & Winckler, Victoria, *Children in severe poverty in Wales: an agenda for action*, Cardiff: Save the Children/Bevan Foundation, February 2008.

Curtis, Ben, 'The Wilson Government and the pit closures in South Wales', 1964–1970', *Llafur* 9, 1, 2004, pp. 59–70.

David, Wayne, *Remaining True: a biography of Ness Edwards*, Caerphilly Local History Society, 2006.

Davidson, Jane, 'Pathway out of Poverty', *Agenda*, summer 2006, pp. 47–49.

Davies, Peter, The rocky road to sustainable development', *Bevan Foundation Review* 9, spring/summer 2007, pp.22–23.

Davies, Steve, *Inside the Laboratory: the new politics of public services in Wales*, London: Catalyst, 2003.

Day, Graham, *Making Sense of Wales*, Cardiff: University of Wales Press 2002.

Drakeford, Mark, *Privatisation and Social Policy*, London: Longman, 2000.

Drakeford, Mark, 'To those that have', *Agenda*, spring 2006, pp. 50–51.

Drakeford, Mark, 'Progressive universalism', *Agenda*, winter 2007, pp. 4–7, available online at www.iwa.org.uk/debate/prog_univers.htm

Dunkerley, David. & Thompson, Andrew (eds), *Wales Today*, Cardiff: University of Wales Press, 1999.

Egan, David, 'Educatiing for Social Justice', *Agenda*, spring 2006, pp.48-49.

England, Joe, *The Wales TUC 1974-2004: Devolution and Industrial Politics*, Cardiff: University of Wales Press, 2004.

Evans, Ceri, 'For Welsh Self-Government', South Wales *Socialist Outlook* discussion document, 1996 www.angelfire.com/alt/ceri_evans/writings/self_government.htm

Evans, Ceri & George, Ed, *Swings and Roundabouts: what really happened on May 6th*, Cardiff: Welsh Labour Action, 1999.

Flynn, Paul, *Dragons Led by Poodles: the inside story of a New Labour stitch-up*, London: Politico's, 1999.

Fothergill, Steve & Grieve Smith, John, *Mobilising Britain's Missing Workforce: unemployment, incapacity benefit and the regions*, London: Catalyst, 2005.

Francis, Hywel & Smith, Dai, *The Fed: a history of the South Wales miners in the twentieth century*, London: Lawrence & Wishart, 1980.

Gannon, Zoe & Lawson, Neal, *Co-production: the modernisation of public services by staff and users*, London: Compass, 2008.

George, Ed, 'A note on Welsh history and politics', published online, October 2002: www.geocities.com/edgeorge2001es/mywritings/Note.html

George, Ed, 'Muddy brown water', *Workers Action* 22, summer 2003. pp.14–17, available online here: www.geocities.com/edgeorge2001es/mywritings/Water.html

Griffiths, Robert, *S.O. Davies: a Socialist Faith*, Llandysul: Gomer, 1983.

Harris, Robert, *The Making of Neil Kinnock*, London: Faber & Faber, 1984.

Hart, Julian Tudor, *The Political Economy of Health Care: A Clinical Perspective*, Bristol: Policy Press 2006.

Harvey, David, *A Brief History of Neoliberalism*, Oxford: OUP, 2005.

Hewlett, Mark, Richard Pring & Margaret Tulloch (eds), *Comprehensive Education: evolution, achievement and new directions*, Northampton: University of Northampton Press, 2006.

Hill, Daran, Edwards, Huw & Jeffes, Leigh. *The Evolution of Devolution: reflections on the operation of our legislative system*, Tredegar: Bevan Foundation, 2008.

Hutton, Will. *The World We're In*. London: Abacus, 2002.

Institute for Welsh Affairs, *Unpacking the Progressive Consensus*, Cardiff: IWA, 2008.

James, Gordon, *Sustaing Spin: an assessment of the mainstreaming of sustainable development by the Welsh Assembly Government and local authorities in Wales*, Friends of the Earth Cymru, 2004.

John, A.H. *The Industrial Development of South Wales, 1750–1850: an Essay*, Cardiff: University of Wales Press, 1950.

John, Angela V. 'The Chartist endurance: industrial South Wales, 1840–1868', *Morgannwg* 15, 1971, pp.23–49.

Jones, Carwyn, *The Future of Welsh Labour*, Cardiff: IWA, 2004.

Jones, David J.V. *Before Rebecca: Popular Protests in Wales, 1793–1835*, London: Allen Lane, 1973.

Jones, David J.V. 'Chartism in Welsh communities', in *Welsh History Review* 6, 3, June 1973, pp. 243–61.

Klein, Naomi, *The Shock Doctrine: the rise of disaster capitalism*, London: Allen Lane, 2007.

Labour Party, *The Labour Party manifesto 2005*, www.labour.org.uk/fileadmin/ manifesto_13042005_a3/flash/ manifesto_2005.swf

Left Economics Advisory Panel. *The Red Papers – 10 Years On: Whatever Happened to Equality?* (London: LEAP, 2007, accessible www.l-r-c.org.uk/policy/leap/LEAPMar07.pdf)

Lister, John, *The NHS after 60: for patients or profits?*, Middlesex University Press, 2008.

Lovering, John, 'New Myths of the Welsh Economy', *Planet* 116, 1996, pp. 6–16.

McAllister, Ian, 'The Labour Party in Wales: the dynamics of one-partyism', *Llafur* 3, 2, spring 1981, pp. 79–89.

McAllister, Laura, *Plaid Cymru: the emergence of a political party*, Bridgend: Seren, 2001.

McDonnell, J. *Another World Is Possible: A Manifesto for 21st Century Socialism*. London: LRC, 2007

McIntosh, Maureen & Wainwright, Hilary (eds), *A Taste of Power: the politics of local economics*, London: Verso, 1987.

Marmot, Michael, *Status Syndrome: how your social standing directly affects your health*, London: Bloomsbury, 2005.

Miliband, Ralph, *Parliamentary Socialism: a study in the politics of Labour*, 2nd edition, London: Merlin, 1972.

Mills, Chris, 'Climate change – the challenge for Wales', *Bevan Foundation Review* 10, spring 2008, pp.6–7.

Morgan, Kenneth O. 'The New Liberalism and the challenge of Labour: the Welsh experience, 1885–1929', in *Welsh History Review* 6, 3, June 1973, pp. 288–312.

Morgan, Kevin & Mungham, Geoff, *Redesigning Democracy: the making of the Welsh Assembly*, Bridgend: Seren, 2000.

Morgan, Rhodri, Speech to the National Centre for Public Policy, Swansea, 11th December 2002, accessible online at www.sochealth.co.uk/Regions/Wales/redwater.htm

Morgan, Rhodri, '21st century socialism – a Welsh recipe', speech to a Compass meeting, Swansea, 30 November 2006, accessible online at: www.compassonline.org.uk/news/item.asp?n=338

Morgan, Rhodri, 'Welsh Labour's future', in Institute of Welsh Affairs, Politics in 21st Century Wales, Cardiff: IWA, 2008.

Morris, David, 'Swimming in clear red water', *Agenda*, spring 2005, pp.33–35.

Nunns, Alex, *The Patchwork Privatisation of Our Health Service: A Users' Guide*, London: Keep Our NHS Public, 2006.

Player, Stewart & Leys, Colin, *Confuse and Conceal: the NHS and Independent Sector Treatment Centres*, Monmouth: Merlin, 2008.

Pollock, Allyson M. *NHS plc: the privatisation of our health care*, London: Verso, 2004.

Price, Adam, 'The red-green grass of hope', *Tribune*, 23 January 2003.

Rees, Gareth & Rees, Teresa L. (eds), *Poverty and Social Inequality in Wales*, London: Croom Helm, 1980.

Smith, David (ed), *A People and a Proletariat: essays in the history of Wales, 1780–1980*, London: Pluto, 1980.

Stead, Peter, 'Working class leadership in South Wales, 1900–1920', in *Welsh History Review* 6, 3, June 1973, pp. 329–53.

Tanner, Duncan, Williams, Chris. & Hopkin, Deian, (eds), *The Labour Party in Wales, 1900–2000*, Cardiff: University of Wales Press, 2000.

Tannock, Stuart & Maiden, James, *St Athan Defence Training Academy and the Future of Wales*, Cardiff: Stop the St Athan Academy Campaign, 2007, online at www.cynefinywerin.org.uk/fileserve.php?mediaid=149

Tomlinson, Sally, *Education in a Post-Welfare Society*, 2nd edition, Maidenhead: Open University Press, 2005.

Wainwright, Hilary, *Reclaim the State: experiments in popular democracy*, London: Verso, 2003.

Webster, Charles, *The National Health Service: a political history*, 2nd edition, Oxford: O.U.P, 2002.

Welsh Assembly Government, *Making the Connections: delivering better services for Wales*, Cardiff: Welsh Assembly Government, October 2004.

Welsh Assembly Government, *A Fair Future for Our Children*, Cardiff: Welsh Assembly Government, February 2005.

Welsh Assembly Government, *Designed for Life: creating world class health and social care for Wales in the 21st century*, Cardiff: Welsh Assembly Government, May 2005.

Welsh Assembly Government, *Making the Connections – Delivering Beyond Boundaries*, Cardiff: Welsh Assembly Government, November 2006.

Welsh Assembly Government, *One Wales: a progressive agenda for the government of Wales*, Cardiff: Welsh Assembly Government, June 2007.

Welsh Assembly Government, *Renewable Energy Route Map for Wales: consultation on way forward to a leaner, greener and cleaner Wales*, February 2008.

Welsh Labour, *Building a Better Wales: Welsh Labour election manifesto 2007*. Cardiff: Welsh Labour, 2007.

Went, Robert, *Globalization: neoliberal challenge, radical responses*, London: Pluto, 2000.

Wilkinson, Richard G. *The Impact of Inequality: how to make sick societies healthier*, London: Routledge, 2005.

Wilks, Ivor, *South Wales and the Rising of 1839*, 2nd edition, Llandysul: Gomer, 1989.

Williams, David, *The Rebecca Riots*, Cardiff: University of Wales Press, 1986 [1955].

Williams, David, 'Chartism in Wales', in A. Briggs, (ed), *Chartist Studies*, London: Macmillan, 1959, pp. 220–48.

Williams, Glyn (ed), *Crisis of Economy and Ideology: Essays on Welsh Society, 1840–1980*, Bangor: SSRC/BSA Sociology of Wales Study Group, 1983.

Williams, Gwyn A. *The Merthyr Rising*, 2nd edition, Cardiff: University of Wales Press, 1988.

Williams, Gwyn A. *When Was Wales? A History of the Welsh*, Harmondsworth: Pelican, 1985.

Williams, John, *Was Wales Industrialised? Essays in modern Welsh history*, Llandysul: Gomer, 1995.

Young, Brendan, 'Wales in Europe: the poor relation?', paper presented to the 'Socialists and a Welsh Assembly' conference, Cardiff, 19 July 1997. Available online here: www.geocities.com/edgeorge2001es/wales/relation.html

Index